Count Lev Nikolayevich Tolstoy (9 September [O.S. 28 August] 1828 – 20 November [O.S. 7 November] 1910), usually referred to in English as Leo Tolstoy, was a Russian writer who is regarded as one of the greatest authors of all time. He received multiple nominations for Nobel Prize in Literature every year from 1902 to 1906, and nominations for Nobel Peace Prize in 1901, 1902 and 1910, and his miss of the prize is a major Nobel prize controversy. Born to an aristocratic Russian family in 1828, he is best known for the novels War and Peace (1869) and Anna Karenina (1877), often cited as pinnacles of realist fiction. He first achieved literary acclaim in his twenties with his semi-autobiographical trilogy, Childhood, Boyhood, and Youth (1852–1856), and Sevastopol Sketches (1855), based upon his experiences in the Crimean War. Tolstoy's fiction includes dozens of short stories and several novellas such as The Death of Ivan Ilyich (1886), Family Happiness (1859), and Hadji Murad (1912). He also wrote plays and numerous philosophical essays. (Source: Wikipedia)

Literary works:
The Autobiographical Trilogy
Childhood (1852)
Boyhood (1854)
Youth (1856)
War and Peace (1869)
Anna Karenina (1877)
Resurrection (1899)
Family Happiness (1859)
The Cossacks (1863)
The Death of Ivan Ilyich (1886)
The Kreutzer Sonata (1889)
The Devil (1911)
The Forged Coupon (1911)
Hadji Murat (1917)

A LETTER TO A HINDU
&
THE AWAKENING; THE RESURRECTION

LEO TOLSTOY

PRINCE CLASSICS

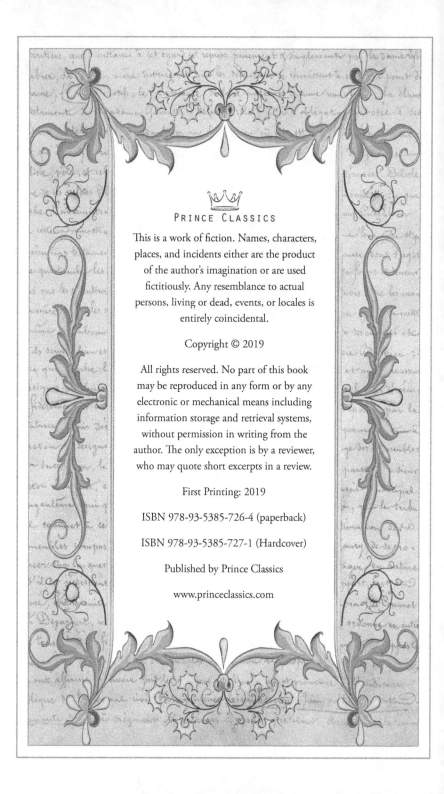

First Printing: 2019

ISBN 978-93-5385-726-4 (paperback)

ISBN 978-93-5385-727-1 (Hardcover)

Published by Prince Classics

www.princeclassics.com

Contents

A LETTER TO A HINDU
&
THE AWAKENING: THE RESURRECTION

A LETTER TO A HINDU

INTRODUCTION

The letter printed below is a translation of Tolstoy's letter written in Russian in reply to one from the Editor of Free Hindustan. After having passed from hand to hand, this letter at last came into my possession through a friend who asked me, as one much interested in Tolstoy's writings, whether I thought it worth publishing. I at once replied in the affirmative, and told him I should translate it myself into Gujarati and induce others' to translate and publish it in various Indian vernaculars.

The letter as received by me was a type-written copy. It was therefore referred to the author, who confirmed it as his and kindly granted me permission to print it.

To me, as a humble follower of that great teacher whom I have long looked upon as one of my guides, it is a matter of honour to be connected with the publication of his letter, such especially as the one which is now being given to the world.

It is a mere statement of fact to say that every Indian, whether he owns up to it or not, has national aspirations. But there are as many opinions as there are Indian nationalists as to the exact meaning of that aspiration, and more especially as to the methods to be used to attain the end.

One of the accepted and 'time-honoured' methods to attain the end is that of violence. The assassination of Sir Curzon Wylie was an illustration of that method in its worst and most detestable form. Tolstoy's life has been devoted to replacing the method of violence for removing tyranny or securing reform by the method of non-resistance to evil. He would meet hatred expressed in violence by love expressed in self-suffering. He admits of no exception to whittle down this great and divine law of love. He applies it to all the problems that trouble mankind.

When a man like Tolstoy, one of the clearest thinkers in the western world, one of the greatest writers, one who as a soldier has known what violence is and what it can do, condemns Japan for having blindly followed the law of modern science, falsely so-called, and fears for that country 'the greatest calamities', it is for us to pause and consider whether, in our impatience of English rule, we do not want to replace one evil by another and a worse. India, which is the nursery of the great faiths of the world, will cease to be nationalist India, whatever else she may become, when she goes through the process of civilization in the shape of reproduction on that sacred soil of gun factories and the hateful industrialism which has reduced the people of Europe to a state of slavery, and all but stifled among them the best instincts which are the heritage of the human family.

If we do not want the English in India we must pay the price. Tolstoy indicates it. 'Do not resist evil, but also do not yourselves participate in evil—in the violent deeds of the administration of the law courts, the collection of taxes and, what is more important, of the soldiers, and no one in the world will enslave you', passionately declares the sage of Yasnaya Polyana. Who can question the truth of what he says in the following: 'A commercial company enslaved a nation comprising two hundred millions. Tell this to a man free from superstition and he will fail to grasp what these words mean. What does it mean that thirty thousand people, not athletes, but rather weak and ordinary people, have enslaved two hundred millions of vigorous, clever, capable, freedom-loving people? Do not the figures make it clear that not the English, but the Indians, have enslaved themselves?'

One need not accept all that Tolstoy says—some of his facts are not accurately stated—to realize the central truth of his indictment of the present system, which is to understand and act upon the irresistible power of the soul over the body, of love, which is an attribute of the soul, over the brute or body force generated by the stirring in us of evil passions.

There is no doubt that there is nothing new in what Tolstoy preaches. But his presentation of the old truth is refreshingly forceful. His logic is unassailable. And above all he endeavours to practise what he preaches. He preaches to convince. He is sincere and in earnest. He commands attention.

[*19th November, 1909*] M. K. GANDHI

All that exists is One. People only call this One by different names. THE VEDAS.

God is love, and he that abideth in love abideth in God, and God abideth in him. I JOHN iv. 16.

God is one whole; we are the parts. EXPOSITION OF THE TEACHING OF THE VEDAS BY VIVEKANANDA.

I

Do not seek quiet and rest in those earthly realms where delusions and desires are engendered, for if thou dost, thou wilt be dragged through the rough wilderness of life, which is far from Me.

Whenever thou feelest that thy feet are becoming entangled in the interlaced roots of life, know that thou has strayed from the path to which I beckon thee: for I have placed thee in broad, smooth paths, which are strewn with flowers. I have put a light before thee, which thou canst follow and thus run without stumbling. KRISHNA.

I have received your letter and two numbers of your periodical, both of which interest me extremely. The oppression of a majority by a minority, and the demoralization inevitably resulting from it, is a phenomenon that has always occupied me and has done so most particularly of late. I will try to explain to you what I think about that subject in general, and particularly about the cause from which the dreadful evils of which you write in your letter, and in the Hindu periodical you have sent me, have arisen and continue to arise.

The reason for the astonishing fact that a majority of working people submit to a handful of idlers who control their labour and their very lives is always and everywhere the same—whether the oppressors and oppressed are of one race or whether, as in India and elsewhere, the oppressors are of a different nation.

This phenomenon seems particularly strange in India, for there more than two hundred million people, highly gifted both physically and mentally, find themselves in the power of a small group of people quite alien to them in thought, and immeasurably inferior to them in religious morality.

From your letter and the articles in Free Hindustan as well as from the very interesting writings of the Hindu Swami Vivekananda and others, it appears that, as is the case in our time with the ills of all nations, the reason lies in the lack of a reasonable religious teaching which by explaining the meaning of life would supply a supreme law for the guidance of conduct and would replace the more than dubious precepts of pseudo-religion and pseudo-science with the immoral conclusions deduced from them and commonly called 'civilization'.

Your letter, as well as the articles in Free Hindustan and Indian political literature generally, shows that most of the leaders of public opinion among your people no longer attach any significance to the religious teachings that were and are professed by the peoples of India, and recognize no possibility of freeing the people from the oppression they endure except by adopting the irreligious and profoundly immoral social arrangements under which the English and other pseudo-Christian nations live to-day.

And yet the chief if not the sole cause of the enslavement of the Indian peoples by the English lies in this very absence of a religious consciousness and of the guidance for conduct which should flow from it—a lack common in our day to all nations East and West, from Japan to England and America alike.

II

O ye, who see perplexities over your heads, beneath your feet, and to the right and left of you; you will be an eternal enigma unto yourselves until ye become humble and joyful as children. Then will ye find Me, and having found Me in yourselves, you will rule over worlds, and looking out from the great world within to the little world without, you will bless everything that is, and find all is well with time and with you. KRISHNA.

To make my thoughts clear to you I must go farther back. We do not, cannot, and I venture to say need not, know how men lived millions of years ago or even ten thousand years ago, but we do know positively that, as far back as we have any knowledge of mankind, it has always lived in special groups of families, tribes, and nations in which the majority, in the conviction that it must be so, submissively and willingly bowed to the rule of one or more persons—that is to a very small minority. Despite all varieties of circumstances and personalities these relations manifested themselves among the various peoples of whose origin we have any knowledge; and the farther back we go the more absolutely necessary did this arrangement appear, both to the rulers and the ruled, to make it possible for people to live peacefully together.

So it was everywhere. But though this external form of life existed for centuries and still exists, very early—thousands of years before our time—amid this life based on coercion, one and the same thought constantly emerged among different nations, namely, that in every individual a spiritual element is manifested that gives life to all that exists, and that this spiritual element strives to unite with everything of a like nature to itself, and attains this aim through love. This thought appeared in most various forms at different times and places, with varying completeness and clarity. It found expression in Brahmanism, Judaism, Mazdaism (the teachings of Zoroaster), in Buddhism, Taoism, Confucianism, and in the writings of the Greek and Roman sages, as well as in Christianity and Mohammedanism. The mere fact that this thought has sprung up among different nations and at different times indicates that it is inherent in human nature and contains the truth. But this truth was made known to people who considered that a community could only be kept together if some of them restrained others, and so it appeared quite irreconcilable with the existing order of society. Moreover it was at first expressed only fragmentarily, and so obscurely that though people admitted its theoretic truth they could not entirely accept it as guidance for their conduct. Then, too, the dissemination of the truth in a society based on coercion was always hindered in one and the same manner, namely, those in power, feeling that the recognition of this truth would undermine their position, consciously or sometimes unconsciously perverted it by explanations and additions quite foreign to it, and also opposed it by open violence. Thus the truth—that his life should be directed by the spiritual element which is its basis, which manifests itself as love, and which is so natural to man—this truth, in order to force a way to man's consciousness, had to struggle not merely against the obscurity with which it was expressed and the intentional and unintentional distortions surrounding it, but also against deliberate violence, which by means of persecutions and punishments sought to compel men to accept religious laws authorized by the rulers and conflicting with the truth. Such a hindrance and misrepresentation of the truth—which had not yet achieved complete clarity—occurred everywhere: in Confucianism and Taoism, in Buddhism and in Christianity, in Mohammedanism and in your Brahmanism.

III

My hand has sowed love everywhere, giving unto all that will receive. Blessings are offered unto all My children, but many times in their blindness they fail to see them. How few there are who gather the gifts which lie in profusion at their feet: how many there are, who, in wilful waywardness, turn their eyes away from them and complain with a wail that they have not that which I have given them; many of them defiantly repudiate not only My gifts, but Me also, Me, the Source of all blessings and the Author of their being. KRISHNA.

I tarry awhile from the turmoil and strife of the world. I will beautify and quicken thy life with love and with joy, for the light of the soul is Love. Where Love is, there is contentment and peace, and where there is contentment and peace, there am I, also, in their midst. KRISHNA.

The aim of the sinless One consists in acting without causing sorrow to others, although he could attain to great power by ignoring their feelings.

The aim of the sinless One lies in not doing evil unto those who have done evil unto him.

If a man causes suffering even to those who hate him without any reason, he will ultimately have grief not to be overcome.

The punishment of evil doers consists in making them feel ashamed of themselves by doing them a great kindness.

Of what use is superior knowledge in the one, if he does not endeavour to relieve his neighbour's want as much as his own?

If, in the morning, a man wishes to do evil unto another, in the evening the evil will return to him.

THE HINDU KURAL.

Thus it went on everywhere. The recognition that love represents the highest morality was nowhere denied or contradicted, but this truth was so interwoven everywhere with all kinds of falsehoods which distorted it, that finally nothing of it remained but words. It was taught that this highest morality was only applicable to private life—for home use, as it were—but that in public life all forms of violence—such as imprisonment, executions, and wars—might be used for the protection of the majority against a minority of evildoers, though such means were diametrically opposed to any vestige of love. And though common sense indicated that if some men claim to decide who is to be subjected to violence of all kinds for the benefit of others, these men to whom violence is applied may, in turn, arrive at a similar conclusion with regard to those who have employed violence to them, and though the great religious teachers of Brahmanism, Buddhism, and above all of Christianity, foreseeing such a perversion of the law of love, have constantly drawn attention to the one invariable condition of love (namely, the enduring of injuries, insults, and violence of all kinds without resisting evil by evil) people continued—regardless of all that leads man forward—to try to unite the incompatibles: the virtue of love, and what is opposed to love, namely, the restraining of evil by violence. And such a teaching, despite its inner contradiction, was so firmly established that the very people who recognize love as a virtue accept as lawful at the same time an order of life based on violence and allowing men not merely to torture but even to kill one another.

For a long time people lived in this obvious contradiction without noticing it. But a time arrived when this contradiction became more and more evident to thinkers of various nations. And the old and simple truth that it is natural for men to help and to love one another, but not to torture and to kill one another, became ever clearer, so that fewer and fewer people were able to believe the sophistries by which the distortion of the truth had been made so plausible.

In former times the chief method of justifying the use of violence and thereby infringing the law of love was by claiming a divine right for the rulers: the Tsars, Sultans, Rajahs, Shahs, and other heads of states. But the longer humanity lived the weaker grew the belief in this peculiar, God—given right of the ruler. That belief withered in the same way and almost simultaneously in the Christian and the Brahman world, as well as in Buddhist and Confucian spheres, and in recent times it has so faded away as to prevail no longer against man's reasonable understanding and the true religious feeling. People saw more and more clearly, and now the majority see quite clearly, the senselessness and immorality of subordinating their wills to those of other people just like themselves, when they are bidden to do what is contrary not only to their interests but also to their moral sense. And so one might suppose that having lost confidence in any religious authority for a belief in the divinity of potentates of various kinds, people would try to free themselves from subjection to it. But unfortunately not only were the rulers, who were considered supernatural beings, benefited by having the peoples in subjection, but as a result of the belief in, and during the rule of, these pseudodivine beings, ever larger and larger circles of people grouped and established themselves around them, and under an appearance of governing took advantage of the people. And when the old deception of a supernatural and God-appointed authority had dwindled away these men were only concerned to devise a new one which like its predecessor should make it possible to hold the people in bondage to a limited number of rulers.

IV

Children, do you want to know by what your hearts should be guided?
Throw aside your longings and strivings after that which is null and void; get rid
of your erroneous thoughts about happiness and wisdom, and your empty and
insincere desires. Dispense with these and you will know Love. KRISHNA.

Be not the destroyers of yourselves. Arise to your true Being, and then you
will have nothing to fear. KRISHNA.

New justifications have now appeared in place of the antiquated, obsolete, religious ones. These new justifications are just as inadequate as the old ones, but as they are new their futility cannot immediately be recognized by the majority of men. Besides this, those who enjoy power propagate these new sophistries and support them so skilfully that they seem irrefutable even to many of those who suffer from the oppression these theories seek to justify. These new justifications are termed 'scientific'. But by the term 'scientific' is understood just what was formerly understood by the term 'religious': just as formerly everything called 'religious' was held to be unquestionable simply because it was called religious, so now all that is called 'scientific' is held to be unquestionable. In the present case the obsolete religious justification of violence which consisted in the recognition of the supernatural personality of the God-ordained ruler ('there is no power but of God') has been superseded by the 'scientific' justification which puts forward, first, the assertion that because the coercion of man by man has existed in all ages, it follows that such coercion must continue to exist. This assertion that people should continue to live as they have done throughout past ages rather than as their reason and conscience indicate, is what 'science' calls 'the historic law'. A further 'scientific' justification lies in the statement that as among plants and wild beasts there is a constant struggle for existence which always results in the survival of the fittest, a similar struggle should be carried on among human beings—beings, that is, who are gifted with intelligence and love; faculties lacking in the creatures subject to the struggle for existence and survival of the fittest. Such is the second 'scientific' justification.

The third, most important, and unfortunately most widespread justification is, at bottom, the age-old religious one just a little altered: that in public life the suppression of some for the protection of the majority cannot be avoided—so that coercion is unavoidable however desirable reliance on love alone might be in human intercourse. The only difference in this justification by pseudo-science consists in the fact that, to the question why such and such people and not others have the right to decide against whom violence may and must be used, pseudo-science now gives a different reply to that given by religion—which declared that the right to decide was valid because it was pronounced by persons possessed of divine power. 'Science' says that these decisions represent the will of the people, which under a constitutional form of government is supposed to find expression in all the decisions and actions of those who are at the helm at the moment.

Such are the scientific justifications of the principle of coercion. They are not merely weak but absolutely invalid, yet they are so much needed by those who occupy privileged positions that they believe in them as blindly as they formerly believed in the immaculate conception, and propagate them just as confidently. And the unfortunate majority of men bound to toil is so dazzled by the pomp with which these 'scientific truths' are presented, that under this new influence it accepts these scientific stupidities for holy truth, just as it formerly accepted the pseudo-religious justifications; and it continues to submit to the present holders of power who are just as hard-hearted but rather more numerous than before.

V

Who am I? I am that which thou hast searched for since thy baby eyes gazed wonderingly upon the world, whose horizon hides this real life from thee. I am that which in thy heart thou hast prayed for, demanded as thy birthright, although thou hast not known what it was. I am that which has lain in thy soul for hundreds and thousands of years. Sometimes I lay in thee grieving because thou didst not recognize me; sometimes I raised my head, opened my eyes, and extended my arms calling thee either tenderly and quietly, or strenuously, demanding that thou shouldst rebel against the iron chains which bound thee to the earth.

KRISHNA.

So matters went on, and still go on, in the Christian world. But we might have hope that in the immense Brahman, Buddhist, and Confucian worlds this new scientific superstition would not establish itself, and that the Chinese, Japanese, and Hindus, once their eyes were opened to the religious fraud justifying violence, would advance directly to a recognition of the law of love inherent in humanity, and which had been so forcibly enunciated by the great Eastern teachers. But what has happened is that the scientific superstition replacing the religious one has been accepted and secured a stronger and stronger hold in the East.

In your periodical you set out as the basic principle which should guide the actions of your people the maxim that: 'Resistance to aggression is not simply justifiable but imperative, nonresistance hurts both Altruism and Egotism.'

Love is the only way to rescue humanity from all ills, and in it you too have the only method of saving your people from enslavement. In very ancient times love was proclaimed with special strength and clearness among your people to be the religious basis of human life. Love, and forcible resistance to evil-doers, involve such a mutual contradiction as to destroy utterly the whole sense and meaning of the conception of love. And what follows? With a light heart and in the twentieth century you, an adherent of a religious people, deny their law, feeling convinced of your scientific enlightenment and your right to do so, and you repeat (do not take this amiss) the amazing stupidity indoctrinated in you by the advocates of the use of violence—the enemies of truth, the servants first of theology and then of science—your European teachers.

You say that the English have enslaved your people and hold them in subjection because the latter have not resisted resolutely enough and have not met force by force.

But the case is just the opposite. If the English have enslaved the people of India it is just because the latter recognized, and still recognize, force as the fundamental principle of the social order. In accord with that principle they submitted to their little rajahs, and on their behalf struggled against one another, fought the Europeans, the English, and are now trying to fight with them again.

A commercial company enslaved a nation comprising two hundred millions. Tell this to a man free from superstition and he will fail to grasp what these words mean. What does it mean that thirty thousand men, not athletes but rather weak and ordinary people, have subdued two hundred million vigorous, clever, capable, and freedom-loving people? Do not the figures make it clear that it is not the English who have enslaved the Indians, but the Indians who have enslaved themselves?

When the Indians complain that the English have enslaved them it is as if drunkards complained that the spirit-dealers who have settled among them have enslaved them. You tell them that they might give up drinking, but they reply that they are so accustomed to it that they cannot abstain, and that they must have alcohol to keep up their energy. Is it not the same thing with the millions of people who submit to thousands' or even to hundreds, of others—of their own or other nations?

If the people of India are enslaved by violence it is only because they themselves live and have lived by violence, and do not recognize the eternal law of love inherent in humanity.

Pitiful and foolish is the man who seeks what he already has, and does not know that he has it. Yes, Pitiful and foolish is he who does not know the bliss of love which surrounds him and which I have given him. KRISHNA.

As soon as men live entirely in accord with the law of love natural to their hearts and now revealed to them, which excludes all resistance by violence, and therefore hold aloof from all participation in violence—as soon as this happens, not only will hundreds be unable to enslave millions, but not even millions will be able to enslave a single individual. Do not resist the evil-doer and take no part in doing so, either in the violent deeds of the administration, in the law courts, the collection of taxes, or above all in soldiering, and no one in the world will be able to enslave you.

VI

O ye who sit in bondage and continually seek and pant for freedom, seek only for love. Love is peace in itself and peace which gives complete satisfaction. I am the key that opens the portal to the rarely discovered land where contentment alone is found. KRISHNA.

What is now happening to the people of the East as of the West is like what happens to every individual when he passes from childhood to adolescence and from youth to manhood. He loses what had hitherto guided his life and lives without direction, not having found a new standard suitable to his age, and so he invents all sorts of occupations, cares, distractions, and stupefactions to divert his attention from the misery and senselessness of his life. Such a condition may last a long time.

When an individual passes from one period of life to another a time comes when he cannot go on in senseless activity and excitement as before, but has to understand that although he has outgrown what before used to direct him, this does not mean that he must live without any reasonable guidance, but rather that he must formulate for himself an understanding of life corresponding to his age, and having elucidated it must be guided by it. And in the same way a similar time must come in the growth and development of humanity. I believe that such a time has now arrived—not in the sense that it has come in the year 1908, but that the inherent contradiction of human life has now reached an extreme degree of tension: on the one side there is the consciousness of the beneficence of the law of love, and on the other the existing order of life which has for centuries occasioned an empty, anxious, restless, and troubled mode of life, conflicting as it does with the law of love and built on the use of violence. This contradiction must be faced, and the solution will evidently not be favourable to the outlived law of violence, but to the truth which has dwelt in the hearts of men from remote antiquity: the truth that the law of love is in accord with the nature of man.

But men can only recognize this truth to its full extent when they have completely freed themselves from all religious and scientific superstitions and from all the consequent misrepresentations and sophistical distortions by which its recognition has been hindered for centuries.

To save a sinking ship it is necessary to throw overboard the ballast, which though it may once have been needed would now cause the ship to sink. And so it is with the scientific superstition which hides the truth of their welfare from mankind. In order that men should embrace the truth—not in the vague way they did in childhood, nor in the one-sided and perverted way presented to them by their religious and scientific teachers, but embrace it as their highest law—the complete liberation of this truth from all and every superstition (both pseudo-religious and pseudo-scientific) by which it is still obscured is essential: not a partial, timid attempt, reckoning with traditions sanctified by age and with the habits of the people—not such as was effected in the religious sphere by Guru-Nanak, the founder of the sect of the Sikhs, and in the Christian world by Luther, and by similar reformers in other religions—but a fundamental cleansing of religious consciousness from all ancient religious and modern scientific superstitions.

If only people freed themselves from their beliefs in all kinds of Ormuzds, Brahmas, Sabbaoths, and their incarnation as Krishnas and Christs, from beliefs in Paradises and Hells, in reincarnations and resurrections, from belief in the interference of the Gods in the external affairs of the universe, and above all, if they freed themselves from belief in the infallibility of all the various Vedas, Bibles, Gospels, Tripitakas, Korans, and the like, and also freed themselves from blind belief in a variety of scientific teachings about infinitely small atoms and molecules and in all the infinitely great and infinitely remote worlds, their movements and origin, as well as from faith in the infallibility of the scientific law to which humanity is at present subjected: the historic law, the economic laws, the law of struggle and survival, and so on—if people only freed themselves from this terrible accumulation of futile exercises of our lower capacities of mind and memory called the 'Sciences', and from the innumerable divisions of all sorts of histories, anthropologies, homiletics, bacteriologics, jurisprudences, cosmographies, strategies—their name is legion—and freed themselves from all this harmful, stupifying ballast—the simple law of love, natural to man, accessible to all and solving all questions and perplexities, would of itself become clear and obligatory.

VII

Children, look at the flowers at your feet; do not trample upon them. Look at the love in your midst and do not repudiate it. KRISHNA.

There is a higher reason which transcends all human minds. It is far and near. It permeates all the worlds and at the same time is infinitely higher than they.

A man who sees that all things are contained in the higher spirit cannot treat any being with contempt.

For him to whom all spiritual beings are equal to the highest there can be no room for deception or grief.

Those who are ignorant and are devoted to the religious rites only, are in a deep gloom, but those who are given up to fruitless meditations are in a still greater darkness.

UPANISHADS, FROM VEDAS.

Yes, in our time all these things must be cleared away in order that mankind may escape from self-inflicted calamities that have reached an extreme intensity. Whether an Indian seeks liberation from subjection to the English, or anyone else struggles with an oppressor either of his own nationality or of another—whether it be a Negro defending himself against the North Americans; or Persians, Russians, or Turks against the Persian, Russian, or Turkish governments, or any man seeking the greatest welfare for himself and for everybody else—they do not need explanations and justifications of old religious superstitions such as have been formulated by your Vivekanandas, Baba Bharatis, and others, or in the Christian world by a number of similar interpreters and exponents of things that nobody needs; nor the innumerable scientific theories about matters not only unnecessary but for the most part harmful. (In the spiritual realm nothing is indifferent: what is not useful is harmful.) What are wanted for the Indian as for the Englishman, the Frenchman, the German, and the Russian, are not Constitutions and Revolutions, nor all sorts of Conferences and Congresses, nor the many ingenious devices for submarine navigation and aerial navigation, nor powerful explosives, nor all sorts of conveniences to add to the enjoyment of the rich, ruling classes; nor new schools and universities with innumerable faculties of science, nor an augmentation of papers and books, nor gramophones and cinematographs, nor those childish and for the most part corrupt stupidities termed art—but one thing only is needful: the knowledge of the simple and clear truth which finds place in every soul that is not stupefied by religious and scientific superstitions—the truth that for our life one law is valid—the law of love, which brings the highest happiness to every individual as well as to all mankind. Free your minds from those overgrown, mountainous imbecilities which hinder your recognition of it, and at once the truth will emerge from amid the pseudo-religious nonsense that has been smothering it: the indubitable, eternal truth inherent in man, which is one and the same in all the great religions of the world. It will in due time emerge and make its way to general recognition, and the nonsense that has obscured it will disappear of itself, and with it will go the evil from which humanity now suffers.

Children, look upwards with your beclouded eyes, and a world full of joy and love will disclose itself to you, a rational world made by My wisdom, the only real world. Then you will know what love has done with you, what love has bestowed upon you, what love demands from you. KRISHNA.

YASNAYA POLYANA.

December 14th, 1908.

THE AWAKENING: THE RESURRECTION

PART FIRST.

CHAPTER I.

All the efforts of several hundred thousand people, crowded in a small space, to disfigure the land on which they lived; all the stone they covered it with to keep it barren; how so diligently every sprouting blade of grass was removed; all the smoke of coal and naphtha; all the cutting down of trees and driving off of cattle could not shut out the spring, even from the city. The sun was shedding its light; the grass, revivified, was blooming forth, where it was left uncut, not only on the greenswards of the boulevard, but between the flag-stones, and the birches, poplars and wild-berry trees were unfolding their viscous leaves; the limes were unfolding their buds; the daws, sparrows and pigeons were joyfully making their customary nests, and the flies were buzzing on the sun-warmed walls. Plants, birds, insects and children were equally joyful. Only men—grown-up men—continued cheating and tormenting themselves and each other. People saw nothing holy in this spring morning, in this beauty of God's world—a gift to all living creatures—inclining to peace, good-will and love, but worshiped their own inventions for imposing their will on each other.

The joy of spring felt by animals and men did not penetrate the office of the county jail, but the one thing of supreme importance there was a document received the previous evening, with title, number and seal, which ordered the bringing into court for trial, this 28th day of April, at nine o'clock in the morning, three prisoners—two women and one man. One of the women, as the more dangerous criminal, was to be brought separately. So, in pursuance of that order, on the 28th day of April, at eight o'clock in the morning, the jail warden entered the dingy corridor of the woman's ward. Immediately behind him came a woman with weary countenance and disheveled gray hair, wearing a crown-laced jacket, and girdled with a blue-edged sash. She was the matron.

"You want Maslova?" she asked the warden, as they neared one of the cells opening into the corridor.

The warden, with a loud clanking of iron, unlocked and opened the door of the cell, releasing an even fouler odor than permeated the corridor, and shouted:

"Maslova to the court!" and again closing the door he waited for her appearance.

The fresh, vivifying air of the fields, carried to the city by the wind, filled even the court-yard of the jail. But in the corridor the oppressive air, laden with the smell of tar and putrescence, saddened and dejected the spirit of every new-comer. The same feeling was experienced by the jail matron, notwithstanding she was accustomed to bad air. On entering the corridor she suddenly felt a weariness coming over her that inclined her to slumber.

There was a bustling in the cell; women's voices and steps of bare feet were heard.

"Hurry up, Maslova! Come on, I say!" shouted the warden into the cell-door.

Presently at the cell-door appeared a middle-sized, full-breasted young woman, dressed in a long, gray coat over a white waist and skirt. She approached with firm step, and, facing about, stood before the warden. Over her linen stockings she wore jail shoes; her head was covered with a white 'kerchief, from under which black curls were evidently purposely brushed over the forehead. The face of the woman was of that whiteness peculiar to people who have been a long time in confinement, and which reminds one of potato-sprouts in a cellar. Her small, wide hands, her white, full neck, showing from under the large collar of the coat, were of a similar hue. On the dull pallor of that face the most striking feature was the black, sparkling eyes, somewhat swollen, but very bright eyes, one of which slightly squinted. She held herself erect, putting forth her full chest. Emerging into the corridor, throwing her head back a little, she looked into the eyes of the warden and stood ready to do his bidding. The warden was about to shut the door, when a pale, severe, wrinkled face of an old woman with disheveled hair was thrust out. The old woman began to say something to Maslova. But the warden pressed the door against the head of the woman, and she disappeared. In the cell a woman's voice burst into laughter. Maslova also smiled, and turned to the grated little opening in the door. The old woman pressed her forehead to the grating, and said in a hoarse voice:

"Above all, don't speak too much; stick to one thing, and that is all."

"Of course. It cannot be any worse," said Maslova.

"You certainly cannot stick to two things," said the chief warden, with official assurance of his own wit. "Follow me, now! Forward! March!"

The eye looking from behind the grating disappeared, and Maslova took to the middle of the corridor, and with short, but rapid strides, followed the warden. They descended the stone stairway, and as they passed the men's ward, noisy and more noisome even than the woman's ward, scores of eyes followed them from behind the gratings. They entered the office, where an armed escort of two soldiers stood. The clerk handed one of the soldiers a document, reeking of tobacco smoke, and, pointing to the prisoner, said:

"Take her."

The soldier, a Nijhni peasant with a red and pock-marked face, placed the paper into the cuff of his coat sleeve, and, smiling, winked to his muscular comrade. The soldiers and prisoner descended the stairs and went in the direction of the main entrance.

A small door in the gate opened, and, crossing the threshold, they passed through the inclosure and took the middle of the paved street.

Drivers, shop-keepers, kitchen maids, laborers and officials halted and gazed with curiosity at the prisoner. Some shook their heads and thought: "There is the result of evil conduct—how unlike ours!" Children looked with horror at the cut-throat, but the presence of the soldiers reassured them, for she was now powerless to do harm. A villager, returning from the mart, where he had disposed of his charcoal and visited an inn, offered her a kopeck. The prisoner blushed, drooped her head and murmured something.

Conscious of the attention that was shown her, without turning her head she looked askance at the onlookers and rather enjoyed it. She also enjoyed the comparatively pure spring air, but the walking on the cobblestones was painful to her feet, unused as they were to walking, and shod in clumsy prison shoes. She looked at her feet and endeavored to step as lightly as possible. Passing by a food store, in front of which some pigeons were picking grain, she came near striking with her foot a dove-colored bird. It rose with a flutter of its wings, and flew past the very ear of the prisoner, fanning her face with its wings. She smiled, then sighed deeply, remembering her own condition.

CHAPTER II.

The history of the prisoner Maslova was a very common one. Maslova was the daughter of an unmarried menial who lived with her mother, a cowherd, on the estate of two spinsters. This unmarried woman gave birth to a child every year, and, as is the custom in the villages, baptized them; then neglected the troublesome newcomers, and they finally starved to death.

Thus five children died. Every one of these was baptized, then it starved and finally died. The sixth child, begotten of a passing gypsy, was a girl, who would have shared the same fate, but it happened that one of the two old maidens entered the cow-shed to reprimand the milkmaids for carelessness in skimming the cream, and there saw the mother with the healthy and beautiful child. The old maiden chided them for the cream and for permitting the woman to lie in the cow-shed, and was on the point of departing, but noticing the child, was moved to pity, and afterward consented to stand godmother to the child. She baptized the child, and in pity for her god-daughter, furnished her with milk, gave the mother some money, and the babe thrived. Wherefore the old maidens called it "the saved one."

The child was three years old when the mother fell ill and died. She was a great burden to her grandmother, so the old maidens adopted her. The dark-eyed girl became unusually lively and pretty, and her presence cheered them.

Of the two old maidens, the younger one—Sophia Ivanovna—was the kindlier, while the older one—Maria Ivanovna—was of austere disposition. Sophia Ivanovna kept the girl in decent clothes, taught her to read and intended to give her an education. Maria Ivanovna said that the girl ought to be taught to work that she might become a useful servant, was exacting, punished, and even beat her when in bad humor. Under such conditions the girl grew up half servant, half lady. Her position was reflected even in her name, for she was not called by the gentle Katinka, nor yet by the disdainful Katka, but Katiousha, which stands sentimentally between the two. She sewed, cleaned the rooms, cleaned the ikons with chalk, ground, cooked and served coffee, washed, and sometimes she read for the ladies.

She was wooed, but would marry no one, feeling that life with any one of her wooers would be hard, spoiled, as she was, more or less, by the comparative ease she enjoyed in the manor.

She had just passed her sixteenth year when the ladies were visited by their nephew, a rich student, and Katiousha, without daring to confess it to him, or even to herself, fell in love with him. Two years afterward, while on his way to the war, he again visited his aunts, and during his four days' stay, consummated her ruin. Before his departure he thrust a hundred ruble bill into her hand.

Thenceforward life ceased to have any charms for her, and her only thought was to escape the shame which awaited her, and not only did she become lax in her duties, but—and she did not know herself how it happened—all of a sudden she gave vent to her ill temper. She said some rude things to the ladies, of which she afterward repented, and left them.

Dissatisfied with her behavior, they did not detain her. She then obtained employment as servant in the house of the commissary of rural police, but was obliged to give up the position at the end of the third month, for the commissary, a fifty-year old man, pursued her with his attentions, and when, on one occasion, he became too persistent, she flared up, called him an old fool, and threw him to the ground. Then she was driven from the house. She was now so far advanced on the road to maternity that to look for a position was out of the question. Hence she took lodgings with an old midwife, who was also a wine dealer. The confinement came off painlessly. But the midwife was attending a sick woman in the village, infected Katiousha with puerperal fever, and the child, a boy, was taken to a foundling asylum where, she was told, he died immediately after his arrival there.

When Katiousha took lodgings with the midwife she had 127 rubles; 27 rubles of which she had earned, and 100 rubles which had been given her by her seducer. When she left her she had but six rubles left. She was not economical, and spent on herself as well as others. She paid 40 rubles to the midwife for two months' board; 25 rubles it cost her to have the child taken away; 40 rubles the midwife borrowed of her to buy a cow with; the balance was spent on dresses, presents, etc., so that after the confinement she was practically penniless, and was compelled to look for a position. She was soon installed in the house of a forester who was married, and who, like the commissary, began to pay court to her. His wife became aware of it, and when, on one occasion, she found them both in the room, she fell on Katiousha and began to beat her. The latter resented it, and the result was a scrimmage, after which she was driven out of the house, without being paid the wages due her. Katiousha went to the city, where she stopped with her aunt. Her aunt's husband was a bookbinder. Formerly he used to earn a competence, but had lost his customers, and was now given to drink, spending everything that came into his hands.

With the aid of a small laundry she was keeping, her aunt supported her children as well as her husband. She offered Maslova work as a washerwoman, but seeing what a hard life the washerwomen at her aunt's establishment were leading, she searched through the intelligence offices for a position as servant. She found such a place with a lady who was living with her two student boys. A week after she had entered upon her duties, the oldest son neglected his studies and made life miserable for Maslova. The mother threw all blame upon Maslova and discharged her. She was some time without any occupation. In one of these intelligence offices she once met a lady richly dressed and adorned with diamonds. This lady, learning of the condition of Maslova, who was looking for a position, gave her her card and invited her to call. The lady received Maslova affectionately, treated her to choice cakes and sweet wine, while she dispatched her servant somewhere with a note. In the evening a tall man with long hair just turning gray, and gray beard, came into the room. The old man immediately seated himself beside Maslova and began to jest. The hostess called him into an adjoining room, and Maslova overheard her say: "As fresh as a rose; just from the country." Then the hostess called in Maslova and told her that the man was an author, very rich, and will be very generous if he takes a liking to her. He did take a liking to her, gave her twenty-five rubles, and promised to call on her often. The money was soon spent in settling for her board at her aunt's, for a new dress, hat and ribbons. A few days afterward the author sent for her a second time. She called. He gave her another twenty-five ruble bill and offered to rent apartments for her where she could reside separately.

While living in the apartments rented by the author, Maslova became infatuated with a jolly clerk living in the same house. She herself told the author of her infatuation, and moved into a smaller apartment. The clerk, who had promised to marry her, without saying anything, left for Nijhni, evidently casting her off, and Maslova remained alone. She wished to remain in the apartment, but the landlord would not permit a single woman to occupy it, and she returned to her aunt. Her fashionable dress, cape and hat won her the respect of her aunt, who no longer dared to offer her work as a washerwoman, considering her present position far above it. The question of working in the laundry did not even occur to Maslova now. She looked with compassion on the life of drudgery led by these pale, emaciated washerwomen, some of whom showed symptoms of consumption, washing and ironing in a stifling, steam-laden atmosphere with the windows open summer and winter, and she was horrified at the thought that she, too, might be driven to such drudgery.

Maslova had for a long time been addicted to cigarette smoking, but of late she had been getting more and more accustomed to drink. The wine attracted her, not because of its taste, but because it enabled her to forget her past life, to comfort herself with ease, and the confidence of her own worth that it gave her. Without wine she was despondent and abashed. There was the choice of two things before her; either the humiliating occupation of a servant, with the certain unwelcome attentions of the men, or a secure, quiet and legitimatized position of everybody's mistress. She wished to revenge herself on her seducer, as well as the clerk, and all those that brought misfortune upon her. Besides, she could not withstand the temptation of having all the dresses her heart desired—dresses made of velvet, gauze and silk—ball dresses, with open neck and short sleeves. And when Maslova imagined herself in a bright yellow silk dress, with velvet trimmings, decolette, she made her choice.

From this day on Maslova began to lead a life to which hundreds of thousands of women are driven, and which, in nine cases out of ten, ends in painful disease, premature decrepitude and death.

After a night's orgies there would come a deep slumber till three or four o'clock in the afternoon; then the weary rising from a dirty couch; seltzer-water to remove the effect of excessive drinking, coffee. Then came the sauntering through the rooms in dressing-gown, looking through the windows; the languid quarrels; then the perfuming of her body and hair, the trying on of dresses, and the quarrels with the mistress which they occasioned; contemplating herself in the mirror, rouging her face, darkening her eyebrows. Then came the sweet, rich food, the bright silk dress, the entry into the brightly lighted parlor, the arrival of the guests, music, dancing, confectionery, wine and cigarettes.

Thus Maslova lived for seven years. On the eighth, when she had reached her twenty-sixth year, there happened that for which she had been jailed, and for which she was now led to the court, after six months of confinement among thieves and murderers.

CHAPTER III.

At the time when Maslova, exhausted by the long walk, was approaching with the armed convoy the building in which court was held, the same nephew of the ladies that brought her up, Prince Dmitri Ivanovitch Nekhludoff, who deceived her, lay on his high, soft, spring feather-bed, in spotless Holland linen, smoking a cigarette. He was gazing before him, contemplating the events of the previous day and considering what he had before him for that day. As he thought of the previous evening, spent at the Korchagins, a wealthy and influential family, whose daughter, rumor had it, he was to marry, he sighed, and throwing away the butt of his cigarette, he was on the point of taking another from the silver cigarette holder, but changed his mind. Half rising, he slipped his smooth, white feet into the slippers, threw a silk morning gown over his broad shoulders, and with quick and heavy stride, walked into the adjoining dressing-room, which was permeated with the artificial odors of elixirs, perfumes, cosmetics. There he washed his partly gold-filled teeth with a tooth-powder, rinsed them with a perfumed mouth-wash, then began to sponge himself and dry his body with Turkish towels. After washing his hands with perfumed soap, carefully brushing his trimmed nails and washing his face and stout neck in a marble basin, he walked into a third room, where a shower-bath was ready. Here he received a cold-water douche, and after rubbing his white and muscular body with coarse towels and donning his white linen, he seated himself before the mirror and began to brush his short, curly beard and the thinning curls of his forehead.

Everything used by him—the linen, clothing, shoes, scarfs, scarf-pins, cuff-buttons, were of the very best quality, simple, tasteful and expensive.

He then picked out the first of a dozen scarfs and pins that came into his hand—it was no more novel and amusing, as it used to be—and he was quite indifferent as to which he put on. He dressed himself in his brushed clothes which lay on the chair and went out, though not quite refreshed, yet clean and fragrant. In the oblong dining-room, the inlaid floor of which had been polished by three of his men the day before, and containing a massive oaken sideboard and a similar extension table, the legs of which were carved in the shape of lion's paws, giving it a pompous appearance, breakfast stood ready for him. A fine, starched cloth with large monograms was spread on the table, on which stood a silver coffee-pot, containing fragrant, steaming coffee, a sugar bowl and cream pitcher to match, fresh rolls and various kinds of biscuits. Beside them lay the last number of the "Revue des deux Mondes," newspapers and his mail. Nekhludoff was about to open the letters, when a middle-aged woman, with a lace head-gear over her unevenly parted hair, glided into the room. This was Agrippina Petrovna, servant of his mother, who died in this very house. She was now stewardess to the son.

Agrippina Petrovna had traveled many years abroad with Nekhludoff's mother, and had acquired the manners of a lady. She had lived in the house of the Nekhludoffs since childhood, and knew Dmitri Ivanovitch when he was called by the diminutive Mitenka.

"Good-morning, Dmitri Ivanovitch."

"How do you do, Agrippina Petrovna? What's the news?" asked Nekhludoff, jesting.

"A letter from the old Princess, or the young one, perhaps. The maid brought it long ago, and is now waiting in my room," said Agrippina Petrovna, handing him the letter with a significant smile.

"Very well; I will attend to it immediately," said Nekhludoff, taking the letter and then, noticing the smile on Agrippina's face, he frowned.

The smile on Agrippina's face signified that the letter came from Princess Korchagin, whom, according to Agrippina Petrovna, he was to marry. And this supposition, expressed by her smile, displeased Nekhludoff.

"Then I will bid her wait," and Agrippina Petrovna glided out of the dining-room, first replacing the crumb-brush, which lay on the table, in its holder.

Nekhludoff opened the perfumed letter and began to read:

"In fulfillment of the duty I assumed of being your memory," the letter ran, "I call to your mind that you have been summoned to serve as juror to-day, the 28th of April, and that, therefore, you cannot accompany us and Kolosoff to the art exhibition, as you promised yesterday in your customary forgetfulness; à moins que vous ne soyez disposé à payer à la cour d'assises les 300 rubles d'amende que vous vous refusez pour votre cheval, for your failure to appear in time. I remembered it yesterday, when you had left. So keep it in mind.

"Princess M. Korchagin."

On the other side was a postscript:

"Maman vous fait dire que votre couvert vous attendra jusqu' à la nuit. Venez absolument à quelle heure que cela soit. M. K."

Nekhludoff knit his brows. The note was the continuation of a skillful strategem whereby the Princess sought, for the last two months, to fasten him with invisible bonds. But Nekhludoff, besides the usual irresoluteness before marriage of people of his age, and who are not passionately in love, had an important reason for withholding his offer of marriage for the time being. The reason was not that ten years before he had ruined and abandoned Katiousha, which incident he had entirely forgotten, but that at this very time he was sustaining relations with a married woman, and though he now considered them at an end, they were not so considered by her.

In the presence of women, Nekhludoff was very shy, but it was this very shyness that determined the married woman to conquer him. This woman was the wife of the commander of the district in which Nekhludoff was one of the electors. She led him into relations with her which held him fast, and at the same time grew more and more repulsive to him. At first Nekhludoff could not resist her wiles, then, feeling himself at fault, he could not break off the relations against her will. This was the reason why Nekhludoff considered that he had no right, even if he desired, to ask for the hand of Korchagin. A letter from the husband of that woman happened to lay on the table. Recognizing the handwriting and the stamp, Nekhludoff flushed and immediately felt an influx of that energy which he always experienced in the face of danger. But there was no cause for his agitation; the husband, as commander of the district where Nekhludoff's estates were situated, informed the latter of a special meeting of the local governing body, and asked him to be present without fail, and donner un coup d'épaule in the important measures to be submitted concerning the schools and roads, and that the reactionary party was expected to offer strong opposition.

The commander was a liberal-minded man, entirely absorbed with the struggles, and knew nothing about his wretched family life.

Nekhludoff recalled all the tortures this man had occasioned him; how on one occasion he thought that the husband had discovered all, and he was preparing to fight a duel with him, intending to use a blank cartridge, and the ensuing scene where she, in despair, ran to the pond, intending to drown herself, while he ran to search for her. "I cannot go now, and can undertake nothing until I have heard from her," thought Nekhludoff. The preceding week he had written to her a decisive letter, acknowledging his guilt, and expressing his readiness to redeem it in any manner she should suggest, but for her own good, considered their relations ended. It is to this letter that he expected a reply. He considered it a favorable sign that no reply came. If she had not consented to a separation, she would have answered long ago, or would have come personally, as she often did before. Nekhludoff had heard that an army officer was courting her, and while he was tormented by jealousy, he was at the same time gladdened by the hope of release from the oppressive lie.

The other letter was from the steward in charge of his estates. Nekhludoff was requested to return and establish his right to the inheritance and also to decide on the future management of the estates; whether the same system of letting out to the peasants, which prevailed during the lifetime of his mother, was to be continued, or, as the steward had strongly advised the deceased Princess, and now advised the young Prince, to augment the stock and work all the land himself. The steward wrote that the land could thus best be exploited. He also apologized for his failure to send the three thousand rubles due on the first of the month, which he would send by the next mail, explaining it by the difficulty of collecting the rents from the peasants whose bad faith had reached a point where it became necessary to resort to the courts to collect them. This letter was partly agreeable and partly disagreeable to Nekhludoff. It was agreeable to feel the power of authority over so vast an estate, and it was disagreeable, because in his youth he was an enthusiastic adherent of Herbert Spencer, and being himself a large land owner, was struck by the proposition in Social Statics that private ownership of land is contrary to the dictates of justice. With the frankness and boldness of youth, he not only then spoke of the injustice of private ownership of land; not only did he compose theses in the university on the subject, but he actually distributed among the peasants the few hundred acres of land left him by his father, not desiring to own land contrary to his convictions. Now that he found himself the owner of vast estates, he was confronted by two alternatives: either to waive his ownership in favor of the peasants, as he did ten years ago with the two hundred acres, or, by tacit acquiescence, confess that all his former ideas were erroneous and false.

He could not carry out the first, because he possessed no resources outside of the land. He did not wish to go into service, and yet he had luxurious habits of life which he thought he could not abandon. Indeed, there was no necessity of abandoning these habits, since he had lost the strength of conviction as well as the resolution, the vanity and the desire to astonish people that he had possessed in his youth. The other alternative—to reject all the arguments against private ownership of land which he gathered from Spencer's Social Statics, and of which he found confirmation in the works of Henry George—he could follow even less.

For this reason the steward's letter was disagreeable to him.

CHAPTER IV.

Having breakfasted, Nekhludoff went to the cabinet to see for what hour he was summoned to appear at court, and to answer the Princess' note. In the work-room stood an easel with a half-finished painting turned face downward, and on the wall hung studies in drawing. On seeing that painting, on which he had worked two years, and those drawings, he called to mind the feeling of impotence, which he experienced of late with greatest force, to make further advance in the art. He explained this feeling by the development of a fine aesthetic taste, and yet this consciousness caused him unpleasant sensations.

Seven years before he had retired from active service he decided that his true vocation in life was painting, and from the height of his artistic activity he looked down upon all other occupations. And now it appeared that he had no right to do so, and every recollection of it was disagreeable to him. He looked on all the luxurious appointments of the work-room with heavy heart, and walked into the cabinet in ill humor. The cabinet was a high room, profusely ornamented, and containing every imaginable device of comfort and necessity.

He produced from one of the drawers of a large table the summons, and, ascertaining that he must appear at eleven o'clock, he sat down and wrote to the Princess, thanking her for the invitation, and saying that he should try to call for dinner. The tone of the note seemed to him too intimate, and he tore it up; he wrote another, but that was too formal, almost offensive. Again he tore it up, and touched a button on the wall. A servant, morose, with flowing side-whiskers and in a gray apron, entered.

"Please send for a carriage."

"Yes, sir."

"And tell the Korchagins' maid that I thank them; I will try to call."

"Yes, sir."

"It is impolite, but I cannot write. But I will see her to-day," thought Nckhludoff, and started to dress himself.

When he emerged from the house a carriage with rubber tires awaited him.

"You had scarcely left Prince Korchagin's house yesterday when I called for you," said the driver, half-turning his stout, sun-burned neck in the white collar of his shirt, "and the footman said that you had just gone."

"Even the drivers know of my relations to the Korchagins," thought Nekhludoff, and the unsolved question which continually occupied his mind of late—whether or not he ought to marry Princess Korchagin—again occurred to him, and, like most questions that he was called upon to decide at that time, it remained unsolved.

He had many reasons for, and as many against, marriage. There was the pleasure of domestic life, which made it possible to lead a moral life, as he called married life; then, and principally, the family and children would infuse his present aimless life with a purpose. This was for marriage generally. On the other hand there was, first, the loss of freedom which all elderly bachelors fear so much; and, second, an unconscious awe of that mysterious creature, woman.

However, in favor of marrying Missy in particular (Korchagin's name was Maria, but, as usual in families of the higher classes, she received a nickname) there was, first, the fact that she came of good stock, and was in everything, from her dress to her manner of speaking, walking and laughing, distinguished not by any exceptional qualities, but by "good breeding"—he knew no other expression for the quality which he prized very highly. Second, she valued him above all other men, hence, he thought she understood him. And this appreciation of him, that is, acknowledging his high qualities, was proof to Nekhludoff of her intelligence and correct judgment. Finally, against marrying Missy in particular, was, first, the extreme probability of his finding a girl of much better qualities than Missy, and, consequently, more worthy of him; and, second, Missy was twenty-seven years old and had probably loved other men before him. This thought tormented him. His pride could not reconcile itself to the thought that she could love some one else, even in the past. Of course, she could not be expected to know that she would meet him, but the very thought that she could have loved some one else before offended him.

So that there were as many reasons for as there were against marriage in general and marrying Missy in particular. At all events the arguments were equally strong on both sides, and Nekhludoff laughed as he compared himself to the ass in the fable who, while deciding which of the two bales of hay before him he should have his meal from, starved himself.

"However, until I have heard from Maria Vasilieona, the wife of the commander, and have done with her for good, I can do nothing," he said to himself.

And the consciousness that he could and must defer his decision pleased him.

"Ah, but I will consider it all later," he said to himself, as his cabriolet silently approached the asphalt pavement of the court-house.

"And now I must do my duty to the community conscientiously, as I always do, and think it one's duty to do. Besides, it is often interesting," he said, and went past the door-keeper into the vestibule of the court.

CHAPTER V.

There was great commotion in the corridors of the court when Nekhludoff entered.

The attendants flitted to and fro breathlessly, delivering orders and documents. Police captains, lawyers and clerks passed now one way, now the other; complainants and defendants under bail leaned sadly against the walls, or were sitting and waiting.

"Where is the Circuit Court?" asked Nekhludoff of one of the attendants.

"Which one? There is a civil division and a criminal one."

"I am a juror."

"Criminal division. You should have said so. This way, to the right, then turn to your left. The second door."

Nekhludoff went as directed.

At the door two men stood waiting. One was a tall, stout merchant, a good-natured man, who had evidently partaken of some liquor and was in very high spirits; the other was a clerk of Jewish extraction. They were talking about the price of wool when Nekhludoff approached them and asked if that was the jury's room.

"Here, sir, here. Are you also one of the jurymen?" mirthfully winking his eyes, the good-natured merchant asked.

"Well, we will drudge together, I suppose," he continued in response to Nekhludoff's affirmative answer. "My name is Baklashoff, merchant of the second guild," he introduced himself, extending his soft, broad hand; "we must do our duty. Whom have I the honor of addressing?"

Nekhludoff gave his name and passed into the jury-room.

In the small jury-room there were about ten men of every description. They had just arrived; some were sitting, others walked about, eyeing, and making each other's acquaintance. One was a retired officer in uniform;

others were in short coats, and but one in peasant garb.

Notwithstanding that they were all complaining that the jury duty was burdensome, and was taking them away from their business, they all seemed to be pleased with the consciousness of performing an important civic duty.

The jurymen talked among themselves of the weather, of the premature spring, of the business before them. Those who were not acquainted with Nekhludoff hastened to become so, evidently considering it an honor. And Nekhludoff, as was usual with him among strangers, received it as his due. If he were asked why he considered himself above the majority of people he would not be able to answer, as there was nothing in his life transcending the commonplace. The fact that he spoke English, French and German fluently; that his linen, clothing, scarf and cuff-buttons were of superior make would not be sufficient reason for assuming his superiority, as he himself well understood. And yet he doubtless acknowledged in himself this superiority, and regarded the respect shown him as his due, and was offended when it was not forthcoming. It just happened that in the jury-room Nekhludoff experienced this disagreeable feeling of being treated with disrespect. Among the jurymen there was an acquaintance of Nekhludoff. This was Peter Gerasimovitch (Nekhludoff never knew, and even boasted of the fact that he did not know his surname), who was at one time tutor to his sister's children. Peter Gerasimovitch was now teacher in a college. Nekhludoff could never bear his familiarity, his self-satisfied laughter—in a word, his "communizing," as Nekhludoff's sister used to put it.

"Ha, ha! So you are also trapped?" he greeted Nekhludoff with a loud burst of laughter. "You did not escape it?"

"I never intended to evade my duty," sternly and gloomily said Nekhludoff.

"That I call civic virtue. But wait till you are hungry and sleepy, you will sing another tune," Peter Gerasimovitch said, laughing still louder.

"This son of an archdeacon will soon begin to 'thou' me," thought Nekhludoff, with an expression of sadness on his face, as though he had just learned of a grievous loss in his family. He turned from the ex-tutor and approached a group of people that had formed around a clean-faced, tall man, of dignified carriage, who were holding a spirited conversation. The man was speaking of a case that was being tried in the civil division, showing his familiarity with the judges and the famous lawyers by referring to them by name. He was telling them of the remarkable turn given to the probable result of the case by the dexterity of a famous lawyer, by which an old lady, who was in the right, would be obliged to pay an enormous sum to the adverse side.

"He is a most ingenious attorney," he said.

He was listened to with respect, and some attempted to interrupt him with some remarks, but he cut them short as if he alone knew the true facts.

Although Nekhludoff arrived late, there was a long wait before him, which was caused by the failure of one of the judges to appear.

CHAPTER VI.

The presiding justice arrived early. He was a tall, stout man, with long, grayish side-whiskers. He was married, but, like his wife, led a very dissolute life. They did not interfere with each other. On the morning in question he received a note from a Swiss governess, who had lived in his house during the summer, and was now passing on her way from the South to St. Petersburg. She wrote that she would be in town between three and six o'clock p. m., and wait for him at the "Hotel Italia." He was, therefore, anxious to end his day's sitting before six o'clock, that he might meet the red-haired Clara Vasilievna.

Entering his private chamber, and locking the door behind him, he produced from the lower shelf of a book-case two dumb-bells, made twenty motions upward, forward, sidewise and downward, and three times lowered himself, holding the bells above his head.

"Nothing so refreshes one as a cold-water bath and exercise," he thought, feeling with his left hand, on the fourth finger of which was a gold ring, the biceps of his right arm. He had to go through two more movements (these exercises he went through every day before court opened), when the door rattled. Some one was attempting to open it. The judge quickly replaced the dumb-bells and opened the door.

"I beg your pardon," he said.

One of the members of the court, wearing gold eye-glasses, of medium height, with high shoulders and frowning countenance, entered.

"Matvei Nikitich is late again," said the newcomer, with an air of displeasure.

"Yes," said the presiding judge, donning his robes. "He is always late."

"It is a shame," said the member, and sat down angrily, then lighted a cigarette.

This member of the court, a very punctilious man, had this morning had an unpleasant encounter with his wife, which was caused by her spending her monthly allowance before the month was up. She asked for a sum of money in advance, and he refused. The result was a quarrel. She said that unless he gave her the money there would be no dinner that night, and that he would have to dine outside. He departed in fear that she would carry out her threat, as anything might be expected from her.

"Is it worth while leading a good, moral life?" he thought, as he looked at the beaming, healthy, joyful and good-natured presiding justice, who, spreading his elbows, stroked his long, gray whiskers; "he is always contented and cheerful, while I am suffering."

The secretary entered and handed the presiding justice a document.

"Thank you," he said, and lighted a cigarette. "Which case shall be taken up first?"

"The poison case, I think," the secretary answered, with feigned indifference.

"Very well; so let it be the poison case," said the justice, considering that that case could be disposed of by four o'clock and make it possible for him to keep the appointment. "Has Matvei Nikitich arrived?"

"Not yet."

"Is Breae here?"

"Yes," answered the secretary.

"Then tell him that we shall try the poisoning case."

Breae was an assistant prosecuting attorney and was assigned to this term of the court.

The secretary met Breae in the corridor. With uplifted shoulders, his robe unbuttoned, and portfolio under his arm, he almost ran, his heels clattering on the floor, and his disengaged hand outstretched in the direction in which he was going.

"Michael Petrovich desires to know if you are ready," said the secretary.

"Certainly; I am always ready," said the assistant prosecutor; "which is the first case?"

"The poisoning case."

"Very well," said the assistant prosecutor, but he did not consider it well at all—he had not slept all night. A send-off had been given to a departing friend, and he drank and played till two in the morning, so that he was entirely unfamiliar with this case, and now hastened to glance over the indictment. The secretary had purposely suggested the case, knowing that the prosecutor had not read it. The secretary was a man of liberal, even radical, ideas. Breae was conservative, and the secretary disliked him, and envied his position.

"And what about the Skoptzy?"[A]

"I have already said that I cannot prosecute them in the absence of witnesses," said the assistant prosecutor, "and I will so declare to the court."

"But you don't need——"

"I cannot," said the assistant prosecutor, and waving his hand, ran to his office.

He was postponing the case against the Skoptzy, although the absent witness was an entirely unnecessary one. The real reason of the postponement was that the prosecutor feared that their trial before an intelligent jury might end in their acquittal. By an understanding with the presiding justice their case was to be transferred to the session of the District Court, where the preponderance of peasants on the jury would insure their conviction.

The commotion in the corridor increased. The greatest crowd was before the Civil Court, where the case of which the portly gentleman was telling the jurymen was being tried. During a recess the same old lady from whom the ingenious attorney managed to win her property in favor of his shrewd client, came out of the court-room. That he was not entitled to the property was known to the judges as well as to the claimant and his attorney, but the mode of their procedure was such that it was impossible to dismiss their claim. The old lady was stout, in smart attire, and with large flowers on her hat. As she passed into the corridor she stopped, and turning to her lawyer, kept repeating:

"How can it be? Great heavens! I don't understand it!"

The lawyer did not listen to her, but looked at the flowers on her hat, making mental calculations.

Behind the old lady, beaming in his wide-open vest, and with a self-sufficient smile on his face, came that same famous lawyer who so managed the case that the lady with the large flowers lost all her property, while his shrewd client, who paid him ten thousand rubles, received over a hundred thousand. All eyes were directed toward him. He was conscious of it and seemed to say by his demeanor:

"Never mind your expressions of devotion," and brushed past the crowd.

FOOTNOTES:

[A] A sect of eunuchs.

CHAPTER VII.

Finally Matvei Nikitich arrived, and the usher, a long-necked and lean man, with a sideling gait and protruding lower lip, entered the jury-room.

The usher was an honest man, with a university education, but he could not hold any employment on account of his tippling habit. A countess, his wife's patroness, had obtained him his present position three months ago; he still retained it, and was exceedingly glad.

"Are you all here, gentlemen?" he asked, putting on his pince-nez and looking through it.

"I think so," said the cheerful merchant.

"Let us see," said the usher, and drawing a sheet of paper from his pocket, began to call the names of the jury, looking at those that responded to their names now through his pince-nez, now over it.

"Counsilor of State E. M. Nikiforoff."

"Here," said the portly gentleman, who was familiar with all the litigations.

"Retired Colonel Ivan Semionovich Ivanoff."

"Present," answered a lank man in the uniform of a retired officer.

"Merchant of the second guild, Peter Baklashoff."

"Here," said the good-natured merchant, smiling from ear to ear. "We are ready."

"Lieutenant of the Guards, Prince Dmitri Nekhludoff."

"Here," answered Nekhludoff.

The usher, looking politely and pleasantly through his pince-nez, bowed, thereby distinguishing him from the rest, as it were.

"Captain Uri Dmitrievich Danchenko; merchant Gregory Ephimovich Kouleshoff," etc., etc., etc.

There were but two missing from the panel.

"You will now, gentlemen, walk into the court," said the usher, pointing to the door with a polite sweep of the hand.

They all rose from their seats, and passing each other through the door, made their way through the corridor to the court-room.

The court was held in a large, oblong room. At one end was a platform, reached by three steps. In the middle of the platform stood a table, covered with green cloth, which was fringed with a dark-green lace. Behind the table stood three arm-chairs with high, carved backs. In an image-case suspended in the right corner was a representation of Christ with a crown of thorns, and beneath it a reading-desk, and on the same side stood the prosecutor's desk. To the left, opposite this desk, was the secretary's table, and dividing these from the seats reserved for spectators was a carved railing, along which stood the prisoners' bench, as yet unoccupied.

On an elevation to the right were two rows of chairs, also with high backs, reserved for the jury; below these were tables for the attorneys. All this was in the front part of the court-room, which was divided in two by a railing. In the rear part of the room benches in lines extended to the wall. In the front row sat four women, either servants or factory employees, and two men, also workmen, who were evidently awed by the grandeur of the ornamentations, and were timidly whispering to each other.

Soon after the jurymen came the usher, who, walking sidewise to the middle of the room, shouted, as if he meant to frighten those present:

"The court is coming!"

Everybody stood up, and the judges ascended the platform. First came the presiding judge with his muscles and beautiful whiskers. Then came the gold-spectacled, gloomy member of the court—now even more gloomy, for before the opening of the session he met his brother-in-law, a candidate for a judicial office, who told him that he had seen his sister, and that she declared that there would be no dinner at home this day.

"So that, it seems, we will have to dine at an inn," said the brother-in-law, laughing.

"What is there droll about it?" said the gloomy member of the court, and sank into a still deeper gloom.

And last of all came the third member of the court, that same Matvei Nikitich, who was always late. He wore a long beard, and had large, kindly eyes, with drooping eyelids. He suffered from catarrh of the stomach, and by the advice of his physician had adopted a new regimen, and this new regimen detained him this morning longer than usual. When he ascended the platform he seemed to be wrapped in thought, but only because he had the habit of making riddles of every question that occurred to him. At this moment he was occupied with the following enigmatical proposition:

If the number of steps in the distance between the cabinet-door and the arm-chair will divide by three without a remainder, then the new regimen will cure him; but if it does not so divide, then it will not. There were twenty-six steps, but he made one short step and reached the chair with the twenty-seventh.

As the judges ascended the elevation in their uniforms, with gold-laced collars, they presented an imposing array. They themselves felt it, and all three, as if confused by their own greatness, modestly lowered their eyes, and hastily seated themselves behind the table on which clean paper and freshly-pointed lead pencils of all sizes had been placed. The prosecutor, who entered with the judges, also hastily walked to his place near the window, his portfolio still under his arm, and waving his hand he began to read the papers in the case, utilizing every moment to prepare himself.

This was his fifth case as prosecuting attorney. He was ambitious, and was determined to make his career, and hence he endeavored to obtain a conviction in every case he prosecuted. He knew the main points of the poisoning case, and had already planned his speech; but he needed to know some particulars of which he was now making extracts from the papers.

The secretary sat on the opposite side of the elevation, and, having prepared all the papers that might be necessary to produce on trial, was glancing over a newspaper article, which he had obtained and read the day before. He was anxious to talk to the member of the court with the long beard, who shared his views, and before doing so wished to better familiarize himself with it.

CHAPTER VIII.

The presiding justice looked over the papers, asked some questions of the usher, and receiving affirmative answers, ordered that the prisoners be brought into court. Immediately a door beyond the grating opened, and two gendarmes with unsheathed swords and caps on their heads, stepped into the court-room. Behind them came a freckled, red-haired man and two women. The man was dressed in prisoner's garb which was too long and too wide for him. As he entered the court-room he held up with outspread fingers the sleeves which were too long. Without looking at the judges or the spectators, his attention was absorbed by the bench around which he was led. When he had passed around he carefully seated himself on the edge, and making room for the others, began to stare at the presiding justice, the muscles of his cheeks moving as if he were whispering something. He was followed by a middle-aged woman, also dressed in a prisoner's coat. A white prison cap covered her head; her face was grayish, and her eyes were devoid of either eye-lashes or eyebrows. She seemed quite composed. As she was passing the railing to take her seat, her coat caught at something; without haste, she carefully disengaged it, then smoothed it and took her seat.

The third prisoner was Maslova.

No sooner did she enter than all the male spectators turned their eyes toward her, attracted by her white face, lustrous black eyes and high breast. Even the gendarme whom she passed gazed at her until she seated herself; then, as if feeling himself guilty, he quickly turned his head from her and straightening himself, he began to gaze into the window directly in front of him.

The presiding justice waited until all the prisoners took their places, and as soon as Maslova was seated, he turned to the secretary.

Then commenced the customary proceeding; calling of the jurymen, fining the absent ones, listening to the claims of exemption from jury duty and filling the panel from a number of reserves. Then the presiding justice folded the slips of paper, placed them in a glass vase, and turning up his gold-laced sleeve drew the slips one by one, unrolled them and read them aloud.

Then he straightened his sleeve and called on the priest to swear in the jury.

An old little priest with a swollen, pale yellow face, in a brown cassock and gold cross on his breast and some small badges pinned to the cassock, slowly moving his swollen feet under the cassock, approached the reading desk under the image.

The jury rose and, crowding each other, came forward.

"Come nearer, please," said the priest, touching with his swollen hand the cross on his breast, and waiting until all the jury were near him.

While the jury were mounting the steps to the elevation where the desk stood, the priest wriggled his bald, hoary head through the opening of the stole, then rearranging his scanty hair, he turned to the jury:

"Raise your right hands and keep your fingers thus," he said, in a slow, feeble voice, raising his bloated hand and pointing at his forehead with the first three of its dimpled fingers. "Now repeat after me: 'I promise and swear by the Almighty God, His Holy Gospel, and by the life-giving cross of our Lord, that in the case'"—he continued, resting after each phrase. "Don't drop your hand; hold it thus," he turned to a young man who let his hand fall— "'that in the case which——'"

The portly, whiskered gentleman, the colonel, merchant and others held their hands as directed by the priest, and seemed to do so with particular pleasure, holding their hands quite high, and their fingers most proper; others seemed to do it against their will, and carelessly. Some repeated the words too loudly, in a provoking manner, with an expression on the face which seemed to say: "I will repeat as I please;" others whispered, fell behind the priest and then, as if frightened, hastened to catch up with him. Some held their fingers tightly closed, as if challenging anyone to part them; others, again, loosened them, now closed them again. After the jury was sworn, the presiding justice directed them to choose a foreman. They arose and, crowding each other, went into the consultation room, where almost every one produced cigarettes and began to smoke. Some one proposed the portly gentleman, who was immediately chosen, then they threw away their cigarettes and returned to the court. The gentleman declared to the presiding justice that he was chosen foreman, and stepping over the feet of each other, the jury again seated themselves in the two rows of high-backed chairs.

Everything proceeded smoothly, quickly and not without solemnity, and the regularity, order and solemnity evidently pleased the participants, confirming their sense of rendering important public service. Nekhludoff also experienced this feeling.

As soon as the jury seated themselves the presiding justice instructed them in their rights, duties and responsibilities. While speaking, he was constantly changing his attitude; now he leaned on his right hand, now on his left; then he reclined in his chair, or rested his hands on the arms of the chair, smoothed the corners of the paper on the table, polished the paper-knife or clutched the lead pencil.

Their rights, according to him, consisted in that they were allowed to question prisoners, through the presiding justice; they might keep pencils and paper, and might also view exhibits. Their duties consisted in not giving a false verdict. And their responsibilities consisted in that if they failed to keep secret their deliberations, or spoke to outsiders, they would be liable to punishment.

They all listened with respectful attention. The merchant, from whom the fumes of wine spread through the jury box, and who was suppressing the noisy rising of gases in his stomach, approvingly nodded at every sentence.

CHAPTER IX.

After he had finished the instructions, the presiding justice turned to the prisoners.

"Simon Kartinkin, rise!" he said.

Simon sprang up nervously. The muscles of his cheeks began to twitch still quicker.

"What is your name?"

"Simon Petroff Kartinkin," he said quickly, in a sharp voice, evidently prepared for the question.

"What estate?"

"Peasant."

"What government, district?"

"Government of Tula, district of Krapivensk, Kupian township, village of Borki."

"How old are you?"

"Thirty-four; born in eighteen hundred——"

"What faith?"

"Of the Russian orthodox faith."

"Are you married?"

"O, no!"

"What is your occupation?"

"I was employed in the Hotel Mauritania."

"Were you ever arrested before?"

"I was never arrested before, because where I lived——"

"You were not arrested?"

"God forbid! Never!"

"Have you received a copy of the indictment?"

"Yes."

"Sit down. Euphemia Ivanovna Bochkova!" The presiding justice turned to the next prisoner.

But Simon remained standing in front of Bochkova.

"Kartinkin, sit down!"

Kartinkin still remained standing.

"Kartinkin, sit down!"

But Kartinkin stood still until the usher, his head leaning to the side, and with wide-open eyes, whispered to him in a tragic tone:

"Sit down, sit down!"

Kartinkin sat down as quickly as he rose, and wrapping himself in his coat began to move his cheeks.

"Your name?" With a sigh of weariness the presiding justice turned to the next prisoner without looking at her, and consulted a paper before him. He was so accustomed to the business that to expedite matters he could try two cases at once.

Bochkova was forty-two years old, a burgess of the town of Koloma; by occupation a servant—in the same Hotel Mauritania. Was never arrested before, and had received a copy of the indictment. She gave the answers very boldly and with an intonation which seemed to add to every answer.

"Yes, Bochkova, Euphemia, have received a copy, and am proud of it, and will permit no one to laugh at me."

Without waiting to be told to sit down, Bochkova sat down immediately after the questioning ceased.

"Your name?" asked the presiding justice of the third prisoner. "You must rise," he added, gently and courteously, seeing Maslova still in her seat.

With quick movement Maslova rose with an air of submissiveness, and throwing back her shoulders, looked into the face of the presiding justice with her smiling, somewhat squinting black eyes.

"What are you called?"

"They used to call me Lubka," she answered, rapidly.

Meanwhile Nekhludoff put on his pince-nez and examined the prisoners while they were questioned.

"It is impossible," he thought, looking intently at the prisoner. "But her name is Lubka," he thought, as he heard her answer.

The presiding justice was about to continue his interrogation when the member with the eye-glasses, angrily whispering something, stopped him. The presiding justice nodded his assent and turned to the prisoner.

"You say 'Lubka,' but a different name is entered here."

The prisoner was silent.

"I ask you what is your real name?"

"What name did you receive at baptism?" asked the angry member.

"Formerly I was called Katherine."

"It is impossible," Nekhludoff continued to repeat, although there was no doubt in his mind now that it was she, that same servant ward with whom he had been in love at one time—yes, in love, real love, and whom in a moment of mental fever he led astray, then abandoned, and to whom he never gave a second thought, because the recollection of it was too painful, revealed too manifestly that he, who prided himself of his good breeding, not only did not treat her decently, but basely deceived her.

Yes, it was she. He saw plainly the mysterious peculiarity that distinguishes every individual from every other individual. Notwithstanding the unnatural whiteness and fullness of her face, this pleasant peculiarity was in the face, in the lips, in the slightly squinting eyes, and, principally, in the naive, smiling glance, and in the expression of submissiveness not only in the face, but in the whole figure.

"You should have said so," again very gently said the presiding justice. "What is your patronymic?"

"I am illegitimate," said Maslova.

"But yet you were named after your godfather?"

"Michailova."

"What crime could she have committed?" Nekhludoff thought meanwhile, his breath almost failing him.

"What is your surname—your family name?" continued the presiding justice.

"Maslova—after my mother."

"Your estate?"

"Burgess."

"Of the orthodox faith?"

"Yes."

"Your occupation? What was your occupation?"

Maslova was silent.

"What was your occupation?" repeated the justiciary.

"You know!" said Maslova. She smiled and quickly glanced around, then looked squarely at the justiciary.

There was something so unusual in the expression of her face—something so terrible and piteous in the meaning of her words, in that smile, that quick glance which she cast over the court-room—that the justiciary hung his head, and for a moment there was perfect silence.

A burst of laughter from some spectator interrupted the silence. Some one hissed. The justiciary raised his head and continued the interrogation.

"Were you ever arrested?"

"No." Maslova said in an undertone, sighing.

"Have you received a copy of the indictment?"

"Yes."

"Sit down."

The prisoner raised her skirt with the customary movement of a fashionable lady, arranging her train, and sat down, folding her hands in the sleeves of her coat, and still looking at the justiciary.

Then began the recounting of witnesses, their removal to a separate room, the decision on the evidence of the medical expert. Then the secretary arose and began to read the indictment, loud and with distinctness, but so rapidly that his incorrect sounding of the letters l and r turned his reading into one continuous, weary drone. The judges leaned now on one side, now on the other side of their arm-chairs, then on the table, and again on the backs of the chairs, or closed their eyes, or opened them and whispered to each other. One of the gendarmes several times stifled a yawn.

The convulsions of Kartinkin's cheeks did not cease. Bochkova sat quietly and erect, now and then scratching with her finger under her cap.

Maslova sat motionless, listening to the reading, and looking at the clerk; at times she shuddered and made a movement as if desiring to object, blushed, then sighed deeply, changed the position of her hands, glanced around and again looked at the clerk.

Nekhludoff sat on the high-backed chair in the front row, second to the aisle, and without removing his pince-nez looked at Maslova, while his soul was being racked by a fierce and complicated struggle.

CHAPTER X.

The indictment read as follows:

"On the 17th of January, 18—, suddenly died in the Hotel Mauritania, merchant of the second guild, Therapont Emelianovich Smelkoff.

"The local police physician certified that the cause of death of said Smelkoff was rupture of the heart, caused by excessive use of liquor.

"The body of Smelkoff was interred.

"On the 21st day of January, a townsman and comrade of Smelkoff, on returning from St. Petersburg, and hearing of the circumstances of his death, declared his suspicion that Smelkoff was poisoned with a view of robbing him of the money he carried about his person.

"This suspicion was confirmed at the preliminary inquest, by which it was established: 1. That Smelkoff had drawn from the bank, some time before his death, three thousand eight hundred rubles; that, after a due and careful inventory of the money of the deceased, only three hundred and twelve rubles and sixteen kopecks were found. 2. That the entire day and evening preceding his death deceased passed in the company of a girl named Lubka (Katherine Maslova) in the Hotel Mauritania, whither said Maslova came at the request of Smelkoff for money; that she obtained the money from Smelkoff's trunk, first unlocking it with a key intrusted to her by Smelkoff; that the money was thus taken in the presence of two servants of the said hotel—Euphemia Bochkova and Simon Kartinkin; that at the opening of said trunk by the said Maslova in the presence of the aforementioned Bochkova and Kartinkin, there were rolls of hundred ruble bills. 3. That on the return of said Smelkoff and Maslova to the said hotel, the said Maslova, on the advice of the said servant Kartinkin, administered to the deceased a glass of brandy, in which she put a white powder given her by said Kartinkin. 4. That on the following morning Lubka (Katherine Maslova) sold to her mistress, Rosanova, a diamond ring belonging to Smelkoff, said ring she alleged to have been presented to her by said Smelkoff. 5. That the servant of said Hotel Mauritania, Euphemia Bochkova, deposited in her name in the local Bank of Commerce the sum of eighteen hundred rubles.

"At the autopsy held on the body of Smelkoff, and after the removal of the intestines, the presence of poison was readily discovered, leaving no doubt that death was caused by poisoning.

"The prisoners, Maslova, Bochkova and Kartinkin pleaded not guilty. Maslova declared that she did go to the Hotel Mauritania, as stated, for the purpose of fetching some money for the merchant, and that opening the trunk with the key given to her by the merchant, she took only forty rubles, as she was directed, but took no more, which fact can be substantiated by Bochkova and Kartinkin, in whose presence she took the money and locked the trunk. She further testified that during her second visit to the room of the merchant she gave him, at the instigation of Kartinkin, several powders in a glass of brandy, which she considered to be narcotic, in order that she might get away from him. The ring was presented to her by Smelkoff when she cried and was about to leave him after he had beaten her.

"Euphemia Bochkova testified that she knew nothing about the missing money, never entered the merchant's room, which Lubka herself kept in order, and that if anything was stolen from the merchant, it was done by Lubka when she came to the room for the money."

At this point Maslova shuddered, and with open mouth looked at Bochkova.

"And when Euphemia Bochkova was shown her bank account of eighteen hundred rubles," continued the secretary, "and asked how she came by the money, she testified that the money was saved from their earnings by herself and Simon Kartinkin, whom she intended to marry.

"Simon Kartinkin, on his part, at the first examination, confessed that, at the instigation of Maslova, who brought the key to the trunk, he and Bochkova stole the money, which was afterwards divided between the three."

At this Maslova shuddered again, sprang to her feet, turned red in the face, and began to say something, but the usher bade her be quiet.

"Finally," continued the secretary, "Kartinkin also confessed to giving Maslova the powders to put the merchant to sleep. On the second examination, however, he denied having either stolen the money, or given Maslova the powders, but charged Maslova with both. As to the money placed by Bochkova in the bank, he declared, in accordance with Bochkova's testimony, that they had saved it during their twelve years' service in the hotel."

The indictment wound up as follows:

"In view of the aforesaid the defendants, Simon Kartinkin, peasant of the village of Borkoff, thirty-three years of age; burgess Euphemia Ivanova Bochkova, forty-two years of age, and burgess Katherine Maslova, twenty-seven years of age, conspired on the 17th day of January, 188—, to administer poison to merchant Smelkoff with intent to kill and rob him, and did on said day administer to said Smelkoff poison, from which poison the said Smelkoff died, and did thereafter rob him of a diamond ring and twenty-five hundred rubles, contrary to the laws in such cases made and provided. Chapter 1453, sections 4 and 5, Penal Code.

"Wherefore, in accordance with chapter 201 of the Code of Criminal Procedure, the said peasant, Simon Kartinkin, burgess Euphemia Bochkova and burgess Katherine Maslova are subject to trial by jury, the case being within the jurisdiction of the Circuit Court."

The clerk having finished the reading of the long indictment, folded the papers, seated himself at his desk and began to arrange his long hair. Every one present gave a sigh of relief, and with the consciousness that the trial had already begun, everything would be cleared up and justice would finally be done, leaned back on their chairs.

Nekhludoff alone did not experience this feeling. He was absorbed in the horrible thought that the same Maslova, whom he knew as an innocent and beautiful girl ten years ago, could be guilty of such a crime.

CHAPTER XI.

When the reading of the indictment was finished, the justiciary, having consulted with his associates, turned to Kartinkin with an expression on his face which plainly betokened confidence in his ability to bring forth all the truth.

"Simon Kartinkin," he called, leaning to the left.

Simon Kartinkin rose, put out his chest, incessantly moving his cheeks.

"You are charged, together with Euphemia Bochkova and Katherine Maslova, with stealing from the trunk of the merchant Smelkoff money belonging to him, and subsequently brought arsenic and induced Maslova to administer it to Smelkoff, by reason of which he came to his death. Are you guilty or not guilty?" he said, leaning to the right.

"It is impossible, because our business is to attend the guests——"

"You will speak afterwards. Are you guilty or not?"

"No, indeed. I only——"

"You can speak later. Do you admit that you are guilty?" calmly but firmly repeated the justiciary.

"I cannot do it because——"

Again the usher sprang toward Simon and with a tragic whisper stopped him.

The justiciary, with an expression showing that the questioning was at an end, moved the hand in which he held a document to another place, and turned to Euphemia Bochkova.

"Euphemia Bochkova, you, with Kartinkin and Maslova, are charged with stealing, on the 17th day of January, 188—, at the Hotel Mauritania, from the trunk of the merchant Smelkoff, money and a ring, and dividing the same among yourselves, and with a view of hiding your crime, administered poison to him, from the effects of which he died. Are you guilty?"

"I am not guilty of anything," boldly and firmly answered the prisoner. "I never entered the room—and as that scurvy woman did go into the room, she, then, did the business——"

"You will speak afterwards," again said the justiciary, with the same gentleness and firmness. "So you are not guilty?"

"I did not take the money, did not give him the poison, did not go into the room. If I were in the room I should have thrown her out."

"You are not guilty, then?"

"Never."

"Very well."

"Katherine Maslova," began the justiciary, turning to the third prisoner. "The charge against you is that, having come to the Hotel Mauritania with the key to Smelkoff's trunk, you stole therefrom money and a ring," he said, like one repeating a lesson learned by rote, and leaning his ear to the associate sitting on his left, who said that he noticed that the phial mentioned in the list of exhibits was missing. "Stole therefrom money and a ring," repeated the justiciary, "and after dividing the money again returned with the merchant Smelkoff to the Hotel Mauritania, and there administered to him poison, from the effects of which he died. Are you guilty or not guilty?"

"I am not guilty of anything," she answered, quickly. "As I said before, so I repeat now: I never, never, never took the money; I did not take anything, and the ring he gave me himself."

"You do not plead guilty of stealing twenty-five hundred rubles?" said the justiciary.

"I say I didn't take anything but forty rubles."

"And do you plead guilty to the charge of giving the merchant Smelkoff powders in his wine?"

"To that I plead guilty. Only I thought, as I was told, that they would put him to sleep, and that no harm could come from them. I did not wish, nor thought of doing him any harm. Before God, I say that I did not," she said.

"So you deny that you are guilty of stealing the money and ring from the merchant Smelkoff," said the justiciary, "but you admit that you gave him the powders?"

"Of course, I admit, only I thought that they were sleeping powders. I only gave them to him that he might fall asleep—never wished, nor thought——"

"Very well," said the justiciary, evidently satisfied with the results of the examinations. "Now tell us how it happened," he said, leaning his elbows on the arms of the chair and putting his hands on the table. "Tell us everything. By confessing frankly you will improve your present condition."

Maslova, still looking straight at the justiciary, was silent.

"Tell us what took place."

"What took place?" suddenly said Maslova. "I came to the hotel; I was taken to the room; he was there, and was already very drunk." (She pronounced the word "he" with a peculiar expression of horror and with wide-open eyes.) "I wished to depart; he would not let me."

She became silent, as if she had lost the thread of the story, or thought of something else.

"What then?"

"What then? Then I remained there awhile and went home."

At this point the assistant public prosecutor half rose from his seat, uncomfortably resting on one elbow.

"Do you wish to question the prisoner?" asked the justiciary, and receiving an affirmative answer, motioned his assent.

"I would like to put this question: Has the prisoner been acquainted with Simon Kartinkin before?" asked the assistant prosecutor without looking at Maslova.

And having asked the question he pressed his lips and frowned.

The justiciary repeated the question. Maslova looked with frightened eyes at the prosecutor.

"With Simon? I was," she said.

"I would like to know now, what was the character of the acquaintance that existed between them. Have they met often?"

"What acquaintance? He invited me to meet guests; there was no acquaintance," answered Maslova, throwing restless glances now at the prosecutor, now at the justiciary.

"I would like to know why did Kartinkin invite Maslova only, and not other girls?" asked the prosecutor, with a Mephistophelian smile, winking his eyes.

"I don't know. How can I tell?" answered Maslova, glancing around her, frightened, and for a moment resting her eyes on Nekhludoff. "He invited whomever he wished."

"Is it possible that she recognized me?" Nekhludoff thought, with horror. He felt his blood rising to his head, but Maslova did not recognize him. She turned away immediately, and with frightened eyes gazed at the prosecutor.

"Then the prisoner denies that she had intimate relations with Kartinkin? Very well. I have no more questions to ask."

He removed his elbow from the desk, and began to make notes. In reality, instead of making notes, he merely drew lines across his notes, having seen prosecutors and attorneys, after an adroit question, making memoranda of questions which were to crush their opponents.

The justiciary did not turn immediately to the prisoner, because he was at the moment asking his associate in the eye-glasses whether he consented to the questions previously outlined and committed to writing.

"What followed?" the justiciary continued.

"I came home," Maslova continued, looking somewhat bolder, "and went to sleep. As soon as I was asleep our girl, Bertha, came and woke me. 'Your merchant is here again. Wake up.' Then he"—again she pronounced it with evident horror—"he wished to send for wine, but was short of money. Then he sent me to the hotel, telling me where the money was and how much to take, and I went."

The justiciary was whispering at the time to his associate on the left, and did not listen to Maslova, but to make it appear that he had heard everything he repeated her last words.

"And you went. Well, what else?" he asked.

"I came there and did as he told me. I went to his room. I did not enter it alone, but called Simon Michaelovich and her," she said, pointing to Bochkova.

"She lies; I never entered——" Bochkova began, but she was stopped.

"In their presence I took four ten ruble bills," she continued.

"And while taking this money, did the prisoner see how much money there was?" asked the prosecutor.

Maslova shuddered as soon as the prosecutor began to speak. She could not tell why, but she felt that he was her enemy.

"I did not count it, but I saw that it was all hundred ruble bills."

"The prisoner saw hundred ruble bills. I have no other questions."

"Well, did you bring back the money?" asked the justiciary, looking at the clock.

"I did."

"Well, what then?"

"Then he again took me with him," said Maslova.

"And how did you give him the powder in the wine?" asked the justiciary.

"How? Poured it into the wine and gave it to him."

"Why did you give it to him?"

Without answering, she sighed deeply. After a short silence she said:

"He would not let me go. He exhausted me. I went into the corridor and said to Simon Michaelovich: 'If he would only let me go; I am so tired.' And Simon Michaelovich said: 'We are also tired of him. We intend to give him sleeping powders. When he is asleep you can go.' 'All right,' I said. I thought that it was a harmless powder. He gave me a package. I entered. He lay behind the partition, and ordered me to bring him some brandy. I took from the table a bottle of feen-champagne, poured into two glasses—for myself and him—threw the powder into his glass and handed it to him. I would not have given it to him if I had known it."

"And how did you come by the ring?" asked the justiciary.

"He presented it to me."

"When did he present it to you?"

"When we reached his room. I wished to depart. Then he struck me on the head and broke my comb. I was angered, and wished to go. Then he took the ring from his finger and gave it to me, asking me to stay," she said.

Here the assistant prosecutor again rose, and with a dissimulating naiveness asked permission to ask a few more questions, which was granted, and leaning his head on his gold-embroidered collar, he asked:

"I would like to know how long was the prisoner in the room with Smelkoff?"

Maslova was again terror-stricken, and with her frightened eyes wandering from the prosecutor to the justiciary, she answered, hurriedly:

"I do not remember how long."

"And does the prisoner remember entering another part of the hotel after she had left Smelkoff?"

Maslova was thinking.

"Into the next room—an empty one," she said.

"Why did you enter that room?" said the assistant prosecutor, impulsively.

"To wait for a cabriolet."

"Was not Kartinkin in the room with the prisoner?"

"He also came in."

"Why did he come in?"

"There was the merchant's feen-champagne left, and we drank it together."

"Oh, drank together. Very well."

"And did the prisoner have any conversation with Simon, and what was the subject of the conversation?"

Maslova suddenly frowned, her face turned red, and she quickly answered:

"What I said? I know nothing more. Do what you please with me. I am innocent, and that is all. I did not say anything. I told everything that happened."

"I have no more questions to ask," said the prosecutor to the court, and uplifting his shoulders he began to add to the memorandums of his speech that the prisoner herself confessed to entering an empty room with Simon.

There was a short silence.

"Have you anything else to say?"

"I have told everything," she said, sighing, and took her seat.

The justiciary then made some notes, and after he had listened to a suggestion whispered by the associate on the left, declared a recess of ten minutes, and, hastily rising, walked out of the court-room.

After the judges had risen, the jury, lawyers and witness also rose, and with the pleasant feeling of having already performed part of an important work, began to move hither and thither.

Nekhludoff walked into the jury-room and took a seat near the window.

CHAPTER XII.

Yes, it was Katiousha.

The relations of Nekhludoff to Katiousha were the following:

Nekhludoff first met Katiousha when he went to stay one summer out at the estate of his aunts in order that he might quietly prepare his thesis on the private ownership of land. Ordinarily he lived on the estate of his mother, near Moskow, with his mother and sister. But that year his sister married, and his mother went abroad. Nekhludoff had to write a composition in the course of his university studies, and decided to pass the summer at his aunts'. There in the woods it was quiet, and there was nothing to distract him from his studies. Besides, the aunts loved their nephew and heir, and he loved them,

74

loved their old-fashioned way of living.

During that summer Nekhludoff experienced that exaltation which youth comes to know not by the teaching of others, but when it naturally begins to recognize the beauty and importance of life, and man's serious place in it; when it sees the possibility of infinite perfection of which the world is capable, and devotes itself to that endeavor, not only with the hope, but with a full conviction of reaching that perfection which it imagines possible. While in the university he had that year read Spencer's Social Statics, and Spencer's reasoning bearing on private ownership of land produced a strong impression on him, especially because he was himself the son of a landed proprietress. His father was not rich, but his mother received as her marriage portion ten thousand acres of land. He then for the first time understood all the injustice of private ownership of land, and being one of those to whom any sacrifice in the name of moral duty was a lofty spiritual enjoyment, he forthwith divided the land he had inherited from his father among the peasants. On this subject he was then composing a disquisition.

His life on the estate of his aunts was ordered in the following way: He rose very early, some times at three o'clock, and till sunrise bathed in the river under a hill, often in the morning mist, and returned when the dew was yet on the grass and flowers. Some mornings he would, after partaking of coffee, sit down to write his composition, or read references bearing on the subject. But, above all, he loved to ramble in the woods. Before dinner he would lie down in the woods and sleep; then, at dinner, he made merry, jesting with his aunts; then went out riding or rowing. In the evening he read again, or joined his aunts, solving riddles for them. On moonlit nights he seldom slept, because of the immense joy of life that pervaded him, and instead of sleeping, he sometimes rambled in the garden till daylight, absorbed in his thoughts and phantasies.

Thus he lived happily the first month under the roof of his aunts' dwelling, paying no attention to the half-servant, half-ward, the black-eyed, nimble-footed Katiousha.

Nekhludoff, raised under the protecting wing of his mother, was at nineteen a perfectly innocent youth. He dreamed of woman, but only as wife. All those women who, according to his view, could not be considered as likely to become his wife, were to him not women, but people. But it happened on Ascension Day that there was visiting his aunts a lady from the neighborhood with her two young daughters, her son and a local artist who was staying with them.

After tea had been served the entire company, as usual, repaired to the meadow, where they played blind man's buff. Katiousha went with them. After some exchanges came Nekhludoff's turn to run with Katiousha. Nekhludoff always liked to see Katiousha, but it had never occurred to him that their relations could ever be any but the most formal.

"It will be difficult to catch them now," said the cheerful artist, whose short and curved legs carried him very swiftly, "unless they stumble."

"You could not catch them."

"One, two, three!"

They clapped their hands three times. Almost bursting into laughter, Katiousha quickly changed places with Nekhludoff, and pressing with her strong, rough little hand his large hand she ran to the left, rustling her starched skirt.

Nekhludoff was a swift runner; he wished to out-distance the artist, and ran with all his might. As he turned around he saw the artist catching up with Katiousha, but with her supple limbs she gained on him and ran to the left. In front of them was a patch of lilac bushes, behind which no one ran, but Katiousha, turning toward Nekhludoff, motioned him with her head to join her there. He understood her, and ran behind the bushes. But here was a ditch overgrown with nettles, whose presence was unknown to Nekhludoff. He stumbled and fell, stinging and wetting his hands in the evening dew that was now falling, but, laughing, he straightened himself and ran into the open.

Katiousha, her black eyes beaming with joy, ran toward him. They met and caught each others' hands.

"You were stung by the nettles, I suppose," she said, arranging with her free hand her loosened braid, breathing heavily, and looking up into his eyes.

"I did not know there was a ditch," he said, also smiling, and still keeping her hand in his.

She advanced a little, and he, without being able to account for it, inclined his face toward hers. She did not draw back. He pressed her hand and kissed her on the lips.

She uttered an exclamation, and with a swift movement, releasing her hand, she ran in the direction of the crowd.

Plucking two lilac twigs from the lilac bush, fanning her flushed face with them, and glancing around toward him, she ran to the players, briskly waving her hands.

From this day on the relations between Nekhludoff and Katiousha were changed, and there were established between them those peculiar relations which are customary between two innocent young people who are attached to each other.

As soon as Katiousha entered the room, or even when Nekhludoff saw her white apron from afar, everything became immediately as if lit by the sun; everything became more interesting, more cheerful, more important; life became more joyful. She experienced the same feeling. But not alone the presence and proximity of Katiousha had such effect upon Nekhludoff; the very thought of her existence had the same power upon him as that of his had upon her. Whether he received an unpleasant letter from his mother, or was backward in his composition, or felt the ceaseless sadness of youth, it would suffice for him to see her and his spirit resumed its wonted good cheer.

Katiousha had to do all the housework, but she managed to do her duty and found spare time for reading. He gave her the works of Dostoievsky and Tourgenieff to read. Those descriptive of the beauties of nature she liked best. Their conversations were but momentary, when they met in the corridor, on the veranda, in the court-yard, or in the room of the aunts' old servant, Matriena Pavlovna, with whom Katiousha roomed, or in the servants' chamber, whither Nekhludoff sometimes went to drink tea. And these conversations in the presence of Matriena Pavlovna were the pleasantest. When they were alone their conversation flagged. Then the eyes would speak something different, more important, than the mouth; the lips were drawn up, they felt uncomfortable, and quickly parted.

These relations continued during the time of his first visit to his aunts. The aunts noticed them, were dismayed, and immediately wrote to the Princess Elena Ivanovna, Nekhludoff's mother. But their anxiety was unfounded; Nekhludoff, without knowing it, loved Katiousha, as innocent people love, and this very love was the principal safeguard against either his or her fall. Not only did he not desire to possess her physically, but the very thought of such relation horrified him. There was more reason in the poetical Sophia Ivanovna's fear that Nekhludoff's having fallen in love with a girl, might take a notion to marry her without regard to her birth or station.

If Nekhludoff were clearly conscious of his love for Katiousha; especially if it were sought to persuade him that he could and must not link his fate to that of the girl, he would very likely have decided in his plumb-line mind that there was no reason why he should not marry her, no matter who she was, provided he loved her. But the aunts did not speak of their fears, and he departed without knowing that he was enamored of Katiousha.

He was certain that his feeling toward Katiousha was but a manifestation of that joy which pervaded his entire being, and which was shared by that lovely, cheerful girl. However, when he was taking leave, and Katiousha, standing on the veranda with the aunts, followed him with her black, tearful and somewhat squinting eyes, he felt that he was leaving behind him something beautiful, precious, which would never recur. And he became very sad.

"Good-by, Katiousha. I thank you for everything," he said, over the cap of Sophia Ivanovna, and seated himself in the cabriolet.

"Good-by, Dmitri Ivanovich," she said, in her pleasant, caressing voice, and holding back the tears which filled her eyes, ran into her room, where she could cry freely.

CHAPTER XIII.

For three years afterward Nekhludoff did not see Katiousha. But when, as staff-officer, he was on his way to his army post, he paid a short visit to his aunts, but an entirely different man. Three years ago he was an honest, self-denying youth, ready to devote himself to every good cause; now he was a corrupt and refined egotist, given over to personal enjoyment. Then, the world appeared to him as a mystery which he joyfully and enthusiastically tried to solve; now, everything in this world was plain and simple, and was determined by those conditions of life in which he found himself. Then, it was necessary and important to hold communion with nature and with those people who lived, thought and felt before him (philosophers, poets); now, human institutions were the only things necessary and important, and communion he held with his comrades. Woman, then, appeared to him a mysterious and charming creature; now, he looked on woman, on every woman, except nearest relations and wives of friends, as a means of gratifying now tried pleasures. Then, he needed no money, and wanted not a third part what his mother gave him, disclaimed title to his father's land, distributing it among the peasants; now, the fifteen hundred rubles' monthly allowance he received from his mother did not suffice for his needs, and he often made it the cause of unpleasant conversation with her. His true self he then considered his spiritual being; now, his healthy, vigorous, animal self was his true ego.

And all this terrible transformation took place in him only because he ceased to have faith in himself, and began to believe in others. To live according to the faith that was in him was burdensome; every question would have to be decided almost always against his animal ego, which was seeking light pleasures; but reposing his faith in others, there remained nothing to decide, everything having been decided, and decided always against the spiritual and in favor of the animal ego. Besides, following his inner faith, he was always subject to the censure of people; in the other case he received the approval of the people that surrounded him.

Thus, when Nekhludoff was thinking, reading, speaking of God, of truth, of wealth, of poverty, everybody considered it out of place and somewhat queer, while his mother and aunt, with good-natured irony, called him notre cher philosophe. When, however, he was reading novels, relating indecent anecdotes or seeing droll vaudevilles in the French theatre, and afterward merrily repeated them, everybody praised and encouraged him. When he considered it necessary to curtail his needs, wore an old coat and gave up wine-drinking, everybody considered it eccentric and vain originality; but when he spent large sums in organizing a chase, or building an unusual, luxurious cabinet, everybody praised his taste and sent him valuable gifts. When he was chaste, and wished to preserve his chastity till marriage, his relatives were anxious about his health, and his mother, so far from being mortified, rather rejoiced when she learned that he had become a real man, and had enticed the French mistress of some friend of his. As to the Katiousha episode—that the thought might occur to him of marrying her, she could not even think of without horror.

Similarly, when Nekhludoff, on reaching his majority, distributed the estate he inherited from his father among the peasants, because he considered the ownership of land unjust, this act of his horrified his mother and relatives, who constantly reproached and ridiculed him for it. He was told unceasingly that so far from enriching it only impoverished the peasants, who opened three liquor stores and stopped working entirely. When, however, Nekhludoff joined the Guards, and spent and gambled away so much money that Elena Ivanovna had to draw from her capital, she scarcely grieved, considering it quite natural and even beneficial to be thus inoculated when young and in good society.

Nekhludoff at first struggled, but the struggle was very hard, for whatever he did, following the faith that was in him, was considered wrong by others, and, contrariwise, whatever he considered wrong was approved of by his relatives. The result was that Nekhludoff ceased to have faith in himself and began to follow others. At first this renunciation of self was unpleasant, but it was short lived, and Nekhludoff, who now began to smoke and drink wine, soon ceased to experience this unpleasant feeling, and was even greatly relieved.

Passionate by nature, Nekhludoff gave himself up entirely to this new life, approved of by all those that surrounded him, and completely stifled in himself that voice which demanded something different. It commenced with his removal to St. Petersburg, and ended with his entry upon active service.

During this period of his life Nekhludoff felt the ecstasy of freedom from all those moral impediments which he had formerly placed before himself, and continued in a chronic condition of insane egotism.

He was in this condition when, three years afterward, he visited his aunts.

CHAPTER XIV.

Nekhludoff called at his aunts because their manor lay on the road through which his regiment had preceded him, and also because they requested him to do so, but principally in order that he might see Katiousha. It may be that in the depth of his soul there was already a mischievous intention toward Katiousha, prompted by his now unbridled animal ego, but he was not aware of it, he merely desired to visit those places in which he lived so happily, and see his somewhat queer, but amiable and good-natured, aunts, who always surrounded the atmosphere around him with love and admiration, and also to see the lovely Katiousha, of whom he had such pleasant recollections.

He arrived toward the end of March, on Good Friday, in the season of bad roads, when the rain was falling in torrents, and was wet all through, and chilled to the marrow of his bones, but courageous and excited, as he always felt at that time of the year.

"I wonder if she is still there?" he thought, as he drove into the familiar court-yard of the old manor, which was covered with snow that fell from the roofs, and was surrounded by a low brick wall. He expected that the ringing of the bell would bring her running to meet him, but on the perron of the servants' quarters appeared two bare-footed women with tucked-up skirts, carrying buckets, who were apparently scrubbing floors. She was not on the front perron, either; only Timon, the lackey, came forth in an apron, also apparently occupied with cleaning. Sophia Ivanovna came into the ante-chamber, attired in a silk dress and cap.

"How glad I am that you came!" said Sophia Ivanovna. "Masheuka[B] is somewhat ill. We were to church, receiving the sacrament. She is very tired."

"I congratulate you, Aunt Sonia,"[C] said Nekhludoff, kissing the hand of Sophia Ivanovna. "Pardon me, I have soiled you."

"Go to your room. You are wet all through. Oh, what a mustache! Katiousha! Katiousha! Bring him some coffee quickly."

"All right!" responded a familiar, pleasant voice. Nekhludoff's heart fluttered. "She is here!" To him it was like the sun rising from behind the clouds, and he cheerfully went with Timon to his old room to change his clothing.

Nekhludoff wished to ask Timon about Katiousha. Was she well? How did she fare? Was she not engaged to be married? But Timon was so respectful, and at the same time so rigid; he so strictly insisted on himself pouring the water from the pitcher over Nekhludoff's hands, that the latter could not decide to ask him about Katiousha, and only inquired about his grand-children, about the old stallion, about the watch-dog Polkan. They were all well, except Polkan, who had gone mad the previous year.

After he had thrown off his wet clothes, and as he was about to dress himself, Nekhludoff heard quick steps and a rapping at the door. He recognized both the steps and the rapping. Only she walked and rapped thus.

It was Katiousha—the same Katiousha—only more lovely than before. The naive, smiling, somewhat squinting black eyes still looked up; she wore a clean white apron, as before. She brought a perfumed piece of soap, just taken from the wrapper, and two towels—one Russian and the other Turkish. The freshly unpacked soap, the towels and she herself, were all equally clean, fresh, pure and pleasant. The lovely, firm, red lips became creased from unrestrainable happiness at sight of him.

"How do you do, Dmitri Ivanovich?" she said, with difficulty, her face becoming flushed.

"How art—how are you?" He did not know whether to "thou" her or not, and became as red in the face as she was.[D] "Are you well?"

"Very well. Your aunt sent you your favorite soap, rose-scented," she said, placing the soap on the table, and the towels on the arms of the chair.

"The gentleman has his own," Timon stood up for the independence of the guest, proudly pointing to the open traveling bag with silver lids, containing a large number of bottles, brushes, perfumes and all sorts of toilet articles.

"My thanks to auntie. But how glad I am that I came," said Nekhludoff, feeling the old brightness and emotions recurring to his soul.

In answer to this she only smiled and left the room.

The aunts, who always loved Nekhludoff, received him this time with greater joy than usual. Dmitri was going to active service, where he might be wounded or killed. This affected the aunts.

Nekhludoff had arranged his trip so that he might spend twenty-four hours with his aunts, but, seeing Katiousha, decided to remain over Easter Sunday, which was two days later, and wired to his friend and commander Shenbok, whom he was to meet at Odessa, to come to his aunts.

From the very first day Nekhludoff experienced the old feeling toward Katiousha. Again he could not see without agitation the white apron of Katiousha; he could not listen without joy to her steps, her voice, her laugh; he could not, without emotion, look into her black eyes, especially when she smiled; he could not, above all, see, without confusion, how she blushed when they met. He felt that he was in love, but not as formerly, when this love was to him a mystery, and he had not the courage to confess it to himself; when he was convinced that one can love only once. Now he loved knowingly, rejoiced at it, and confusedly knowing, though he concealed it from himself, what it consisted of, and what might come of it.

In Nekhludoff, as in all people, there were two beings; one spiritual, who sought only such happiness for himself as also benefited others; and the animal being, seeking his own happiness for the sake of which he is willing to sacrifice that of the world. During this period of his insane egotism, called forth by the life in the army and in St. Petersburg, the animal man dominated him and completely suppressed the spiritual man. But, seeing Katiousha, and being again imbued with the feelings he formerly experienced toward her, the spiritual man raised his head and began to assert his rights. And during the two days preceding Easter an incessant struggle was going on within Nekhludoff of which he was quite unconscious.

In the depth of his soul he knew that he had to depart; that his stay at his aunts was unnecessary, that nothing good could come of it, but it was so joyous and pleasant that he did not heed it, and remained.

On the eve of Easter Sunday, the priest and deacon who, as they afterward related, with difficulty covered the three miles from the church to the aunts' manor, arrived on a sleigh to perform the morning services.

Nekhludoff, with his aunts and the servants, went through the motions, without ceasing to look on Katiousha, who brought a censer and was standing at the door; then, in the customary fashion, kissed the priest and the aunts, and was about to retire to his room when he heard Matriena Pavlovna, the old servant of Maria Ivanovna, making preparations with Katiousha to go to church and witness the consecration of the paschal bread. "I will go there, too," he thought.

There was no wagon or sleigh road to the church, so Nekhludoff gave command, as he would in his own house, to have a horse saddled, and, instead of going to bed, donned a brilliant uniform and tight knee-breeches, threw on his military coat, and, mounting the snorting and constantly neighing, heavy stallion, he drove off to the church in the dark, over pools and snow mounds.

FOOTNOTES:

[B] Diminutive of Maria.

[C] Diminutive of Sophia.

[D] The Russian thou cannot be rendered into English with any degree of accuracy. The greeting to which the impulsive Nekhludoff was about to give expression is that used toward a beloved person.

CHAPTER XV.

That morning service formed the brightest and most impressive reminiscence of Nekhludoff's after life.

The darkness of the night was only relieved here and there by white patches of snow, and as the stallion, splashing through the mud-pools, and his ears pricked up at the sight of the fire-pots surrounding the church, entered its inclosure, the service had already begun.

The peasants, recognizing Maria Ivanovna's nephew, led his horse to the driest spot, where he dismounted, then they escorted him to the church filled with a holiday crowd.

To the right were the male peasants; old men in homespun coats and bast shoes, and young men in new cloth caftans, bright-colored belts and boots. To the left the women, with red silk 'kerchiefs on their heads, shag caftans with bright red sleeves, and blue, green, red, striped and dotted skirts and iron-heeled shoes. Behind them stood the more modest women in white 'kerchiefs and gray caftans and ancient skirts, in shoes or bast slippers. Among these and the others were dressed-up children with oiled hair. The peasants made the sign of the cross and bowed, disheveling their hair; the women, especially the old women, gazing with their lustreless eyes on one image, before which candles burned, pressed hard with the tips of their fingers on the 'kerchief of the forehead, the shoulders and the abdomen, and, mumbling something, bent forward standing, or fell on their knees. The children, imitating their elders, prayed fervently when they were looked at. The gold iconostasis was aflame with innumerable candles, which surrounded a large one in the centre wound in a narrow strip of gilt paper. The church lustre was dotted with candles, joyful melodies of volunteer singers with roaring bass and piercing contralto mingled with the chant of the choir.

Nekhludoff went forward. In the middle of the church stood the aristocracy; a country squire with his wife and son in a sailor blouse, the commissary of the rural police, a telegraph operator, a merchant in high boots, the local syndic with a medal on his breast, and to the right of the tribune, behind the squire's wife, Matriena Pavlovna, in a lilac-colored chatoyant dress and white shawl with colored border, and beside her was Katiousha in a white dress, gathered in folds at the waist, a blue belt, and a red bow in her black hair.

Everything was solemn, joyous and beautiful; the priest in his bright, silver chasuble, dotted with gilt crosses, the deacon, the chanters in holiday surplice of gold and silver, the spruce volunteer singers with oiled hair, the joyous melodies of holiday songs, the ceaseless blessing of the throng by the priests with flower-bedecked tern candles with the constantly repeated exclamations: "Christ has risen! Christ has risen!" Everything was beautiful, but more beautiful than all was Katiousha, in her white dress, blue belt and red bow in her hair, and her eyes radiant with delight.

Nekhludoff felt that she saw him without turning round. He saw it while passing near her to the altar. He had nothing to tell her, but tried to think of something, and said, when passing her:

"Auntie said that she would receive the sacrament after mass."

Her young blood, as it always happened when she looked at him, rose to her cheeks, and her black eyes, naively looking up, fixed themselves on Nekhludoff.

"I know it," she said, smiling.

At that moment a chanter with a copper coffee-pot in his hand passed close to Katiousha, and, without looking at her, grazed her with the skirt of the surplice. The chanter, evidently out of respect for Nekhludoff, wished to sweep around him, and thus it happened that he grazed Katiousha.

Nekhludoff, however, was surprised that that chanter did not understand that everything in the church, and in the whole world, for that matter, existed only for Katiousha, and that one might spurn the entire world, but must not slight her, because she was the centre of it. It was for her that the gold iconostasis shone brightly, and these candles in the church-lustre burned; for her were the joyful chants: "Be happy, man; it is the Lord's Easter." All the good in the world was for her. And it seemed to him that Katiousha understood that all this was for her. It seemed to Nekhludoff, when he looked at her erect figure in the white dress with little folds at the waist, and by the expression of her happy face, that the very thing that filled his soul with song, also filled hers.

In the interval between early and late mass Nekhludoff left the church. The people made way for him and bowed. Some recognized him; others asked: "Who is he?" He stopped at the porch. Beggars surrounded him, and, distributing such change as he had in his pocket, he descended the stairs.

The day began to break, but the sun was yet beyond the horizon. The people seated themselves on the grass around the church-yard, but Katiousha remained in the church, and Nekhludoff waited on the porch for her appearance.

The crowd was still pouring out of the church, their hob-nailed shoes clattering against the stone pavement, and spread about the cemetery.

An old man, confectioner to Maria Ivanovna, stopped Nekhludoff and kissed him, and his wife, an old woman with a wrinkled Adam's apple under a silk 'kerchief, unrolled a yellow saffron egg from her handkerchief and gave it to him. At the same time a young, smiling and muscular peasant, in a new caftan, approached.

"Christ has risen!" he said, with smiling eyes and, nearing Nekhludoff, spread around him a peculiar, pleasant, peasant odor, and, tickling him with his curly beard, three times kissed him on the lips.

While Nekhludoff was thus exchanging the customary kisses with the peasant and taking from him a dark-brown egg, he noticed the chatoyant dress of Matriena Pavlovna and the lovely head with the red bow.

No sooner did she catch sight of him over the heads of those in front of her, than her face brightened up.

On reaching the porch they also stopped, distributing alms. One of the beggars, with a red, cicatrized slough instead of a nose, approached Katiousha. She produced some coins from her handkerchief, gave them to him, and without the slightest expression of disgust, but, on the contrary, her eyes beaming with delight, kissed him three times. While she was thus kissing with the beggar, her eyes met those of Nekhludoff, and she seemed to ask him: "Is it not right? Is it not proper?"

"Yes, yes, darling; it is right; everything is beautiful. I love you."

As they descended the stairs he came near her. He did not wish to kiss her, but merely wished to be by her side.

"Christ has risen!" said Matriena Pavlovna, leaning her head forward and smiling. By the intonation of her voice she seemed to say, "All are equal to-day," and wiping her mouth with a bandana handkerchief which she kept under her arm-pit, she extended her lips.

"He has risen, indeed," answered Nekhludoff, and they kissed each other.

He turned to look at Katiousha. She flushed and at the same moment approached him.

"Christ has risen, Dmitri Ivanovich."

"He has risen, indeed," he said. They kissed each other twice, and seemed to be reflecting whether or not it was necessary to kiss a third time, and having decided, as it were, that it was necessary, they kissed again.

"Will you go to the priest?" asked Nekhludoff.

"No, we will stay here, Dmitri Ivanovich," answered Katiousha, laboriously, as though after hard, pleasant exertion, breathing with her full breast and looking straight in his eyes, with her submissive, chaste, loving and slightly squinting eyes.

There is a point in the love between man and woman when that love reaches its zenith; when it is free from consciousness, reason and sensuality. Such a moment arrived for Nekhludoff that Easter morn.

Now, whenever he thought of Katiousha, her appearance at that moment obscured every other recollection of her. The dark, smooth, resplendent head; the white dress with folds clinging to her graceful bust and undulating breast;

those vermilion cheeks, those brilliant black eyes, and two main traits in all her being: the virgin purity of her love, not only for himself, but for everything and everybody—he knew it—not only the good and beautiful, but even that beggar whom she had kissed.

He knew that she possessed that love, because that night and that morning he felt it within him, and felt that in that love his soul mingled into one with hers.

Ah, if that feeling had continued unchanged! "Yes, that awful affair occurred after that notable commemoration of Christ's resurrection!" he thought now, sitting at the window of the jury-room.

CHAPTER XVI.

Returning from the church, Nekhludoff broke his fast with the aunts, and to repair his strength, drank some brandy and wine—a habit he acquired in the army—and going to his room immediately fell asleep with his clothes on. He was awakened by a rap at the door. By the rap he knew that it was she, so he rose, rubbing his eyes and stretching himself.

"Is it you, Katiousha? Come in," he said, rising.

She opened the door.

"You are wanted to breakfast," she said. She was in the same white dress, but without the bow in her hair.

As she looked in his eyes she brightened up, as if she had announced something unusually pleasant.

"I shall come immediately," he answered, taking a comb to rearrange his hair.

She lingered for a moment. He noticed it, and putting down the comb, he moved toward her. But at the same moment she quickly turned and walked off with her customary light and agile step along the narrow mat of the corridor.

"What a fool I am!" Nekhludoff said to himself. "Why did I not detain her?" And he ran after her.

He did not know himself what he wished of her, but it seemed to him that when she entered his room he ought to have done something that any one in his place would have done, but which he failed to do.

"Wait, Katiousha," he said.

She looked around.

"What is it?" she said, stopping.

"Nothing. I only——"

With some effort he overcame his shyness, and remembering how people generally act in such a case, he put his arm about Katiousha's waist.

She stopped and looked in his eyes.

"Don't, Ivanovich, don't," she said, blushing until her eyes filled with tears. Then with her rough, strong hands she removed his arm.

Nekhludoff released her, and for a moment felt not only awkward and ashamed, but seemed odious to himself. He should have believed in himself, but he failed to understand that this awkwardness and shame were the noblest feelings of his soul begging for recognition, and, on the contrary, it seemed to him that it was his foolishness that was speaking within him, that he ought to have done as everybody does in a similar case.

He overtook her again, again embraced her and kissed her on the neck. This kiss was entirely unlike the other two kisses. The first was given unconsciously, behind the lilac bush; the second, in the morning in church. The last one was terrible, and she felt it.

"But what are you doing?" she exclaimed in such a voice, as if he had irrecoverably destroyed something infinitely precious, and ran away from him.

He went to the dining-room. His aunts in holiday attire, the doctor and a neighbor were taking lunch standing. Everything was as usual, but a storm raged in Nekhludoff's soul. He did not understand what was said to him, his answers were inappropriate, and he was thinking only of Katiousha, recalling the sensation of the last kiss he gave her when he overtook her in the corridor. He could think of nothing else. When she entered the room, without looking at her, he felt her presence with all his being, and had to make an effort not to look at her.

After lunch he went immediately to his room, and in great agitation walked to and fro, listening to the sounds in the house and waiting to hear her steps. The animal man that dwelled in him not only raised his head, but crushed under foot the spiritual man that he was when he first arrived at the manor, and was even this very morning in church, and that terrible animal man now held sway in his soul. Although Nekhludoff was watching an opportunity to meet Katiousha that day, he did not succeed in seeing her face to face even once. She was probably avoiding him. But in the evening it happened that she had to enter a room adjoining his. The physician was to remain over night, and Katiousha had to make the bed for him. Hearing her steps, Nekhludoff, stepping on tip-toe and holding his breath, as though preparing to commit a crime, followed her into the room.

Thrusting both her hands into a white pillow-case, and taking hold of two corners of the pillow, she turned her head and looked at him smiling, but it was not the old, cheerful, happy smile, but a frightened, piteous smile. The smile seemed to tell him that what he was doing was wrong. For a moment he stood still. There was still the possibility of a struggle. Though weak, the voice of his true love to her was still heard; it spoke of her, of her feelings, of her life. The other voice reminded him of his enjoyment, his happiness. And this second voice stifled the first. He approached her with determination. And the terrible, irresistible animal feeling mastered him.

Without releasing her from his embrace, Nekhludoff seated her on the bed, and feeling that something else ought to be done, seated himself beside her.

"Dmitri Ivanovich, darling, please let me go," she said in a piteous voice. "Matriena Pavlovna is coming!" she suddenly exclaimed, tearing herself away.

91

Matriena Pavlovna was really approaching the door. She entered the room, holding a quilt on her arm, and, looking reproachfully at Nekhludoff, angrily rebuked Katiousha for taking the wrong quilt.

Nekhludoff went out in silence. He was not even ashamed. By the expression of Matriena Pavlovna's face he saw that she condemned him, and justly so; he knew that what he was doing was wrong, but the animal feeling, which succeeded his former feeling of pure love to her, seized him and held sole sway over him; recognizing no other feeling. He knew now what was necessary to do in order to satisfy that feeling, and was looking for means to that end.

He was out of sorts all that night. Now he would go to his aunts; now he returned to his room, or went to the perron, thinking but of one thing: how to meet her alone. But she avoided him, and Matriena Pavlovna strove not to lose sight of her.

CHAPTER XVII.

Thus the entire evening passed, and when night came the doctor went to bed. The aunts were also preparing to retire. Nekhludoff knew that Matriena Pavlovna was in the aunts' dormitory, and that Katiousha was in the servants' quarters—alone. He again went out on the perron. It was dark, damp and warm, and that white mist which in the spring thaws the last snow, filled the air. Strange noises came from the river, which was a hundred feet from the house. It was the breaking up of the ice.

Nekhludoff came down from the perron, and stepping over pools and the thin ice-covering formed on the snow, walked toward the window of the servants' quarters. His heart beat so violently that he could hear it; his breathing at times stopped, at others it escaped in a heavy sigh. A small lamp was burning in the maid-servants' room.

Katiousha was sitting at the table alone, musing and looking at the wall before her. Without moving Nekhludoff for some time stood gazing at her, wishing to know what she would do while thinking herself unobserved. For about two minutes she sat motionless, then raised her eyes, smiled, reproachfully shook her head, at herself apparently, and, changing her position, with a start placed both hands on the table and fixed her eyes before her.

He remained looking at her, and involuntarily listened to the beating of his heart and the strange sounds coming from the river. There, on the misty river some incessant, slow work was going on. Now something snuffled, then it crackled, and again the thin layer of ice resounded like a mass of crushed glass.

He stood looking at the thoughtful face of Katiousha, tormented by an internal struggle, and he pitied her. But, strange to say, this pity only increased his longing for her.

He rapped at the window. She trembled from head to foot, as if an electric current had passed through her, and terror was reflected on her face. Then she sprang up, and, going to the window, placed her face against the window-pane. The expression of terror did not leave her even when, shading her eyes with the palms of her hands, she recognized him. Her face was unusually grave—he had never seen such an expression on it. When he smiled she smiled also—she smiled as if only in submission to him, but in her soul, instead of a smile, there was terror. He motioned her with his hand to come out. But she shook her head and remained at the window. Again he leaned toward the window and was about to speak when she turned toward the door. Some one had apparently called her. Nekhludoff moved away from the window. The fog was so dense that when five feet away he saw only a darkening mass from which a red, seemingly large, light of the lamp was reflected. From the river came the same strange sounds of snuffling, crackling and grinding of the ice. In the court-yard a cock crowed, others near by responded; then from the village, first singly, interrupting each other, then mingling into one chorus, was heard the crowing of all the cocks. Except for the noise of the river, it was perfectly quiet all around.

After walking twice around the corner of the house, and stepping several times into mud-pools, Nekhludoff returned to the window of the maid-servants' quarters. The lamp was still burning, and Katiousha sat alone at the table as if in indecision. As soon as he came near the window she looked at him. He rapped. Without stopping to see who had rapped, she immediately ran from the room, and he heard the opening and closing of the door. He was already waiting for her in the passage, and immediately silently embraced her. She pressed against his bosom, lifted her head, and with her lips met his kiss.

When Nekhludoff returned to his room it was getting brighter. Below, the noises on the river increased, and a buzzing was added to the other sounds. The mist began to settle, and from behind the wall of mist the waning moon appeared, gloomily, lighting up something dark and terrible.

"Is it good fortune or a great misfortune that has happened to me?" he asked himself. "It is always thus; they all act in that way," and he returned to his room.

CHAPTER XVIII.

On the following day the brilliant and jovial Shenbok called at the aunts for Nekhludoff, and completely charmed them with his elegance, amiability, cheerfulness, liberality, and his love for Dmitri. Though his liberality pleased the aunts, they were somewhat perplexed by the excess to which he carried it. He gave a ruble to a blind beggar; the servants received as tips fifteen rubles, and when Sophia Ivanovna's lap-dog, Suzette, hurt her leg so that it bled, he volunteered to bandage it, and without a moment's consideration tore his fine linen handkerchief (Sophia Ivanovna knew that those handkerchiefs were worth fifteen rubles a dozen) and made bandages of it for the dog. The aunts had never seen such men, nor did they know that his debts ran up to two hundred thousand rubles, which—he knew—would never be paid, and that therefore twenty-five rubles more or less made no appreciable difference in his accounts.

Shenbok remained but one day, and the following evening departed with Nekhludoff. They could remain no longer, for the time for joining their regiment had arrived.

On this last day spent at the aunts, when the events of the preceding evening were fresh in his memory, two antagonistic feelings struggled in Nekhludoff's soul; one was the burning, sensual recollection of love, although it failed to fulfill its promises, and some satisfaction of having gained his ends;

94

the other, a consciousness of having committed a wrong, and that that wrong must be righted—not for her sake, but for his own sake.

In that condition of insane egotism Nekhludoff thought only of himself—whether he would be condemned, and how far, if his act should be discovered, but never gave a thought to the question, "How does she feel about it, and what will become of her?"

He thought that Shenbok divined his relations to Katiousha, and his ambition was flattered.

"That's why you so suddenly began to like your aunts," Shenbok said to him when he saw Katiousha. "In your place I should stay here even longer. She is charming!"

He also thought that while it was a pity to leave now, without enjoying his love in its fullness, the necessity of going was advantageous in that he was able to break the relations which it were difficult to keep up. He further thought it was necessary to give her money, not because she might need it, but because it was customary to do so. So he gave as much money as he thought was proper, considering their respective positions.

On the day of his departure, after dinner he waited in the passage until she came by. She flushed as she saw him, and wished to pass on, pointing with her eyes to the door of her room, but he detained her.

"I came to bid you farewell," he said, crumpling an envelope containing a hundred ruble bill. "How is——"

She suspected it, frowned, shook her head and thrust aside his hand.

"Yes, take it," he murmured, thrusting the envelope in the bosom of her waist, and, as if it had burned his fingers, he ran to his room.

For a long time he paced his room to and fro, frowning, and even jumping, and moaning aloud as if from physical pain, as he thought of the scene.

But what is to be done? It is always thus. Thus it was with Shenbok and the governess whom he had told about; it was thus with Uncle Gregory; with his father, when he lived in the country, and the illegitimate son Miteuka, who is still living, was born to him. And if everybody acts thus, consequently it ought to be so. Thus he was consoling himself, but he could not be consoled. The recollection of it stung his conscience.

In the depth of his soul he knew that his action was so base, abominable and cruel that, with that action upon his conscience, not only would he have no right to condemn others but he should not be able to look others in the face, to say nothing of considering himself the good, noble, magnanimous man he esteemed himself. And he had to esteem himself as such in order to be able to continue to lead a valiant and joyous life. And there was but one way of doing so, and that was not to think of it. This he endeavored to do.

The life into which he had just entered—new scenes, comrades, and active service—helped him on. The more he lived, the less he thought of it, and in the end really forgot it entirely.

Only once, on his return from active service, when, in the hope of seeing her, he paid a visit to his aunts, he was told that Katiousha, soon after his departure, had left them; that she had given birth to a child, and, as the aunts were informed, had gone to the bad. As he heard it his heart was oppressed with grief. From the statement of the time when she gave birth to the child it might be his, and it might not be his. The aunts said that she was vicious and of a depraved nature, just like her mother. And this opinion of the aunts pleased him, because it exculpated him, as it were. At first he intended to find her and the child, but as it pained him very much, and he was ashamed to think of it, he did not make the necessary efforts, and gradually ceased to think of his sin.

But now, this fortuitous meeting brought everything to his mind, and compelled the acknowledgment of his heartlessness, cruelty and baseness which made it possible for him to live undisturbed by the sin which lay on his conscience. He was yet far from such acknowledgment, and at this moment was only thinking how to avoid disclosure which might be made by her, or her attorney, and thus disgrace him before everybody.

CHAPTER XIX.

Nekhludoff was in this state of mind when he left the court-room and entered the jury-room. He sat near the window, listening to the conversations of his fellow jurymen, and smoked incessantly.

The cheerful merchant evidently sympathized with Merchant Smelkoff's manner of passing his time.

"Well, well! He went on his spree just like a Siberian! Seems to have known a good thing when he saw it. What a beauty!"

The foreman expressed the opinion that the whole case depended on the expert evidence. Peter Gerasimovich was jesting with the Jewish clerk, and both of them burst out laughing. Nekhludoff answered all questions in monosyllables, and only wished to be left in peace.

When the usher with the sidling gait called the jury into court Nekhludoff was seized with fear, as if judgment was to be passed on him, and not he to pass judgment on others.

In the depth of his soul he already felt that he was a rascal, who ought to be ashamed to look people in the face, and yet, by force of habit, he walked to the elevation with his customary air of self-confidence, and took his seat next to the foreman, crossed his legs and began to play with his pince-nez.

The prisoners, who had also been removed from the court, were brought in again.

The new faces of witnesses were now seen in the court-room, and Nekhludoff noticed Maslova constantly turning her head in the direction of a smartly attired, stout woman in silk and plush, with an elegant reticule hanging on her half-bare arm. This was, as Nekhludoff afterward learned, Maslova's mistress and a witness against her.

The examination of the witnesses began as to their names, age, religion, et cetera. After being questioned as to whether they preferred to testify under oath, the same old priest, with difficulty moving his legs, came, and again arranging the gold cross on his silk-covered breast, with the same calmness and confidence, began to administer the oath to the witnesses and the expert. When the swearing in was over, the witnesses were removed to an adjoining room, leaving only Kitaeva, Maslova's mistress. She was asked what she knew of the affair. Kitaeva, with a feigned smile, a German accent, and straightening her hat at every sentence, fluently and circumstantially related the following:

Simon came first to her house for Liubasha. [E] In a little while Liubasha returned with the merchant. "The merchant was already in ecstasy," slightly smiling, said Kitaeva, "and he continued to drink and treat himself, but as he was short of money he sent to his room this same Liubasha, for whom he acquired a predilection," she said, looking at Maslova.

It seemed to Nekhludoff that Maslova smiled at this, and the smile seemed to him disgusting. A strange feeling of squeamishness mingled with compassion rose in his breast.

"What opinion did you entertain of Maslova?" timidly and blushingly asked the attorney assigned by the court to defend Maslova.

"Very excellent," answered Kitaeva. "The girl is very well educated and elegant in her manners. She was raised in a very good family, and could read French. She sometimes drank a little too much, but she never forgot herself. She is a very good girl."

Katiousha looked at her mistress, then suddenly turned her eyes on the jury and rested them on Nekhludoff, her face becoming serious and even stern. One of the stern eyes squinted. These strangely gazing eyes were turned on Nekhludoff for a considerable time. Notwithstanding the terror that seized him, he could not remove his own gaze from those squinting eyes with their shining whites. He recalled that awful night with the breaking ice, the fog, and especially that waning, upturned moon which rose in the morning and lit up something dark and terrible. These two black eyes which looked at and at the same time by him reminded him of something dark and terrible.

"She recognized me!" he thought. And Nekhludoff shrank, as it were, waiting for the blow. But she did not recognize him. She sighed calmly and again fixed her eyes on the justiciary. Nekhludoff also sighed. "Ah, if they would only hasten it through," he thought. He felt now as he did once when out game shooting, when he was obliged to kill a wounded bird—he was filled with disgust, pity and vexation. The wounded bird is struggling in the game bag; he feels disgust and pity, and wishes to kill it quickly and forget it.

Such mingled feelings filled Nekhludoff's breast as he sat listening to the examination of the witnesses.

FOOTNOTES:

[E] A contemptuous diminutive of Liuba. Tr.

CHAPTER XX.

As if to spite him, the case dragged out to a weary length. After the examination of the witnesses and the expert, and after all the unnecessary questions by the prosecutor and the attorneys, usually made with an important air, the justiciary told the jury to look at the exhibits, which consisted of an enormous ring with a diamond rosette, evidently made for the forefinger, and a glass tube containing the poison. These were sealed and labeled.

The jury were preparing to view these things, when the prosecutor rose again and demanded that before the exhibits were examined the medical report of the condition of the body be read.

The justiciary was hurrying the case, and though he knew that the reading of the report would only bring ennui and delay the dinner, and that the prosecutor demanded it only because he had the right to do so, he could not refuse the request and gave his consent. The secretary produced the report, and, lisping the letters l and r, began to read in a sad voice.

The external examination disclosed:

1. The height of Therapout Smelkoff was six feet five inches.

"But what a huge fellow," the merchant whispered in Nekhludoff's ear with solicitude.

2. From external appearances he seemed to be about forty years of age.

3. The body had a swollen appearance.

4. The color of the pall was green, streaked with dark spots.

5. The skin on the surface of the body rose in bubbles of various sizes, and in places hung in patches.

6. The hair was dark and thick, and fell off at a slight touch.

7. The eyes came out of their orbits, and the pupils were dull.

8. A frothy, serous fluid flowed continuously from the cavity of the mouth, the nostrils and ears. The mouth was half open.

9. The neck almost disappeared in the swelling of the face and breast, et cetera, et cetera.

Thus, over four pages and twenty-seven clauses, ran the description of the external appearance of the terrible, large, stout, swollen and decomposing body of the merchant who amused himself in the city. The loathing which Nekhludoff felt increased with the reading of the description. Katiousha's life, the sanies running from the nostrils, the eyes that came out of their sockets, and his conduct toward her—all seemed to him to belong to the same order, and he was surrounded and swallowed up by these things. When the reading was finally over, the justiciary sighed deeply and raised his head in the hope that it was all over, but the secretary immediately began to read the report on the internal condition of the body.

The justiciary again bent his head, and, leaning on his hand, closed his eyes. The merchant, who sat near Nekhludoff, barely kept awake, and from time to time swayed his body. The prisoners as well as the gendarmes behind them sat motionless.

The internal examination disclosed:

1. The skin covering of the skull easily detached, and no hemorrhage was noticeable. 2. The skull bones were of average thickness and uninjured. 3. On the hard membrane of the skull there were two small discolored spots of about the size of four centimetres, the membrane itself being of a dull gray color, et cetera, et cetera, to the end of thirteen more clauses.

Then came the names of the witnesses, the signature and deduction of the physician, from which it appeared that the changes found in the stomach, intestines and kidneys justified the conclusion "to a large degree probable" that the death of Smelkoff was due to poison taken into the stomach with a quantity of wine. That it was impossible to tell by the changes in the stomach and intestines the name of the poison; and that the poison came into the stomach mixed with wine could be inferred from the fact that Smelkoff's stomach contained a large quantity of wine.

"He must have drank like a fish," again whispered the awakened merchant.

The reading of this official report, which lasted about two hours, did not satisfy, however, the prosecutor. When it was over the justiciary turned to him, saying:

"I suppose it is superfluous to read the record of the examination of the intestines."

"I would ask that it be read," sternly said the prosecutor without looking at the justiciary, sidewise raising himself, and impressing by the tone of his voice that it was his right to demand it, that he would insist on it, and that a refusal would be ground for appeal.

The associate with the long beard and kind, drooping eyes, who was suffering from catarrh, feeling very weak, turned to the justiciary:

"What is the good of reading it? It will only drag the matter out. These new brooms only take a longer time to sweep, but do not sweep any cleaner."

The associate in the gold eye-glasses said nothing, and gloomily and determinedly looked in front of him, expecting nothing good either from his wife or from the world.

The report commenced thus: "February 15th, 188—. The undersigned, in pursuance of an order, No. 638, of the Medical Department," began the secretary with resolution, raising the pitch of his voice, as if to dispel the drowsiness that seized upon every one present, "and in the presence of the assistant medical director, examined the following intestines:

"1. The right lung and heart (contained in a five-pound glass vial).

"2. The contents of the stomach (contained in a five-pound glass vial).

"3. The stomach itself (contained in a five-pound glass vial).

"4. The kidneys, liver and spleen (contained in a two-and-a-half-pound glass vial).

"5. The entrails (contained in a five-pound earthen jar)."

As the reading of this report began the justiciary leaned over to one of his associates and whispered something, then to the other, and, receiving affirmative answers, interrupted the reading at this point.

"The Court finds the reading of the report superfluous," he said.

The secretary closed reading and gathered up his papers, while the prosecutor angrily began to make notes.

"The gentlemen of the jury may now view the exhibits," said the justiciary.

The foreman and some of the jury rose from their seats, and, holding their hands in awkward positions, approached the table and looked in turn on the ring, vials and jars. The merchant even tried the ring on his finger.

"What a finger he had," he said, returning to his seat. "It must have been the size of a large cucumber," he added, evidently amused by the giant figure of the merchant, as he imagined him.

CHAPTER XXI.

When the examination of the exhibits was over, the justiciary announced the investigation closed, and, desiring to end the session, gave the word to the prosecutor, in the hope that as he, too, was mortal, he might also wish to smoke or dine, and would have pity on the others. But the prosecutor pitied neither himself nor them. When the word was given him, he rose slowly, displaying his elegant figure, and, placing both hands on the desk, and slightly bending his head, he cast a glance around the court-room, his eyes avoiding the prisoners.

102

"Gentlemen of the jury, the case which is now to be submitted to your consideration," he began his speech, prepared while the indictment and reports were being read, "is a characteristic crime, if I may so express myself."

The speech of a prosecuting attorney, according to his idea, had to be invested with a social significance, according to the manner of those lawyers who became famous. True, among his hearers were three women; a seamstress, a cook and Simon's sister, also a driver, but that made no difference. Those celebrities also began on a small scale. The prosecutor made it a rule to view the situation from the eminence of his position, i. e., to penetrate into the profound psychological meaning of crime, and bare the ulcers of society.

"Here is before you, gentlemen of the jury, a crime characteristic, if I may so express myself, of the end of our century, bearing, as it were, all the specific features of the first symptoms of decomposition, to which those elements of our society, which are exposed, as it were, to the more scorching rays of that process, are subject."

The prosecutor spoke at great length, endeavoring on the one hand to remember all those wise sayings which he had prepared for the occasion, and on the other, most important, hand, not to stop for a moment, but to make his speech flow uninterruptedly for an hour and a quarter. He stopped only once, for a long time swallowing his saliva, but he immediately mastered himself and made up for the lost time by a greater flow of eloquence. He spoke in a gentle, insinuating voice, resting now on one foot, now on the other, and looking at the jury; then changed to a calm, business tone, consulting his note-book, and again he thundered accusations, turning now to the spectators, now to the jury. But he never looked at the prisoners, all three of whom stared at him. He incorporated into his speech all the latest ideas then in vogue in the circle of his acquaintances, and what was then and is now received as the last word of scientific wisdom. He spoke of heredity, of innate criminality, of Lombroso, of Charcot, of evolution, of the struggle for existence, of hypnotism, of hypnotic suggestion, and of decadence.

The merchant Smelkoff, according to the prosecutor, was a type of the great, pure Russian, with his broad nature, who, in consequence of his trusting nature and generosity, had become a victim of a gang of corrupt people, into whose hands he had fallen.

Simon Kartinkin was the atavistic production of serfdom, stupid, without education, and even without religion. Euphemia was his mistress, and a victim of heredity. All the symptoms of degenerate life were in her. But the ruling spirit in this crime was Maslova, who was the mouthpiece of the lowest phenomenon of decadence. "This woman," said the prosecutor without looking at her, "received an education—you have heard here the evidence of her mistress. Not only can she read and write, but she can speak French. She is an orphan, and probably bears the germs of criminality in her. She was raised in an intelligent, noble family, and could make her living by honest toil, but she leaves them, yields to her passions, and displays an intelligence, and especially, as you have heard here, gentlemen of the jury, an ability to exert influence on people by that mysterious, lately discovered by science, especially by the school of Charcot, power known by the name of hypnotic suggestion. By the aid of this power she gets control over this hero—a kind, trustful, rich guest, and uses his confidence first to rob him, and then to pitilessly murder him."

"But he is wandering away," said the justiciary, smiling and leaning over to the stern associate.

"What an awful blockhead!" said the stern associate.

"Gentlemen of the jury!" the prosecutor continued meanwhile, gracefully swaying his slim body. "The fate of these people is in your hands, as is to some extent the fate of society, which is influenced by your verdict. You must fathom the significance of this crime, the danger to society that lurks in such pathological, as it were, individuals as Maslova. You must guard it against infection; it is your duty to guard the innocent, healthy elements of society against contagion, if not destruction."

And as if himself impressed with the importance of the verdict, and evidently greatly delighted with his speech, the prosecutor took his seat.

The burden of his speech, if we eliminate the flights of eloquence, was to the effect that Maslova, after gaining the merchant's confidence, hypnotized him, and that, arriving at the inn with the key to the merchant's trunk, she intended to steal the money herself, but, being discovered by Simon and Euphemia, was obliged to divide with them. That afterward, desiring to conceal the traces of her crime, she returned with the merchant to the inn and administered poison to him.

When the prosecutor had finished his speech, a middle-aged man, in a dress coat and wide semi-circle of starched shirt front, rose from the lawyer's bench, and boldly began to deliver a speech in defense of Kartinkin and Bochkova. He was a lawyer hired by them for three hundred rubles. He declared them both innocent, and threw all the blame on Maslova.

He belittled the deposition of Maslova relating to the presence of Bochkova and Kartinkin when she took the money, and insisted that, as she had confessed to poisoning the merchant, her evidence could have no weight. The twenty-five hundred rubles could have been earned by two hard working and honest persons, who were receiving in tips three to four rubles a day from guests. The merchant's money was stolen by Maslova, who either gave it to some one for safe keeping, or lost it, which was not unlikely, as she was not in a normal condition. The poisoning was done by Maslova alone.

For these reasons he asked the jury to acquit Kartinkin and Bochkova of stealing the money; or, if they found them guilty of stealing he asked for a verdict of theft, but without participation in the poisoning, and without conspiracy.

In conclusion, this lawyer made a thrust at the prosecuting attorney by remarking that, although the splendid reasonings of the prosecutor on heredity explain the scientific questions of heredity, they hardly hold good in the case of Bochkova, since her parentage was unknown.

The prosecutor, growling, began to make notes, and shrugged his shoulders in contemptuous surprise.

Next rose Maslova's lawyer, and timidly and falteringly began his speech in her defense. Without denying that Maslova participated in the theft, he insisted that she had no intention of poisoning Smelkoff, but gave him the powder in order to make him sleep. When he described Maslova's unfortunate life, telling how she had been drawn into a life of vice by a man who went unpunished, while she was left to bear the whole burden of her fall, he attempted to become eloquent, but his excursion into the domain of psychology failed, so that everybody felt awkward. When he began to mutter about man's cruelty and woman's helplessness, the justiciary, desiring to help him, asked him to confine himself to the facts of the case.

After this lawyer had finished the prosecutor rose again and defended his position on the question of heredity against the first lawyer, stating that the fact that Bochkova's parentage was unknown did not invalidate the truth of the theory of heredity; that the law of heredity is so well established by science that not only can one deduce the crime from heredity, but heredity from the crime. As to the statement of the defense that Maslova was drawn into a vicious life by an imaginary (he pronounced the word imaginary with particular virulence) man, he could say that all facts rather pointed to her being the seducer of many victims who were unfortunate enough to fall into her hands. Saying which he sat down in triumph.

The prisoners were then allowed to make any statements they wished in their behalf.

Euphemia Bochkova repeated her statement that she knew nothing, had not taken part in anything, and persistently pointed at Maslova as the only guilty person. Simon only repeated several times:

"Do what you please with me, only it is all for nothing."

Maslova was silent. When asked what she had to say in her defense, she only lifted her eyes on the justiciary, looked around like a hunted animal, and immediately lowering them began to sob aloud.

"What is the matter?" asked the merchant of Nekhludoff, hearing a strange sound escaping the latter's lips. It was a suppressed sob.

Nekhludoff did not yet realize the significance of his present position, and the scarcely suppressed sob and the tears that welled up in his eyes he ascribed to the weakness of his nerves. He put on his pince-nez to hide them, and, drawing a handkerchief from his pocket, began to blow his nose.

His fear of the disgrace that would fall upon him if everybody in the court-room were to find out his conduct toward her stifled the struggle that was going on within him. At this time fear outweighed in him every other feeling.

CHAPTER XXII.

After the last words of the prisoners had been heard, and the lengthy arguments over the form in which the questions were to be put to the jury were over, the questions were finally agreed upon, and the justiciary began to deliver his instructions to the jury.

Although he was anxious to finish the case, he was so carried away that when he started to speak he could not stop himself. He told the jury at great length that if they found the prisoners guilty, they had the right to return a verdict of guilty, and if they found them not guilty, they had the right to return a verdict of not guilty. If, however they found them guilty of one charge, and not guilty of the other, they might bring in a verdict of guilty of the one and not guilty of the other. He further explained to them that they must exercise this power intelligently. He also intended to explain to them that if they gave an affirmative answer to a question, they would thereby affirm everything involved in the question, and that if they did not desire to affirm everything involved in the question, they must distinguish the part they affirmed from the part they disaffirmed. But, seeing on the clock that it was five minutes of three, he decided to pass over to a statement of the case.

"The facts of this case are the following," he began, repeating everything that had been stated over and over again by the defendants' attorneys, the prosecutor and the witnesses. While the justiciary was charging the jury his associates thoughtfully listened, and now and then glanced at the clock. They thought that although his charge was sound, i. e., as it should be, it was too long. Of the same opinion was the prosecutor, as well as all those connected with the court, including the spectators. The justiciary concluded his charge.

It was thought he had finished. But the justiciary found it necessary to add a few words concerning the importance of the power given to the jury; that it should be used with care, and should not be abused; that they had taken an oath; that they were the conscience of society, and that the secrecy of the consultation room was sacred, etc., etc.

From the moment the justiciary began to speak, Maslova kept her eyes on him, as if she feared to miss a word, so that Nekhludoff was not afraid to meet her gaze, and constantly looked at her. And before his imagination arose that common phenomenon of the appearance of a long absent, beloved face, which, after the first shock produced by the external changes which have taken place during the long absence, gradually becomes the same as it was many years ago—all the past changes disappear, and before the spiritual eyes stands forth the main expression of the peculiar spiritual individuality. This happened with Nekhludoff.

Yes, notwithstanding the prison garb, the bloated body and the high breast; notwithstanding the distended lower part of the face, the wrinkles on the forehead and the temples, and the swelling under the eyes, it was undoubtedly that same Katiousha who on Easter Sunday looked up to him, her beloved, with her enamored, smiling, happy, lively eyes.

"What a remarkable coincidence! That this case should be tried during my term! That, without seeing her for ten years, I should meet her here in the prisoner's dock! And what will be the end? Ah, I wish it were over!"

He would not yield to the feeling of repentance which spoke within him. He considered it an incident which would soon pass away without disturbing his life. He felt himself in the position of a puppy who had misbehaved in his master's rooms, and whom his master, taking him by the neck, thrust into the dirt he had made. The puppy squeals, pulls back in his effort to escape the consequences of his deed, which he wishes to forget, but the inexorable master holds him fast. Thus Nekhludoff felt the foulness of his act, and he also felt the powerful hand of the master, but did not yet understand the significance of his act, did not recognize the master. He did not wish to believe that what he saw before him was the result of his own deed. But the inexorable, invisible hand held him fast, and he had a foreboding that he should not escape. He summoned up his courage, crossed his legs, as was his wont, and, negligently playing with his pince-nez, he sat with an air of self-confidence on the second chair of the front row. Meanwhile he already felt in the depth of his soul all the cruelty, dastardliness and baseness not only of that act of his, but of his whole idle, dissolute, cruel and wayward life. And the terrible veil, which during these twelve years in such marvelous manner had hidden from him that crime and all his subsequent life, already began to stir, and now and then he caught a glimpse behind it.

CHAPTER XXIII.

The justiciary finally finished his speech and handed the list of questions to the foreman. The jury rose from their seats, glad of an opportunity to leave the court-room, and, not knowing what to do with their hands, as if ashamed of something, they filed into the consultation-room. As soon as the door closed behind them a gendarme, with drawn sword resting on his shoulder, placed himself in front of it. The judges rose and went out. The prisoners also were led away.

On entering the consultation-room the jury immediately produced cigarettes and began to smoke. The sense of their unnatural and false position, of which they were to a greater or less degree cognizant, while sitting in the court-room, passed away as soon as they entered their room and lighted their cigarettes, and, with a feeling of relief, they seated themselves and immediately started an animated conversation.

"The girl is not guilty, she was confused," said the kind-hearted merchant.

"That is what we are going to consider," retorted the foreman. "We must not yield to our personal impressions."

"The judge's summing up was good," said the colonel.

"Do you call it good? It nearly sent me to sleep."

"The important point is that the servants could not have known that there was money in the room if Maslova had no understanding with them," said the clerk with the Jewish face.

"So you think that she stole it?" asked one of the jury.

"I will never believe that," shouted the kind-hearted merchant. "It is all the work of that red-eyed wench."

"They are all alike," said the colonel.

"But she said that she did not go into the room."

"Do you believe her more than the other? I should never believe that worthless woman."

"That does not decide the question," said the clerk.

"She had the key."

"What if she had?" answered the merchant.

"And the ring?"

"She explained it," again shouted the merchant. "It is quite likely that being drunk he struck her. Well, and then he was sorry, of course. 'There, don't cry! Take this ring.' And what a big man! They said he weighed about two hundred and fifty pounds, I believe."

"That is not the point," interrupted Peter Gerasimovich. "The question is, Was she the instigator, or were the servants?"

"The servants could not have done it without her. She had the key."

This incoherent conversation lasted for a long time.

"Excuse me, gentlemen," said the foreman. "Let us sit down and consider the matter. Take your seats," he added, seating himself in the foreman's chair.

"These girls are rogues," said the clerk, and to sustain his opinion that Maslova was the chief culprit, he related how one of those girls once stole a watch from a friend of his.

As a case in point the colonel related the bolder theft of a silver samovar.

"Gentlemen, let us take up the questions," said the foreman, rapping on the table with a pencil.

They became silent. The questions submitted were:

1. Is the peasant of the village of Barkoff, district of Krapivensk, Simon Petroff Kartinkin, thirty-three years of age, guilty of having, with the design of taking the life of Smelkoff and robbing him, administered to him poison in a glass of brandy, which caused the death of Smelkoff, and of afterward robbing him of twenty-five hundred rubles and a diamond ring?

2. Is the burgess Euphemia Ivanovna Bochkova, forty-seven years of age, guilty of the crime mentioned in the first question?

3. Is the burgess Katherine Michaelovna Maslova, twenty-seven years of age, guilty of the crime mentioned in the first question?

4. If the prisoner Euphemia Bochkova is not guilty of the crime set forth in the first question, is she not guilty of secretly stealing, while employed in the Hotel Mauritania, on the 17th day of January, 188—, twenty-five hundred rubles from the trunk of the merchant Smelkoff, to which end she opened the trunk in the hotel with a key brought and fitted by her?

The foreman read the first question.

"Well, gentlemen, what do you think?"

This question was quickly answered. They all agreed to answer "Guilty." The only one that dissented was an old laborer, whose answer to all questions was "Not guilty."

The foreman thought that he did not understand the questions and proceeded to explain that from all the facts it was evident that Kartinkin and Bochkova were guilty, but the laborer answered that he did understand them, and that he thought that they ought to be charitable. "We are not saints ourselves," he said, and did not change his opinion.

The second question, relating to Bochkova, after many arguments and elucidations, was answered "Not guilty," because there was no clear proof that she participated in the poisoning—a fact on which her lawyer put much stress.

The merchant, desiring to acquit Maslova, insisted that Bochkova was the author of the conspiracy. Many of the jurymen agreed with him, but the foreman, desiring to conform strictly to the law, said that there was no foundation for the charge of poisoning against her. After a lengthy argument the foreman's opinion triumphed.

The fourth question, relating to Bochkova, was answered "Guilty," but at the insistence of the laborer, she was recommended to the mercy of the court.

The third question called forth fierce argument. The foreman insisted that she was guilty of both the poisoning and robbery; the merchant, colonel, clerk and laborer opposed this view, while the others hesitated, but the opinion of the foreman began to predominate, principally because the jury were tired out, and they willingly joined the side which promised to prevail the sooner, and consequently release them quicker.

From all that occurred at the trial and his knowledge of Maslova, Nekhludoff was convinced that she was innocent, and at first was confident that the other jurors would so find her, but when he saw that because of the merchant's bungling defense of Maslova, evidently prompted by his undisguised liking for her, and the foreman's resistance which it caused, but chiefly because of the weariness of the jury, there was likely to be a verdict of guilty, he wished to make objection, but feared to speak in her favor lest his relations toward her should be disclosed. At the same time he felt that he could not let things go on without making his objections. He blushed and grew pale in turn, and was about to speak, when Peter Gerasimovich, heretofore silent, evidently exasperated by the authoritative manner of the foreman, suddenly began to make the very objections Nekhludoff intended to make.

"Permit me to say a few words," he began. "You say that she stole the money because she had the key; but the servants could have opened the trunk with a false key after she was gone."

"Of course, of course," the merchant came to his support.

"She could not have taken the money because she would have nowhere to hide it."

"That is what I said," the merchant encouraged him.

"It is more likely that her coming to the hotel for the money suggested to the servants the idea of stealing it; that they stole it and then threw it all upon her."

Peter Gerasimovich spoke provokingly, which communicated itself to the foreman. As a result the latter began to defend his position more persistently. But Peter Gerasimovich spoke so convincingly that he won over the majority, and it was finally decided that she was not guilty of the theft. When, however, they began to discuss the part she had taken in the poisoning, her warm supporter, the merchant, argued that this charge must also be dismissed, as she had no motive for poisoning him. The foreman insisted that she could not be declared innocent on that charge, because she herself confessed to giving him the powder.

"But she thought that it was opium," said the merchant.

"She could have killed him even with the opium," retorted the colonel, who liked to make digressions, and he began to relate the case of his brother-in-law's wife, who had been poisoned by opium and would have died had not antidotes promptly been administered by a physician who happened to be in the neighborhood. The colonel spoke so impressively and with such self-confidence and dignity that no one dared to interrupt him. Only the clerk, infected by the example set by the colonel, thought of telling a story of his own.

"Some people get so accustomed to opium," he began, "that they can take forty drops at a time. A relative of mine——"

But the colonel would brook no interruption, and went on to tell of the effect of the opium on his brother-in-law's wife.

"It is five o'clock, gentlemen," said one of the jury.

"What do you say, gentlemen," said the foreman. "We find her guilty, but without the intent to rob, and without stealing any property—is that correct?"

Peter Gerasimovich, pleased with the victory he had gained, agreed to the verdict.

"And we recommend her to the mercy of the court," added the merchant.

Every one agreed except the laborer, who insisted on a verdict of "Not guilty."

"But that is the meaning of the verdict," explained the foreman. "Without the intent to rob, and without stealing any property—hence she is not guilty."

"Don't forget to throw in the recommendation to mercy. If there be anything left that will wipe it out," joyfully said the merchant. They were so tired and the arguments had so confused them that it did not occur to any one to add "but without the intent to cause the death of the merchant."

Nekhludoff was so excited that he did not notice it. The answers were in this form taken to the court.

Rabelais relates the story of a jurist who was trying a case, and who, after citing innumerable laws and reading twenty pages of incomprehensible judicial Latin, made an offer to the litigants to throw dice; if an even number fell then the plaintiff was right; if an odd number the defendant was right.

It was the same here. The verdict was reached not because the majority of the jury agreed to it, but first because the justiciary had so drawn out his speech that he failed to properly instruct the jury; second, because the colonel's story about his brother-in-law's wife was tedious; third, because Nekhludoff was so excited that he did not notice the omission of the clause limiting the intent in the answer, and thought that the words "without intent to rob" negatively answered the question; fourth, because Peter Gerasimovich was not in the room when the foreman read the questions and answers, and chiefly because the jury were tired out and were anxious to get away, and therefore agreed to the verdict which it was easiest to reach.

They rang the bell. The gendarme sheathed his sword and stood aside. The judges, one by one, took their seats and the jury filed out.

114

The foreman held the list with a solemn air. He approached the justiciary and handed it to him. The justiciary read it, and, with evident surprise, turned to consult with his associates. He was surprised that the jury, in limiting the charge by the words, "without intent to rob," should fail to add also "without intent to cause death." It followed from the decision of the jury, that Maslova had not stolen or robbed, but had poisoned a man without any apparent reason.

"Just see what an absurd decision they have reached," he said to the associate on his left. "This means hard labor for her, and she is not guilty."

"Why not guilty?" said the stern associate.

"She is simply not guilty. I think that chapter 818 might properly be applied to this case." (Chapter 818 gives the court the power to set aside an unjust verdict.)

"What do you think?" he asked the kind associate.

"I agree with you."

"And you?" he asked the choleric associate.

"By no means," he answered, decidedly. "As it is, the papers say that too many criminals are discharged by juries. What will they say, then, if the court should discharge them? I will not agree under any circumstances."

The justiciary looked at the clock.

"It is a pity, but what can I do?" and he handed the questions to the foreman.

They all rose, and the foreman, standing now on one foot, now on the other, cleared his throat and read the questions and answers. All the officers of the court—the secretary, the lawyers and even the prosecutor—expressed surprise.

The prisoners, who evidently did not understand the significance of the answers, were serene. When the reading was over, the justiciary asked the prosecutor what punishment he thought should be imposed on the prisoners.

The prosecutor, elated by the successful verdict against Maslova, which he ascribed to his eloquence, consulted some books, then rose and said:

"Simon Kartinkin, I think, should be punished according to chapter 1,452, sec. 4, and chapter 1,453; Euphemia Bochkova according to chapter 1,659, and Katherine Maslova according to chapter 1,454."

All these were the severest punishments that could be imposed for the crimes.

"The court will retire to consider their decision," said the justiciary, rising.

Everybody then rose, and, with a relieved and pleasant feeling of having fulfilled an important duty, walked around the court-room.

"What a shameful mess we have made of it," said Peter Gerasimovitch, approaching Nekhludoff, to whom the foreman was telling a story. "Why, we have sentenced her to hard labor."

"Is it possible?" exclaimed Nekhludoff, taking no notice at all this time of the unpleasant familiarity of the tutor.

"Why, of course," he said. "We have not inserted in the answer, 'Guilty, but without intent to cause death.' The secretary has just told me that the law cited by the prosecutor provides fifteen years' hard labor."

"But that was our verdict," said the foreman.

Peter Gerasimovitch began to argue that it was self-evident that as she did not steal the money she could not have intended to take the merchant's life.

"But I read the questions before we left the room," the foreman justified himself, "and no one objected."

"I was leaving the room at the time," said Peter Gerasimovitch. "But how did you come to miss it?"

"I did not think of it," answered Nekhludoff.

"You did not!"

"We can right it yet," said Nekhludoff.

"No, we cannot—it is all over now."

Nekhludoff looked at the prisoners. While their fate was being decided, they sat motionless behind the grating in front of the soldiers. Maslova was smiling.

Nekhludoff's soul was stirred by evil thoughts. When he thought that she would be freed and remain in the city, he was undecided how he should act toward her, and it was a difficult matter. But Siberia and penal servitude at once destroyed the possibility of their meeting again. The wounded bird would stop struggling in the game-bag, and would no longer remind him of its existence.

CHAPTER XXIV.

The apprehensions of Peter Gerasimovitch were justified.

On returning from the consultation-room the justiciary produced a document and read the following:

"By order of His Imperial Majesty, the Criminal Division of the ——— Circuit Court, in conformity with the finding of the jury, and in accordance with ch. 771, s. 3, and ch. 776, s. 3, and ch. 777 of the Code of Criminal Procedure, this 28th day of April, 188—, decrees that Simon Kartinkin, thirty-three years of age, and Katherine Maslova, twenty-seven years of age, be deprived of all civil rights, and sent to penal servitude, Kartinkin for eight, Maslova for the term of four years, under conditions prescribed by ch. 25 of the Code. Euphemia Bochkova is deprived of all civil and special rights and privileges, and is to be confined in jail for the period of three years under conditions prescribed by ch. 49 of the Code, with the costs of the trial to be borne by all three, and in case of their inability to pay, to be paid out of the treasury.

"The exhibits are to be sold, the ring returned, and the vials destroyed."

Kartinkin stood like a post, and with outstretched fingers held up the sleeves of his coat, moving his jaws. Bochkova seemed to be calm. When Maslova heard the decision, she turned red in the face.

"I am innocent, I am innocent!" she suddenly cried. "It is a sin. I am innocent. I never wished; never thought. It is the truth." And sinking to the bench, she began to cry aloud.

When Kartinkin and Bochkova left the court-room she was still standing and crying, so that the gendarme had to touch the sleeve of her coat.

"She cannot be left to her fate," said Nekhludoff to himself, entirely forgetting his evil thoughts, and, without knowing why, he ran into the corridor to look at her again. He was detained at the door for a few minutes by the jostling, animated crowd of jurors and lawyers, who were glad that the case was over, so that when he reached the corridor Maslova was some distance away. Without thinking of the attention he was attracting, with quick step he overtook her, walked a little ahead of her and stopped. She had ceased to cry, only a sob escaped her now and then while she wiped her tears with a corner of her 'kerchief. She passed him without turning to look at him. He then hastily returned to see the justiciary. The latter had left his room, and Nekhludoff found him in the porter's lodge.

"Judge," said Nekhludoff, approaching him at the moment when he was putting on a light overcoat and taking a silver-handled cane which the porter handed him, "may I speak to you about the case that has just been tried? I am a juror."

"Why, of course, Prince Nekhludoff! I am delighted to see you. We have met before," said the justiciary, pressing his hand, and recalling with pleasure that he was the jolliest fellow and best dancer of all the young men on the evening he had met him. "What can I do for you?"

"There was a mistake in the jury's finding against Maslova. She is not guilty of poisoning, and yet she is sent to penal servitude," he said, with a gloomy countenance.

"The court gave its decision in accordance with your own finding," answered the justiciary, moving toward the door, "although the answers did not seem to suit the case."

He remembered that he intended to explain to the jury that an answer of guilty without a denial of intent to kill involved an intent to kill, but, as he was hastening to terminate the proceedings, he failed to do so.

"But could not the mistake be rectified?"

"Cause for appeal can always be found. You must see a lawyer," said the justiciary, putting on his hat a little on one side and continuing to move toward the door.

"But this is terrible."

"You see, one of two things confronted Maslova," the justiciary said, evidently desiring to be as pleasant and polite with Nekhludoff as possible. Then, arranging his side-whiskers over his coat collar, and taking Nekhludoff's arm, he led him toward the door. "You are also going?" he continued.

"Yes," said Nekhludoff, hastily donning his overcoat and following him.

They came out into the bright, cheerful sunlight, where the rattling of wheels on the pavement made it necessary to raise their voices.

"The situation, you see, is a very curious one," continued the justiciary. "Maslova was confronted by one of two things: either a short term in jail, in which case her lengthy confinement would have been taken into consideration, or penal servitude; no other sentence was possible. Had you added the words, 'without intent to kill,' she would have been discharged."

"It is unpardonable neglect on my part," said Nekhludoff.

"That is the whole trouble," the justiciary said, smiling and looking at his watch.

There was only three-quarters of an hour left to the latest hour fixed in Clara's appointment.

"You can apply to a lawyer, if you wish. It is necessary to find grounds for appeal. But that can always be found. To the Dvorianskaia," he said to the cab-driver. "Thirty kopecks—I never pay more."

"All right, Your Excellency."

"Good-day. If I can be of any service to you, please let me know. You will easily remember my address: Dvornikoff's house, on the Dvorinskaia."

And, making a graceful bow, he rode off.

CHAPTER XXV.

The conversation with the justiciary and the pure air somewhat calmed Nekhludoff. The feeling he experienced he now ascribed to the fact that he had passed the day amid surroundings to which he was unaccustomed.

"It is certainly a remarkable coincidence! I must do what is necessary to alleviate her lot, and do it quickly. Yes, I must find out here where Fanarin or Mikishin lives." Nekhludoff called to mind these two well-known lawyers.

Nekhludoff returned to the court-house, took off his overcoat and walked up the stairs. In the very first corridor he met Fanarin. He stopped him and told him that he had some business with him. Fanarin knew him by sight, and also his name. He told Nekhludoff that he would be glad to do anything to please him.

"I am rather tired, but, if it won't take long, I will listen to your case. Let us walk into that room."

And Fanarin led Nekhludoff into a room, probably the cabinet of some judge. They seated themselves at a table.

"Well, state your case."

"First of all, I will ask you," said Nekhludoff, "not to disclose that I am interesting myself in this case."

"That is understood. Well?"

"I was on a jury to-day, and we sent an innocent woman to Siberia. It torments me."

To his own surprise, Nekhludoff blushed and hesitated. Fanarin glanced at him, then lowered his eyes and listened.

120

"Well?"

"We condemned an innocent woman, and I would like to have the case appealed to a higher court."

"To the Senate?" Fanarin corrected him.

"And I wish you to take the case."

Nekhludoff wanted to get through the most difficult part, and therefore immediately added:

"I take all expenses on myself, whatever they may be," he said, blushing.

"Well, we will arrange all that," said the lawyer, condescendingly smiling at Nekhludoff's inexperience.

"What are the facts of the case?"

Nekhludoff related them.

"Very well; I will examine the record to-morrow. Call at my office the day after—no, better on Thursday, at six o'clock in the evening, and I will give you an answer. And now let us go; I must make some inquiries here."

Nekhludoff bade him good-by, and departed.

His conversation with the lawyer, and the fact that he had already taken steps to defend Maslova, still more calmed his spirit. The weather was fine, and when Nekhludoff found himself on the street, he gladly inhaled the spring air. Cab drivers offered their services, but he preferred to walk, and a swarm of thoughts and recollections of Katiousha and his conduct toward her immediately filled his head. He became sad, and everything appeared to him gloomy. "No, I will consider it later," he said to himself, "and now I must have some diversion from these painful impressions."

The dinner at the Korchagin's came to his mind, and he looked at his watch. It was not too late to reach there for dinner. A tram-car passed by. He ran after it, and boarded it at a bound. On the square he jumped off, took one of the best cabs, and ten minutes later he alighted in front of Korchagin's large dwelling.

CHAPTER XXVI.

"Walk in, Your Excellency, you are expected," said the fat porter, pushing open the swinging, oaken door of the entrance. "They are dining, but I was told to admit you."

The porter walked to the stairway and rang the bell.

"Are there any guests?" Nekhludoff asked, while taking off his coat.

"Mr. Kolosoff, also Michael Sergeievich, besides the family," answered the porter.

A fine-looking lackey in dress coat and white gloves looked down from the top of the stairs.

"Please to walk in, Your Excellency," he said.

Nekhludoff mounted the stairs, and through the spacious and magnificent parlor he entered the dining-room. Around the table were seated the entire family, except Princess Sophia Vasilievna, who never left her own apartments. At the head of the table sat old Korchagin, on his left the physician; on his right, a visitor, Ivan Ivanovich Kolosoff, an ex-district commander, and now a bank manager, who was a friend of the family, and of liberal tendencies; further to the left was Miss Rader, governess to Missy's four-year-old sister, with the little girl herself; then to the right, Missy's only brother, Peter, a high-school pupil, on account of whose forthcoming examinations the entire family remained in the city, and his tutor, also a student; then again to the left, Katherine Alexeievna, a forty-year-old girl Slavophile; opposite to her was Michael Sergeievich, or Misha Telegin, Missy's cousin, and at the foot of the table, Missy herself, and beside her, on the table, lay an extra cover.

"Ah, very glad you came! Take a seat! We are still at the fish," chewing carefully with his false teeth old Korchagin said, lifting his bloodshot eyes on Nekhludoff. "Stepan!" he turned with a full mouth to the fat, majestic servant, pointing with his eyes to Nekhludoff's plate. Although Nekhludoff had often dined with and knew Korchagin well, this evening his old face, his sensual, smacking lips, the napkin stuck under his vest, the fat neck, and especially the well-fed, military figure made an unpleasant impression on him.

"It is all ready, Your Excellency," said Stepan, taking a soup ladle from the sideboard and nodding to the fine-looking servant with the side-whiskers, who immediately began to set the table beside Missy.

Nekhludoff went around the table shaking hands with every one. All, except Korchagin and the ladies, rose from their seats when he approached them. And this walking around the table and his handshaking, although most of the people were comparative strangers to him, this evening seemed to Nekhludoff particularly unpleasant and ridiculous. He excused himself for his late coming, and was about to seat himself at the end of the table between Missy and Katherine Alexeievna, when old Korchagin demanded that, since he would not take any brandy, he should first take a bite at the table, on which were lobster, caviare, cheese and herring. Nekhludoff did not know he was as hungry as he turned out to be, and when he tasted of some cheese and bread he could not stop eating, and ate ravenously.

"Well? Have you been undermining the bases of society?" asked Kolosoff, ironically, using an expression of a retrogressive newspaper, which was attacking the jury system. "You have acquitted the guilty and condemned the innocent? Have you?"

"Undermining the bases—undermining the bases"—smilingly repeated the Prince, who had boundless confidence in the intelligence and honesty of his liberal comrade and friend.

Nekhludoff, at the risk of being impolite, did not answer Kolosoff, and, seating himself before the steaming soup, continued to eat.

"Do let him eat," said Missy, smiling. By the pronoun "him," she meant to call attention to her intimacy with Nekhludoff.

Meanwhile Kolosoff was energetically and loudly discussing the article against trial by jury which had roused his indignation. Michael Sergeievich supported his contentions and quoted the contents of another similar article.

Missy, as usual, was very distingue and unobtrusively well dressed. She waited until Nekhludoff had swallowed the mouthful he was chewing, and then said: "You must be very tired and hungry."

"Not particularly. Are you? Have you been to the exhibition?" he asked.

"No, we postponed it. But we went to play lawn tennis at the Salamatoff's. Mister Crooks is really a remarkable player."

Nekhludoff had came here for recreation, and it was always pleasant to him to be in this house, not only because of the elegant luxury, which acted pleasantly on his senses, but because of the adulating kindnesses with which they invisibly surrounded him. To-day, however—it is wonderful to relate— everything in this house disgusted him; the porter, the broad stairway, the flowers, the lackeys, the table decorations, and even Missy herself, who, just now, seemed to him unattractive and unnatural. He was disgusted with that self-confident, vulgar, liberal tone of Kolosoff, the bull-like, sensual, figure of old Korchagin, the French phrases of the Slavophile maiden, the ceremonious faces of the governess and the tutor. But above all, he was disgusted with the pronoun "him" that Missy had used. Nekhludoff was always wavering between two different relations he sustained toward Missy. Sometimes he looked at her as through blinking eyes or by moonlight, and then she seemed to him beautiful, fresh, pretty, clever and natural. At other times he looked at her as if under a bright sun, and then he saw only her defects. To-day was such a day. He saw the wrinkles on her face; saw the artificial arrangement of her hair; the pointed elbows, and, above all, her large thumb nail, resembling that of her father.

"It is the dullest game," Kolosoff said, speaking of tennis, "baseball, as we played it when we were boys, is much more amusing."

"You have not tried it. It is awfully interesting," retorted Missy, unnaturally accentuating the word "awfully," as it seemed to Nekhludoff.

A discussion arose in which Michael Sergeievich and Katherine Alexeievna took part. Only the governess, the tutor and the children were silent, evidently from ennui.

"They are eternally disputing!" laughing aloud, said old Korchagin. He

124

pulled the napkin from his vest, and, noisily pushing back his chair, which was immediately removed by a servant, rose from the table. They all rose after him and went to a small table, on which stood figured bowls filled with perfumed water; then they washed their finger-tips and rinsed their mouths, and continued their conversation, in which no one took any interest.

"Is it not true?" Missy said to Nekhludoff, desiring to receive confirmation of her opinion that man's character can best be learned in play. She noticed on his thoughtful face an expression of reproach, which inspired her with fear, and she wished to know the cause of it.

"I really don't know. I never thought of it," answered Nekhludoff.

"Will you go to mamma?" asked Missy.

"Yes, yes," he said, producing a cigarette. The tone of his voice plainly betrayed that he did not wish to go.

She looked at him inquiringly, but was silent. He felt ashamed. "It is hardly proper for me to come here to put people out of temper," he thought, and, in an effort to be pleasant, he said that he would go with pleasure if the Princess were in a mood to receive him.

"Yes, yes; mamma will be glad. You can smoke there also. And Ivan Ivanovich is with her."

The mistress of the house, Sophia Vasilievna, was an invalid. For eight years she had reclined in laces and ribbons, amid velvet, gilding, ivory, bronzes and flowers. She never drove out, and received only her "friends," i. e., whoever, according to her view, in any way distinguished himself from the crowd. Nekhludoff was one of these friends, not only because he was considered a clever young man, but also because his mother was a close friend of the family and he was a desirable match for Missy.

Her room was beyond the small and large drawing-rooms. In the large drawing-room Missy, who preceded Nekhludoff, suddenly stopped, and placing her hands on the back of a gilt chair, looked at him.

Missy was very anxious to be married, and Nekhludoff was a desirable party. Besides, she liked him, and had become accustomed to the thought that he would belong to her, and not she to him, and, with the unconscious but persistent craftiness of heart-sick persons, she gained her end. She addressed him now with the intention of bringing forth an explanation.

"I see that something has happened to you," she said. "What is the matter with you?"

The meeting in the court came to his mind, and he frowned and blushed.

"Yes, something has happened," he said, desiring to be truthful. "It was a strange, extraordinary and important event."

"What was it? Can't you tell me?"

"Not now. Don't press me for an answer. I have not had the time to think over the matter," he said, blushing still more.

"And you will not tell me?" The muscles on her cheek quivered, and she pushed away the chair.

"No, I cannot," he answered, feeling that answering her thus he answered himself—admitted to himself that something very important had really happened to him.

"Well, then, come!"

She shook her head as if desiring to drive away undesirable thoughts, and walked forward with a quicker step than usual.

It seemed to him that she unnaturally compressed her lips in order to suppress her tears. It was painful to him to grieve her, but he knew that the slightest weakness would ruin him, i. e., bind him. And this he feared more than anything else to-day, so he silently followed her to the door of the Princess' apartments.

CHAPTER XXVII.

Princess Sophia Vasilievna had finished her meal of choice and nourishing dishes, which she always took alone, that no one might see her performing that unpoetical function. A cup of coffee stood on a small table near her couch, and she was smoking a cigarette. Princess Sophia Vasilievna was a lean and tall brunette, with long teeth and large black eyes, who desired to pass for a young woman.

People were making unpleasant remarks about her relations with the doctor. Formerly Nekhludoff had paid no attention to them. But to-day, the sight of the doctor, with his oily, sleek head, which was parted in the middle, sitting near her couch, was repulsive to him.

Beside the Princess sat Kolosoff, stirring the coffee. A glass of liquor was on the table.

Missy entered, together with Nekhludoff, but she did not remain in the room.

"When mamma gets tired of you and drives you away, come to my room," she said, turning to Nekhludoff, as if nothing had happened, and, smiling cheerfully, she walked out of the room, her steps deadened by the heavy carpet.

"Well, how do you do, my friend? Sit down and tell us the news," said Sophia Vasilievna, with an artful, feigned, resembling a perfectly natural, smile, which displayed her beautiful, long, skillfully made, almost natural-looking teeth. "I am told that you returned from the court in very gloomy spirits. It must be very painful to people with a heart," she said in French.

"Yes, that is true," said Nekhludoff. "One often feels his—feels that he has no right to judge others."

"Comme c'est vrai!" she exclaimed, as if struck by the truth of the remark, and, as usual, artfully flattering her friend.

"And what about your picture? It interests me very much," she added. "Were it not for my indisposition, I should have visited you long ago."

"I have given up painting entirely," he answered dryly. Her unjust flattery was as apparent to him to-day as was her age, which she attempted to conceal. Try as he would, he could not force himself to be pleasant.

"It is too bad! You know, Riepin himself told me that Nekhludoff possesses undoubted talent," she said, turning to Kolosoff.

"What a shameless liar!" Nekhludoff thought, frowning.

Seeing that Nekhludoff was in ill humor, and could not be drawn into pleasant and clear conversation, Sophia Vasilievna turned to Kolosoff for his opinion of the new drama, with an air as if Kolosoff's opinion would dispel all doubt and every word of his was destined to become immortalized. Kolosoff condemned the drama and took occasion to state his views on art. The correctness of his views seemed to impress her; she attempted to defend the author of the drama, but immediately yielded, or found a middle ground. Nekhludoff looked and listened and yet saw and heard but little.

Listening now to Sophia Vasilievna, now to Kolosoff, Nekhludoff saw, first, that neither of them cared either for the drama or for each other, and that they were talking merely to satisfy a physiological craving to exercise, after dinner, the muscles of the tongue and throat. Secondly, he saw that Kolosoff, who had drunk brandy, wine and liquors, was somewhat tipsy— not as drunk as a drinking peasant, but like a man to whom wine-drinking has become a habit. He did not reel, nor did he talk nonsense, but was in an abnormal, excited and contented condition. Thirdly, Nekhludoff saw that Princess Sophia Vasilievna, during the conversation, now and again anxiously glanced at the window, through which a slanting ray of the sun was creeping toward her, threatening to throw too much light on her aged face.

"How true it is," she said of some remark of Kolosoff, and pressed a button on the wall near the couch.

At this moment the doctor rose with as little ceremony as one of the family, and walked out of the room. Sophia Vasilievna followed him with her eyes.

"Please, Phillip, let down that curtain," she said to the fine-looking servant who responded to the bell, her eyes pointing to the window.

"Say what you will, but there is something mystical about him, and without mysticism there is no poetry," she said, with one black eye angrily following the movements of the servant who was lowering the curtain.

"Mysticism without poetry is superstition, and poetry without mysticism is prose," she continued, smiling sadly, still keeping her eye on the servant, who was smoothing down the curtain.

"Not that curtain, Phillip—the one at the large window," she said in a sad voice, evidently pitying herself for the efforts she was compelled to make to say these words, and to calm herself, with her ring-bedecked hand, she lifted to her lips the fragrant, smoking cigarette.

The broad-chested, muscular Phillip bowed slightly, as if excusing himself, and submissively and silently stepped over to the next window, and, carefully looking at the Princess, so arranged the curtain that no stray ray should fall on her. It was again unsatisfactory, and again the exhausted Princess was obliged to interrupt her conversation about mysticism and correct the unintelligent Phillip, who was pitilessly tormenting her. For a moment Phillip's eyes flashed fire.

"'The devil knows what you want,' he is probably saying to himself," Nekhludoff thought, as he watched this play. But the handsome, strong Phillip concealed his impatience, and calmly carried out the instructions of the enervated, weak, artificial Princess Sophia Vasilievna.

"Of course there is considerable truth in Darwin's theory," said the returning Kolosoff, stretching himself on a low arm-chair and looking through sleepy eyes at the Princess, "but he goes too far."

"And do you believe in heredity?" she asked Nekhludoff, oppressed by his silence.

"In heredity?" repeated Nekhludoff. "No, I do not," he said, being entirely absorbed at the moment by those strange forms which, for some reason, appeared to his imagination. Alongside of the strong, handsome Phillip, whom he looked upon as a model, he imagined Kolosoff, naked, his abdomen like a water-melon, bald-headed, and his arms hanging like two cords. He also dimly imagined what the silk-covered shoulders of Sophia Vasilievna would appear like in reality, but the picture was too terrible, and he drove it from his mind.

Sophia Vasilievna scanned him from head to foot.

"Missy is waiting for you," she said. "Go to her room; she wished to play for you a new composition by Schuman. It is very interesting."

"It isn't true. Why should she lie so!" Nekhludoff thought, rising and pressing her transparent, bony, ring-bedecked hand.

In the drawing-room he met Katherine Alexeievna, returning to her mother's apartments. As usual, she greeted him in French.

"I see that the duties of juryman act depressingly upon you," she said.

"Yes, pardon me. I am in low spirits to-day, and I have no right to bore people," answered Nekhludoff.

"Why are you in low spirits?"

"Permit me not to speak of it," he said, looking for his hat as they entered the Princess' cabinet.

"And do you remember telling us that one ought to tell the truth? And what cruel truths you used to tell us! Why don't you tell us now? Do you remember, Missy?" the Princess turned to Missy, who had just entered.

"Because that was in play," answered Nekhludoff gravely. "In play it is permissible, but in reality we are so bad, that is, I am so bad, that I, at least, cannot tell the truth."

"Don't correct yourself, but rather say that we are so bad," said Katherine Alexeievna, playing with the words, and pretending not to see Nekhludoff's gravity.

"There is nothing worse than to confess being in low spirits," said Missy. "I never confess it to myself, and that is why I am always cheerful. Well, come to my room. We shall try to drive away your mauvais humeur."

Nekhludoff experienced the feeling which a horse must feel when brushed down before the bridle is put on and it is led to be harnessed to the wagon. But to-day he was not at all disposed to draw. He excused himself and began to take leave. Missy kept his hand longer than usual.

"Remember that what is important to you is important to your friends," she said. "Will you come to-morrow?"

"I don't think I will," said Nekhludoff. And feeling ashamed, without knowing himself whether for her or for himself, he blushed and hastily departed.

"What does it mean? Comme cela m'intrigue," said Katherine Alexeievna, when Nekhludoff had left. "I must find it out. Some affaire d'amour propre; il est très susceptible notre cher Mitia."

"Plutôt une affaire d'amour sale," Missy was going to say. Her face was now wan and pale. But she did not give expression to that passage, and only said: "We all have our bright days and gloomy days."

"Is it possible that he, too, should deceive me?" she thought. "After all that has happened, it would be very wrong of him."

If Missy had had to explain what she meant by the words, "After all that has happened," she could have told nothing definite, and yet she undoubtedly knew that not only had he given her cause to hope, but he had almost made his promise—not in so many words, but by his glances, his smiles, his innuendos, his silence. She considered him her own, and to lose him would be very painful to her.

CHAPTER XXVIII.

"It is shameful and disgusting," Nekhludoff meditated, while returning home on foot along the familiar streets. The oppressive feeling which he had experienced while speaking to Missy clung to him. He understood that nominally, if one may so express himself, he was in the right; he had never said anything to bind himself to her; had made no offer, but in reality he felt that he had bound himself to her, that he had promised to be hers. Yet he felt in all his being that he could not marry her.

"It is shameful and disgusting," he repeated, not only of his relations to Missy, but of everything. "Everything is disgusting and shameful," he

131

repeated to himself, as he ascended the steps of his house.

"I shall take no supper," he said to Kornei, who followed him into the dining-room, where the table was set for his supper. "You may go."

"All right," said Kornei, but did not go, and began to clear the table. Nekhludoff looked at Kornei and an ill feeling sprung up in his heart toward him. He wished to be left in peace, and it seemed as if everybody were spitefully worrying him. When Kornei had left, Nekhludoff went over to the samovar, intending to make some tea, but, hearing the footsteps of Agrippina Petrovna, he hastily walked into the drawing-room, closing the door behind him. This was the room in which, three months ago, his mother had died. Now, as he entered this room, lighted by two lamps with reflectors—one near a portrait of his father, the other near a portrait of his mother—he thought of his relations toward his mother, and these relations seemed to him unnatural and repulsive. These, too, were shameful and disgusting. He remembered how, during her last sickness, he wished her to die. He said to himself that he wished it so that she might be spared the suffering, but in reality he wished to spare himself the sight of her suffering.

Desiring to call forth pleasant recollections about her, he looked at her portrait, painted by a famous artist for five thousand rubles. She was represented in a black velvet dress with bared breast. The artist had evidently drawn with particular care the breast and the beautiful shoulders and neck. That was particularly shameful and disgusting. There was something revolting and sacriligious to him in this representation of his mother as a denuded beauty, the more so because three months ago she lay in this very room shrunken like a mummy, and filling the entire house with an oppressive odor. He thought he could smell the odor now. He remembered how, on the day before she died, she took his strong, white hand into her own emaciated, discolored one, and, looking into his eyes, said: "Do not judge me, Mitia, if I have not done as I should," and her faded eyes filled with tears.

"How disgusting!" he again repeated to himself, glancing at the half-nude woman with splendid marble shoulders and arms and a triumphant smile on her lips. The bared bosom of that portrait reminded him of another young woman whom he had seen dressed in a similar way a few days before. It was Missy, who had invited him to the house under some pretext, in order to display before him her ball-dress. He recalled with disgust her beautiful shoulders and arms; and her coarse, brutal father, with his dark past, his cruelties, and her mother with her doubtful reputation. All this was disgusting and at the same time shameful.

"No, no; I must free myself from all these false relations with the Korchagins, with Maria Vasilievna, with the inheritance and all the rest," he thought. "Yes, to breathe freely; to go abroad—to Rome—and continue to work on my picture." He remembered his doubts about his talent. "Well, it is all the same; I will simply breathe freely. First, I will go to Constantinople, then to Rome—away from this jury duty. Yes, and to fix matters with the lawyer——"

And suddenly, before his imagination, appeared with uncommon vividness the picture of the prisoner with the black, squinting eyes. And how she wept when the last words of the prisoners were spoken! He hastily crushed the cigarette he was smoking, lit another, and began pacing up and down the room. One after another the scenes he had lived through with her rose up in his mind. He recalled their last meeting, the passion which seized him at the time, and the disappointment that followed. He recalled the white dress with the blue ribbon; he recalled the morning mass. "Why, I loved her with a pure love that night; I loved her even before, and how I loved her when I first came to my aunts and was writing my composition!" That freshness, youth, fullness of life swept over him and he became painfully sad.

The difference between him as he was then and as he was now was great; it was equally great, if not greater, than the difference between Katiousha in the church and that girl whom they had tried this morning. Then he was a courageous, free man, before whom opened endless possibilities; now he felt himself caught in the tenets of a stupid, idle, aimless, miserable life, from which there was no escape; aye, from which, for the most part, he would not escape. He remembered how he once had prided himself upon his rectitude; how he always made it a rule to tell the truth, and was in reality truthful, and how he was now steeped in falsehood—falsehood which was recognized as truth by all those around him.

And there was no escape from this falsehood; at all events, he did not see any escape. He had sunk in it, became accustomed to it, and indulged himself in it.

The questions that absorbed him now were: How to break loose from Maria Vasilievna and her husband, so that he might be able to look them in the face? How, without falsehood, to disentangle his relations with Missy? How to get out of the inconsistency of considering the private holding of land unjust and keeping his inheritance? How to blot out his sin against Katiousha? "I cannot abandon the woman whom I have loved and content myself with paying money to the lawyer to save her from penal servitude, which she does not even deserve." To blot out the sin, as he did then, when he thought that he was atoning for his wrong by giving her money! Impossible!

He vividly recalled the moment when he ran after her in the corridor, thrust money in her bosom, and ran away from her. "Oh, that money!" With the same horror and disgust he recalled that moment. "Oh, how disgusting!" he said aloud, as he did then. "Only a scoundrel and rascal could do it! And I am that scoundrel, that rascal!" he said aloud. "It is possible that I—" and he stopped in the middle of the room—"Is it possible that I am really a scoundrel? Who but I?" he answered himself. "And is this the only thing?" he continued, still censuring himself. "Are not my relations toward Maria Vasilievna base and detestable? And my position with regard to property? Under the plea that I inherited it from my mother I am using wealth, the ownership of which I consider unlawful. And the whole of this idle, abominable life? And to crown all, my conduct toward Katiousha? Scoundrel! Villain! Let people judge me as they please—I can deceive them, but I cannot deceive myself."

And he suddenly understood that the disgust which he had lately felt toward everybody, and especially to-day toward the Prince and Maria Vasilievna, and Missy, and Kornei, was disgust with himself. And in this confession of his own baseness there was something painful, and at the same time joyous and calming.

In the course of his life Nekhludoff often experienced what he called a "cleansing of the soul." This happened when, after a long period of retardation, or, perhaps, entire cessation of his inner life, he suddenly became aware of it, and proceeded to cleanse his soul of all the accumulated filth that caused this standstill.

After such awakenings Nekhludoff always laid down some rules for himself which he intended to follow all the rest of his life; kept a diary and began a new life, which he hoped he should never change again—"turning a new leaf," he used to call it. But the temptations of life entrapped him anew, after every awakening, and, without knowing it, he sank again, often to a lower depth than he was in before.

Thus he cleansed himself and revived several times. His first cleansing happened when he visited his aunts. That was the brightest and most enthusiastic awakening. And it lasted a long time. The next happened when he left the civil service, and, desiring to sacrifice his life, he entered, during the war, the military service. Here he began to sink quickly. The next awakening occurred when he retired from the military service, and, going abroad, gave himself up to painting.

From that day to this there was a long period of uncleanliness, the longest he had gone through yet, and, therefore, he had never sunk so deep, and never before was there such discord between the demands of his conscience and the life which he was leading. So, when he saw the chasm which separated the two, he was horrified.

The discord was so great, the defilement so thorough, that at first he despaired of the possibility of a complete cleansing. "Why, you have tried to improve before, and failed," the tempter in his soul whispered. "What is the good of trying again? You are not the only one—all are alike. Such is life." But the free, spiritual being which alone is true, alone powerful, alone eternal, was already awake in Nekhludoff. And he could not help believing it. However great the difference between that which he was and that which he wished to be, for the awakened spiritual being everything was possible.

"I shall break this lie that binds me at any cost. I will confess the truth to everybody, and will act the truth," he said aloud, resolutely. "I will tell Missy

135

the truth—that I am a profligate and cannot marry her; that I have trifled with her. I will tell Maria Vasilevna (the wife of the marshal of nobility)—but no, what is the good of telling her? I will tell her husband that I am a scoundrel, that I have deceived him. I will dispose of my inheritance in accordance with the demands of justice. I will tell her, Katiousha, that I am a knave, that I have wronged her, and will do everything in my power to alleviate her condition. Yes, I shall see her, and beg her forgiveness—I will beg like a child."

He stopped.

"I will marry her, if necessary."

He crossed his hands on his breast, as he used to do when a child, raised his eyes and said:

"Lord, help me, teach me; come and enter within me and purify me of all this abomination."

He prayed, asked God to help him and purify him, while that which he was praying for had already happened. Not only did he feel the freedom, vigor and gladness of life, but he also felt the power of good. He felt himself capable of doing the best that man can do.

There were tears in his eyes when he said these things—tears of joy—on the awakening within him of that spiritual being, and tears of emotion over his own virtue.

He felt warm and opened a window which looked into a garden. It was a moonlit, fresh and quiet night. Past the street rattled some vehicle, and then everything was quiet. Directly beneath the window a tall, denuded poplar threw its shadow on the gravel of the landing-place, distinctly showing all the ramifications of its bare branches. To the left the roof of a shed seemed white under the bright light of the moon; in front were the tangled branches of the trees, through which was seen the dark shadow of the garden inclosure.

Nekhludoff looked at the moonlit garden and roof, the shadows of the poplar, and drank in the fresh, invigorating air.

"How delightful! My God, how delightful!" he said of that which was in his soul.

CHAPTER XXIX.

It was six o'clock when Maslova returned to her cell, weary and foot-sore from the long tramp over the stone pavement. Besides, she was crushed by the unexpectedly severe sentence, and was also hungry.

When, during a recess, her guards had lunched on bread and hard-boiled eggs her mouth watered and she felt that she was hungry, but considered it humiliating to ask them for some food. Three hours after that her hunger had passed, and she only felt weak. In this condition she heard the sentence. At first she thought that she misunderstood it; she could not believe what she heard, and could not reconcile herself to the idea that she was a convict. But, seeing the calm, serious faces of the judges and the jury, who received the verdict as something quite natural, she revolted and cried out that she was innocent. And when she saw also that her outcry, too, was taken as something natural and anticipated, and which could not alter the case, she began to weep. She felt that she must submit to the cruel injustice which was perpetrated on her. What surprised her most was that she should be so cruelly condemned by men—not old men, but those same young men who looked at her so kindly.

The prosecuting attorney was the only man whose glances were other than kind. While she was sitting in the prisoners' room, and during recesses she saw these men passing by her and entering the room under various pretexts, but with the obvious intention of looking at her. And now these same men, for some reason, sentenced her to hard labor, although she was innocent of the crime. For some time she wept, then became calm, and in a condition of complete exhaustion she waited to be taken away. She desired but one thing now—a cigarette. She was in this frame of mind when Bochkova and Kartinkin were brought into the room. Bochkova immediately began to curse her.

"You are innocent, aren't you? Why weren't you discharged, you vile thing? You got your deserts! You will drop your fineries in Siberia!"

Maslova sat with lowered head, her hands folded in the sleeves of her coat, and gazed on the smoothly trampled ground.

"I am not interfering with you, so leave me in peace," she repeated several times, then became silent. She became enlivened again when, after Bochkova and Kartinkin had been removed from the room, the guard entered, bringing her three rubles.

"Are you Maslova?" he asked.

"Yes."

"Here is some money which a lady sent you," he said.

"What lady?"

"Take it, and ask no questions."

The money was sent by Kitaeva. When leaving the court she asked the usher if she could send some money to Maslova, and, receiving an affirmative answer, she removed a chamois glove, and, from the back folds of her silk dress, produced a stylish pocket-book, and counted out the money into the hands of the usher who, in her presence, handed it to the guard.

"Please be sure to give it to her," said Karolina Albertoona to the guard.

The guard was offended by this distrust shown to him, which was the cause of his speaking angrily to Maslova.

Maslova was overjoyed by the receipt of the money, for it could give her the one thing she wished for now.

All her thoughts were now centered on her desire to inhale the smoke of a cigarette. So strong was this desire that she greedily inhaled the smoke-laden air which was wafted in from the corridor and through the cabinet door. But there was a long wait before her, for the secretary, who was to deliver to the guard the order for her removal, forgetting the prisoners, engaged one of the lawyers in the discussion of an editorial that had appeared in a newspaper.

At five o'clock she was finally led down through the rear door. While in the waiting-room she gave one of the guards twenty kopecks, asking him to buy for her two lunch rolls and some cigarettes. The guard laughed, took the money, honestly made the purchase and returned the change to her. She could not smoke on the road, so Maslova arrived at the jail with the same unsatisfied craving for a cigarette. At that moment about a hundred prisoners were brought from the railroad station. Maslova met them in the passageway.

The prisoners, bearded, clean-shaven, old, young, Russians and foreigners—some with half-shaved heads, and with a clinking of iron fetters, filled the passage with dust, tramping of feet, conversation and a sharp odor of perspiration. The prisoners, as they passed Maslova, scanned her from head to foot; some approached and teased her.

"Fine girl, that!" said one. "My compliments, auntie," said another, winking one eye. A dark man with a shaven, blue neck and long mustache, tangling in his fetters, sprang toward her and embraced her.

"Don't you recognize your friend? Come, don't put on such style!" he exclaimed, grinning as she pushed him away.

"What are you doing, you rascal?" shouted the officer in charge of the prisoners.

The prisoner hastily hid himself in the crowd. The officer fell upon Maslova.

"What are you doing here?"

Maslova was going to say that she had been brought from the court, but she was very tired and too lazy to speak.

"She is just from the court, sir," said one of the guards, elbowing his way through the passing crowd, and raising his hand to his cap.

"Then take her to the warden. What indecencies!"

"Very well, sir!"

"Sokoloff! Take her away!" shouted the officer.

Sokoloff came and angrily pushed Maslova by the shoulder, and, motioning to her to follow him, he led her into the woman's corridor. There she was thoroughly searched, and as nothing was found upon her (the box of cigarettes was hidden in the lunch roll), she was admitted into the same cell from which she had emerged in the morning.

CHAPTER XXX.

The cell in which Maslova was confined was an oblong room, twenty feet by fifteen. The kalsomining of the walls was peeled off, and the dry boards of the cots occupied two-thirds of the space. In the middle of the room, opposite the door, was a dark iron, with a wax candle stuck on it, and a dusty bouquet of immortelles hanging under it. To the left, behind the door, on a darkened spot of the floor, stood an ill-smelling vat. The women had been locked up for the night.

There were fifteen inmates of this cell, twelve women and three children.

It was not dark yet, and only two women lay in their cots; one a foolish little woman—she was constantly crying—who had been arrested because she had no written evidence of her identity, had her head covered with her coat; the other, a consumptive, was serving a sentence for theft. She was not sleeping, but lay, her coat under her head, with wide-open eyes, and with difficulty retaining in her throat the tickling, gurgling phlegm, so as not to cough. The other women were with bare heads and skirts of coarse linen; some sat on their cots sewing; others stood at the window gazing on the passing prisoners. Of the three women who were sewing, one, Korableva, was the one who had given Maslova the instructions when the latter left the cell. She was a tall, strong woman, with a frowning, gloomy face, all wrinkled, a bag of skin hanging under her chin, a short braid of light hair, turning gray at the temples, and a hairy wart on her cheek. This old woman was sentenced to penal servitude for killing her husband with an axe. The killing was committed because he annoyed her daughter with improper advances. She was the overseer of the cell, and also sold wine to the inmates. She was sewing with eye-glasses, and held the needle, after the fashion of the peasants, with three fingers, the sharp point turned toward her breast. Beside her, also sewing, sat a little woman, good-natured and talkative, dark, snub-nosed and with little black eyes. She was the watch-woman at a flag-station, and was sentenced to three months' imprisonment for negligently causing an accident on the railroad. The third of the women who were occupied with sewing was Theodosia—called Fenichka by her fellow-prisoners—of light complexion, and with rosy cheeks; young, lovely, with bright, childish blue eyes, and two long, flaxen braids rolled up on her small head. She was imprisoned for attempting to poison her husband. She was sixteen years old when she was married, and she made the attempt immediately after her marriage. During the eight months that she was out on bail, she not only became reconciled to her husband, but became so fond of him that the court officers found them living in perfect harmony. In spite of all the efforts of her husband, her father-in-law, and especially her mother-in-law, who had grown very fond of her, to obtain her discharge, she was sentenced to hard labor in Siberia. The kind, cheerful and smiling Theodosia, whose cot was next to Maslova's, not only took a liking to her, but considered it her duty to help her in every possible way. Two other women were sitting idly on their cots; one of about forty years, who seemed to have been pretty in her youth, but was now pale and slim, was feeding a child with her long, white breast. Her crime consisted in that, when the people of the village she belonged to attempted to stop a recruiting officer who had drafted, illegally, as they thought, her nephew, she was the first to take hold of the bridle of his horse. There was another little white-haired, wrinkled woman, good-natured and hunch-backed, who sat near the oven and pretended to be catching a four-year-old, short-haired and stout boy, who, in a short little shirt, was running past her, laughing and repeating: "You tan't tatch me!" This old woman, who, with her son, was charged with incendiarism, bore her confinement good-naturedly, grieving only over her son, who was also in jail, but above all, her heart was breaking for her old man who, she feared, would be eaten up by lice, as her daughter-in-law had returned to her parents, and there was no one to wash him.

Besides these seven women, there were four others who stood near the open windows, their hands resting on the iron gratings, and conversing by signs and shouts with the prisoners whom Maslova had met in the passageway. One of these, who was serving a sentence for theft, was a flabby, large, heavy, red-haired woman with white-yellow freckles over her face, and a stout neck which was exposed by the open waist collar. In a hoarse voice she shouted indecent words through the window. Beside her stood a woman of the size of a ten-year-old girl, very dark, with a long back and very short legs. Her face was red and blotched; her black eyes wide open, and her short, thick lips failed to hide her white, protruding teeth. She laughed in shrill tones at the antics of the prisoners. This prisoner, who was nicknamed Miss Dandy, because of her stylishness, was under indictment for theft and incendiarism. Behind them, in a very dirty, gray shirt, stood a wretched-looking woman, big with child, who was charged with concealing stolen property. This woman was silent, but she approvingly smiled at the actions of the prisoners without. The fourth of the women who stood at the window, and was undergoing sentence for illicit trading in spirits, was a squat little country woman with bulging eyes and kindly face. She was the mother of the boy who was playing with the old woman, and of another seven-year-old girl, both of whom were in jail with her, because they had no one else to take care of them. Knitting a stocking, she was looking through the window and disapprovingly frowned and closed her eyes at the language used by the passing prisoners. The girl who stood near the red-haired woman, with only a shirt on her back, and clinging with one hand to the woman's skirt, attentively listened to the abusive words the men were exchanging with the women, and repeated them in a whisper, as if committing them to memory. The twelfth was the daughter of a church clerk and chanter who had drowned her child in a well. She was a tall and stately girl, with large eyes and tangled hair sticking out of her short, thick, flaxen braid. She paid no attention to what was going on around her, but paced, bare-footed, and in a dirty gray shirt, over the floor of the cell, making sharp and quick turns when she reached the wall.

CHAPTER XXXI.

When with a rattling of chains the cell door was unlocked and Maslova admitted, all eyes were turned toward her. Even the chanter's daughter stopped for a moment and looked at her with raised eyebrows, but immediately resumed walking with long, resolute strides. Korableva stuck her needle into the sack she was sewing and gazed inquiringly through her glasses at Maslova.

"Ah me! So she has returned," she said in a hoarse basso voice. "And I was sure she would be set right. She must have got it."

She removed her glasses and placed them with her sewing beside her.

"I have been talking with auntie, dear, and we thought that they might discharge you at once. They say it happens. And they sometimes give you money, if you strike the right time," the watch-woman started in a singing

142

voice. "What ill-luck! It seems we were wrong. God has His own way, dear," she went on in her caressing and melodious voice.

"It is possible that they convicted you?" asked Theodosia, with gentle compassion, looking at Maslova with her childish, light-blue eyes, and her cheerful, young face changed, and she seemed to be ready to cry.

Maslova made no answer, but silently went to her place, next to Korableva's, and sat down.

"You have probably not eaten anything," said Theodosia, rising and going over to Maslova.

Again Maslova did not answer, but placed the two lunch-rolls at the head of the cot and began to undress. She took off the dusty coat, and the 'kerchief from her curling black hair and sat down.

The hunch-backed old woman also came and stopped in front of Maslova, compassionately shaking her head.

The boy came behind the old woman, and, with a protruding corner of the upper lip and wide-open eyes, gazed on the rolls brought by Maslova. Seeing all these compassionate faces, after what had happened, Maslova almost cried and her lips began to twitch. She tried to and did restrain herself until the old woman and the child approached. When, however, she heard the kind, compassionate exclamation of pity from the old woman, and, especially, when her eyes met the serious eyes of the boy who looked now at her, now at the rolls, she could restrain herself no longer. Her whole face began to twitch and she burst into sobs.

"I told her to take a good lawyer," said Korableva. "Well? To Siberia?" she asked.

Maslova wished to answer but could not, and, crying, she produced from the roll the box of cigarettes, on which a picture of a red lady with a high chignon and triangle-shaped, low cut neck was printed, and gave it to Korableva. The latter looked at the picture, disapprovingly shook her head, chiefly because Maslova spent money so foolishly, and, lighting a cigarette over the lamp, inhaled the smoke several times, then thrust it at Maslova. Maslova, without ceasing to cry, eagerly began to inhale the smoke.

"Penal servitude," she murmured, sobbing.

"They have no fear of God, these cursed blood-suckers!" said Korableva. "They have condemned an innocent girl."

At this moment there was a loud outburst of laughter among those standing near the window. The delicate laughter of the little girl mingled with the hoarse and shrill laughter of the women. This merriment was caused by some act of a prisoner without.

"Oh, the scoundrel! See what he is doing!" said the red-headed woman, pressing her face against the grating, her whole massive frame shaking.

"What is that drum-hide shouting about?" said Korableva, shaking her head at the red-haired woman, and then again turning to Maslova. "How many years?"

"Four," said Maslova, and the flow of her tears was so copious that one of them fell on the cigarette. She angrily crushed it, threw it away and took another.

The watch-woman, although she was no smoker, immediately picked up the cigarette-end and began to straighten it, talking at the same time.

"As I said to Matveievna, dear," she said, "it is ill-luck. They do what they please. And we thought they would discharge you. Matveievna said you would be discharged, and I said that you would not, I said. 'My heart tells me,' I said, 'that they will condemn her,' and so it happened," she went on, evidently listening to the sounds of her own voice with particular pleasure.

The prisoners had now passed through the court-yard, and the four women left the window and approached Maslova. The larged-eyed illicit seller of spirits was the first to speak.

"Well, is the sentence very severe?" she asked, seating herself near Maslova and continuing to knit her stocking.

"It is severe because she has no money. If she had money to hire a good lawyer, I am sure they would not have held her," said Korableva. "That lawyer—what's his name?—that clumsy, big-nosed one can, my dear madam, lead one out of the water dry. That's the man you should take."

"To hire him!" grinned Miss Dandy. "Why, he would not look at you for less than a thousand rubles."

"It seems to be your fate," said the old woman who was charged with incendiarism. "I should say he is severe! He drove my boy's wife from her; put him in jail, and me, too, in my old age," for the hundredth time she began to repeat her story. "Prison and poverty are our lot. If it is not prison, it is poverty."

"Yes, it is always the same with them," said the woman-moonshiner, and, closely inspecting the girl's head, she put her stocking aside, drew the girl over between her overhanging legs and with dexterous fingers began to search in her head. "Why do you deal in wine? But I have to feed my children," she said, continuing her search.

These words reminded Maslova of wine.

"Oh, for a drop of wine," she said to Korableva, wiping her tears with the sleeve of her shirt and sobbing from time to time.

"Some booze? Why, of course!" said Korableva.

CHAPTER XXXII.

Maslova produced the money from one of the lunch-rolls and gave it to Korableva, who climbed up to the draught-hole of the oven for a flask of wine she had hidden there. Seeing which, those women who were not her immediate neighbors went to their places. Meantime Maslova shook the dust from her 'kerchief and coat, climbed up on her cot and began to eat a roll.

"I saved some tea for you, but I fear it is cold," said Theodosia, bringing down from a shelf a pot, wrapped in a rag, and a tin cup.

The beverage was perfectly cold, and tasted more of tin than of tea, but Maslova poured out a cupful and began to drink.

145

"Here, Finashka!" she called, and breaking a piece from the roll thrust it toward the boy, who gazed at her open-mouthed.

Korableva, meanwhile, brought the flask of wine. Maslova offered some to Korableva and Miss Dandy. These three prisoners constituted the aristocracy of the cell, because they had money and divided among themselves what they had.

In a few minutes Maslova became brighter and energetically began to relate what had transpired at the court, mockingly imitating the prosecutor and rehearsing such parts as had appealed to her most. She was particularly impressed by the fact that the men paid considerable attention to her wherever she went. In the court-room every one looked at her, she said, and for that purpose constantly came into the prisoners' room.

"Even the guard said: 'It is to look at you that they come here.' Some one would come and ask for some document or something, but I saw that it was not for the document that he came. He would devour me with his eyes," she said, smiling and shaking her head as if perplexed. "They are good ones!"

"Yes, that is how it is," chimed in the watch-woman in her melodious voice. "They are like flies on sugar. If you needed them for any other purpose, be sure they would not come so quickly. They know a good thing when they see it."

"It was the same here," interrupted Maslova. "As soon as I was brought here I met with a party coming from the depot. They gave me no rest, and I could hardly get rid of them. Luckily the warden drove them off. One of them bothered me particularly."

"How did he look?" asked Miss Dandy.

"He had a dark complexion, and wore a mustache."

"It is he."

"Who?"

"Stchegloff. He passed here just now."

146

"Who is Stchegloff?"

"She don't know Stchegloff! He twice escaped from Siberia. Now he has been caught, but he will escape again. Even the officers fear him," said Miss Dandy, who delivered notes to prisoners, and knew everything that transpired in the jail. "He will surely escape."

"If he does he won't take either of us with him," said Korableva. "You'd better tell me this: What did the lawyer say to you about a petition—you must send one now."

Maslova said that she did not know anything about a petition.

At this moment the red-haired woman, burying her two freckled hands into her tangled, thick hair, and scratching her head with her nails, approached the wine-drinking aristocrats.

"I will tell you, Katherine, everything," she began. "First of all, you must write on paper: 'I am not satisfied with the trial,' and then hand it to the prosecutor."

"What do you want here?" Korableva turned to her, speaking in an angry basso. "You have smelled the wine! We know you. We don't need your advice; we know what we have to do."

"Who is talking to you?"

"You want some wine—that's what you want."

"Let her alone. Give her some," said Maslova, who always divided with others what she had.

"Yes, I will give her," and Korableva clenched her fist.

"Try it! Try it!" moving toward Korableva, said the red-haired woman. "I am not afraid of you."

"You jail bird!"

"You are another!"

"You gutter rake!"

"I am a rake—am I? You convict, murderess!" shrieked the red-haired woman.

"Go away, I tell you!" said Korableva frowning.

But the red-haired woman only came nearer, and Korableva gave her a push on the open, fat breast. The other seemingly only waited for this, for with an unexpected, quick movement of one hand she seized Korableva's hair and was about to strike her in the face with the other, when Korableva seized this hand. Maslova and Miss Dandy sprang up and took hold of the hands of the red-haired woman, endeavoring to release her hold on Korableva, but the hand that clutched the hair would not open. For a moment she released the hair, but only to wind it around her fist. Korableva, her head bent, with one hand kept striking her antagonist over the body and catching the latter's hand with her teeth. The women crowded around the fighters, parting them and shouting. Even the consumptive came near them, and, coughing, looked on. The children huddled together and cried. The noise attracted the warden and the matron. They were finally parted. Korableva loosened her gray braid and began to pick out the pieces of torn hair, while the other held the tattered remnant of her shirt to her breast—both shouting, explaining and complaining against one another.

"I know it is the wine—I can smell it," said the matron. "I will tell the superintendent to-morrow. Now, remove everything, or there will be trouble. There is no time to listen to you. To your places, and be silent!"

But for a long time there was no silence. The women continued to curse each other; they began to relate how it all commenced, and whose fault it was. The warden and matron finally departed; the women quieted down and took to their cots. The old woman stood up before the image and began to pray.

"Two Siberian convicts," suddenly said the red-haired woman in a hoarse voice, accompanying every word with a torrent of abuse.

"Look out, or you will get it again," quickly answered Korableva, adding similar revilement. Then they became silent.

"If they had not prevented me, I should have knocked out your eyes," the red-haired one began again, and again came a quick and sharp retort.

Then came another interval of silence, followed by more abuse. The intervals became longer and longer, and finally silence settled over the cell.

They were all falling asleep; some began to snore; only the old woman, who always prayed for a long time, was still bowing before the image, while the chanter's daughter, as soon as the matron left the cell, came down from her cot and began to walk up and down the cell.

Maslova was awake and incessantly thinking of herself as a convict, the word which had been twice applied to her—once by Bochkova, and again by the red-haired woman. She could not be reconciled to the thought. Korableva, who was lying with her back turned toward Maslova, turned around.

"I never dreamed of such a thing," she said, in a low voice. "Others commit heaven knows what crimes, and they go scot free, while I must suffer for nothing."

"Don't worry, girl. People live also in Siberia. You will not be lost even there," Korableva consoled her.

"I know that I will not be lost, but it is painful to be treated that way. I deserved a better fate. I am used to a comfortable life."

"You can do nothing against God's will," Korableva said, with a sigh. "You can do nothing against His will."

"I know, auntie, but it is hard, nevertheless."

They became silent.

"Listen to that wanton," said Korableva, calling Maslova's attention to the strange sounds that came from the other end of the cell.

These sounds were the suppressed sobbing of the red-haired woman. She wept because she had just been abused, beaten, and got no wine, for which she so yearned. She also wept because her whole life was one round of abuse, scorn, insults and blows. She meant to draw some consolation from the recollection of her first love for the factory hand, Fedka Molodenkoff, but, recalling this first love, she also recalled the manner of its ending. The end of it was that this Molodenkoff, while in his cups, by way of jest, smeared her face with vitriol, and afterward laughed with his comrades as he watched her writhing in pain. She remembered this, and she pitied herself; and, thinking that no one heard her, she began to weep, and wept like a child—moaning, snuffling and swallowing salty tears.

CHAPTER XXXIII.

Nekhludoff rose the following morning with a consciousness that some change had taken place within him, and before he could recall what it was he already knew that it was good and important.

"Katiousha—the trial. Yes, and I must stop lying, and tell all the truth." And what a remarkable coincidence! That very morning finally came the long-expected letter of Maria Vasilievna, the wife of the marshal of the nobility—that same letter that he wanted so badly now. She gave him his liberty and wished him happiness in his proposed marriage.

"Marriage!" he repeated ironically. "How far I am from it!"

And his determination of the day before to tell everything to her husband, to confess his sin before him, and to hold himself ready for any satisfaction he might demand, came to his mind. But this morning it did not seem to him so easy as it had yesterday. "And then, what is the good of making a man miserable? If he asks me, I will tell him; but to call on him specially for that purpose—— No, it is not necessary."

It seemed to him equally difficult this morning to tell all the truth to Missy. He thought it would be offering an insult. It was inevitable, as in all worldly affairs, that there should remain something unexpressed but understood. One thing, however, he decided upon this morning—that he would not go there, and would tell the truth when asked. But in his relations toward Katiousha there was to be nothing unsaid.

"I will go to the jail—will tell her, beg of her to forgive me. And, if necessary—yes, if necessary—I will marry her," he thought.

The idea that for the sake of moral satisfaction he would sacrifice everything and marry her this morning particularly affected him.

It was a long time since he had risen with so much energy in him. When Agrippina Petrovna entered his room he declared to her with a determination which he himself did not expect, that he had no further need of the house, and that he would dispense with her services. There was a tacit understanding that the large house was kept up for his contemplated marriage. The closing up of the house consequently had some particular significance. Agrippina Petrovna looked at him with surprise.

"I thank you very much, Agrippina Petrovna, for your solicitude in my behalf, but I do not now need such a large house, or any of the servants. If you wish to help me, then be so kind as to pack away the things as you used to do in mamma's lifetime. Natasha will dispose of them when she arrives." Natasha was Nekhludoff's sister.

Agrippina Petrovna shook her head.

"Dispose of them? Why, they will be needed," she said.

"No, they will not, Agrippina Petrovna—they will positively not be needed," said Nekhludoff, answering what she meant by shaking his head. "Please tell Kornei that his salary will be paid for two months in advance, but that I do not need him."

"You are wrong in doing this, Dmitri Ivanovich," she said. "You will need a house even if you go abroad."

"You misunderstand me, Agrippina Petrovna. I will not go abroad, and if I do go, it will be to an entirely different place."

His face suddenly turned a purple color.

"Yes, it is necessary to tell her," he thought. "I must tell all to everybody."

"A very strange and important thing has happened to me. Do you remember Katiousha, who lived with Aunt Maria Ivanovna?"

"Of course; I taught her to sew."

"Well, then, she was tried in court yesterday, and I was one of the jury."

"Ah, good Lord! what a pity!" said Agrippina Petrovna. "What was she tried for?"

"Murder, and it was all caused by me."

"How could you have caused it? You are talking very strangely," said Agrippina Petrovna, and fire sparkled in her old eyes.

She knew of the incident with Katiousha.

"Yes, it is my fault. And this causes me to change my plans."

"What change can this cause in your plans?" said Agrippina Petrovna, suppressing a smile.

"This: That since it was through my fault that she is in her present condition, I consider it my duty to help her to the extent of my ability."

"That is your affair, but I cannot see that you are so much in fault. It happens to everybody, and if one is guided by common sense the matter is usually arranged and forgotten, and one lives on like the rest of the world," said Agrippina Petrovna, sternly and seriously. "There is no reason why you should take it so much to heart. I heard long ago that she had gone to the bad, so whose fault is it?"

"It is my fault, and that is why I wish to make amends."

"Well, it is hard to set that right."

"That is my affair. If you are thinking of yourself, then that which mother wished——"

"I am not thinking of myself. Your deceased mother showed me so many favors that I do not desire anything. My niece, Lizauka, wishes me to come to her, so I will go as soon as you need me no longer. Only you are taking it too much to heart; it happens with everybody."

"Well, I do not think so. I still ask you to help me rent the house and pack away the things. And do not be angry with me. I am very, very thankful to you for everything."

It is remarkable that since Nekhludoff understood that he was disgusted

152

with himself, others ceased to be repulsive to him. On the contrary, he had a kindly and respectful feeling for Agrippina Petrovna and Kornei. He wished to confess also before Kornei, but the latter was so impressively respectful that he could not make up his mind to do it.

On his way to the court, passing along the familiar streets and in the same carriage, Nekhludoff was himself surprised what a different man he felt himself to-day.

His marriage to Missy, which but yesterday seemed to be so near, to-day appeared to him absolutely impossible. Yesterday he understood his position to be such that there could be no doubt that she would be happy to marry him; to-day he felt himself unworthy not only of marrying her, but of being her friend. "If she only knew who I was, she would never receive me, and yet I taunted her with coquetting with that gentleman. But no, even if she married me I should never have peace, even though I were happy, while that one is in jail, and may any day be sent under escort to Siberia. While the woman whom I have ruined is tramping the weary road to penal servitude, I will be receiving congratulations, and paying visits with my young wife. Or I will be counting the votes for and against school inspection, etc., with the marshal, whom I have shamefully deceived, and afterward make appointments with his wife (what abomination!). Or I will work on my picture, which will, evidently, never be finished, for I had no business to occupy myself with such trifles. And I can do neither of these things now," he said to himself, happy at the inward change which he felt.

"First of all," he thought, "I must see the lawyer, and then—then see her in jail—the convict of yesterday—and tell her everything."

And when he thought how he would see her, confess his guilt before her, how he would declare to her that he would do everything in his power, marry her in order to wipe out his guilt, he became enraptured, and tears filled his eyes.

CHAPTER XXXIV.

Arriving at the court-house, Nekhludoff met the usher in the corridor and asked him where the prisoners already sentenced were kept, and from whom permission could be obtained to see them. The usher told him that the prisoners were kept in various places, and that before final judgment the public prosecutor was the only person from whom permission to see them could be obtained. "The prosecutor has not arrived yet; when he does I will let you know, and will escort you myself to him after the session. And now, please to walk into the court. The session is commencing."

Nekhludoff thanked the usher, who seemed to him particularly pitiful to-day, and went into the jury-room.

As Nekhludoff was approaching the jury-room his fellow jurors were coming out, repairing to the court-room. The merchant was as cheerful, had lunched as well as yesterday, and greeted Nekhludoff like an old friend. The loud laughter and familiarity of Peter Gerasimovitch did not give rise to-day in Nekhludoff of the unpleasant sensation of yesterday.

Nekhludoff wished to tell all the jurymen of his relations to the woman whom they had convicted yesterday. "It would have been proper," he thought, "yesterday to rise in court and publicly confess my guilt." But when with the other jurymen he entered the court-room and witnessed the same procedure, the same "Hear ye! Hear ye!" the three judges in high collars on the elevation, the silence, the seating of the jury on high-backed chairs, the gendarmes, the priest—he felt that, though it was necessary to do it, he would not have been able even yesterday to break this solemnity.

They went through the same preliminaries, except the swearing in of the jury and the justiciary's speech to them.

A case of burglary was before the court. The prisoner, who was guarded by two gendarmes with unsheathed swords, was a twenty-year-old boy with a bloodless face and in a gray coat. He sat alone on the prisoners' bench and scanned from under his eyebrows all those that entered the court-room. This boy and another were charged with breaking the lock of a shed and stealing therefrom mats of the value of three rubles and sixty-seven kopecks. It appeared from the indictment that a policeman caught the boy when he was walking with the other, who carried the mats on his shoulder. Both of them immediately confessed, and they were put in jail. The comrade of this boy, a locksmith, died in jail, and he was tried alone. The old mats lay on the table reserved for exhibits.

The case was conducted in the same order as yesterday, with all the proofs, witnesses, experts, oath-taking, examinations and cross-examinations. The policeman, when questioned by the justiciary, complainant and the defense, made listless answers—"Yes, sir," "Can't tell," and again "Yes, sir"— but notwithstanding this, it was apparent that he pitied the boy and testified involuntarily against him.

Another witness, a splenetic old man who owned those mats, when asked if they belonged to him, unwillingly testified that they were his. When, however, the prosecutor asked him what use he intended to make of them, and whether he needed them much, he became angry and answered: "I wish they had been lost entirely, these mats. I don't need them at all. And if I had known that you would make so much fuss about them, I would gladly have given ten rubles, or twenty, rather than be dragged into court. I have spent five rubles on carriages coming here and going back again. And I am sick; I am suffering from rupture and rheumatism."

The prisoner admitted the charge against him, and, like a trapped animal, stupidly looked now to one side, now to the other, and in a halting voice related everything as it happened.

It was a clear case, but the prosecutor, as he did yesterday, raised his shoulders and propounded subtle questions which were calculated to entrap the clever criminal.

In his speech he argued that the theft was committed in a dwelling-house by breaking and entering it, and that therefore the severest punishment should be meted out to him.

Counsel for the defense, appointed by the court, argued that the theft was committed not in a dwelling-house, and that, though the prisoner pleaded guilty, he was not as dangerous to society as the prosecutor would have them believe.

The justiciary was the personification of impartiality and justice, and endeavored to impress on the jury that which they already knew and could not help knowing. Again they took recesses and smoked cigarettes, and again the usher shouted "Hear ye!" and the two gendarmes sat trying to keep awake.

It developed during the trial that this boy had been apprenticed in a tobacco factory, in which he worked five years. This year he was discharged by his employer after a misunderstanding with the employees, and, going idly about the city, he spent all he had on drink. At an inn he met a locksmith who had also been discharged and was drinking hard, and the two went at night, while drunk, to that shed, broke the lock, and took the first thing they saw. They were caught, and as they confessed they were imprisoned. The locksmith, while waiting for a trial, died. The boy was now being tried as a dangerous creature from whom it was necessary to protect society.

"As dangerous a creature as the prisoner of yesterday," Nekhludoff thought while watching the proceedings. "They are dangerous, but are we not dangerous? I am a libertine, an impostor; and all of us, all those that know me as I am, not only do not detest but respect me."

It is evident that this boy is no villain, but a very ordinary person—every one sees that—and that he became what he is only because he lived amid conditions that beget such people. It is therefore plain that such boys will exist as long as the conditions producing these unfortunates remain unchanged. If any one had taken pity on this boy, Nekhludoff thought while looking at the sickly, frightened face of the boy, before want had driven him from the village to the city, and relieved that want, or, when, after twelve hours' work in the factory, he was visiting inns with grown-up comrades, some one had told him, "Don't go, Vania; it is bad," the boy would not have gone, or got drunk, and the burglary would never have occurred.

But no one pitied the boy during the time that he, like an animal, spent his school years in the city, and, with close-cropped hair, to prevent his getting vermin, ran errands for the workmen. On the contrary, the only thing he had heard from the workmen and his comrades was to the effect that a brave fellow was he who cheated, drank, reviled, fought, or led a depraved life.

And when, sickly and depraved from the unhealthy work, from drink and lewdness, foolish and capricious, he aimlessly prowled around the city, as in a dream, entered some shed and abstracted a few worthless mats, then, instead of destroying the causes that led this boy into his present condition, we intend to mend matters by punishing him!

It is dreadful!

Thus Nekhludoff thought, and no longer listened to what was going on around him. He was himself terrified at this revelation. He wondered why he had not seen it before—how others failed to see it.

CHAPTER XXXV.

As soon as the first recess was taken, Nekhludoff rose and went out of the court, intending to return no more. They might do with him what they pleased, but he could no longer take part in that farce.

Having inquired where the prosecutor's room was, he directed his steps toward that dignitary. The messenger would not admit him, declaring that the prosecutor was busy, but Nekhludoff brushed past him and asked an officer who met him to announce him to the prosecutor, saying that he was on important business. His title and dress helped Nekhludoff. The officer announced him, and he was admitted. The prosecutor received him standing, evidently dissatisfied with Nekhludoff's persistence in seeking an audience with him.

"What do you wish?" the prosecutor asked, sternly.

"I am a juryman, my name is Nekhludoff, and I want to see the prisoner Maslova," he said, resolutely and quickly. He blushed, and felt that his act would have a decisive influence on his life.

The prosecutor was a tall, swarthy man with short hair just turning gray, bright eyes and a trimmed, bushy beard on the protruding lower jaw.

"Maslova? Yes, I know her. She was charged with poisoning," he said calmly. "Why do you want to see her?" And then, as if desiring to soften his harsh demeanor, he added: "I cannot give you the permission before I know what you want to see her for."

"It is very important for me to see her," Nekhludoff burst out.

"I see," said the prosecutor, and, raising his eyes, looked intently at Nekhludoff. "Has her case been tried?"

"She was tried yesterday and sentenced to four years' penal servitude. The conviction was irregular; she is innocent."

"I see. If she has only been sentenced yesterday," said the prosecutor without paying attention to Nekhludoff's declaration about her innocence, "then she will be detained until final judgment in the place where she is now. The jail is open to visitors on certain days only. I advise you to apply there."

"But I must see her as soon as possible," with trembling lower jaw Nekhludoff said, feeling that a critical moment was approaching.

"Why are you so anxious about seeing her?" the prosecutor asked, raising his eyebrows with some alarm.

"Because she is innocent of the crime for which she was sentenced to penal servitude. The guilt is mine, not hers," Nekhludoff said in a trembling voice, feeling that he was saying what he should not.

"How so?" asked the prosecutor.

"I deceived her, and brought her to the condition in which she is now. If I had not driven her to the position in which she was, she would not have been charged here with such a crime."

"Still I fail to see what all this has to do with visiting her."

"It has, because I want to follow her and—marry her," said Nekhludoff. And, as it usually happened when he spoke of this, his eyes filled with tears.

"Ah, is that so?" said the prosecutor. "This is really an exceptional case. Are you not a member of the Krasnopersk town council?" asked the prosecutor, as if recalling that he had heard of this Nekhludoff who was now making such a strange statement.

"Excuse me, but I fail to see what this has to do with my request," fuming, Nekhludoff answered with rancor.

"Nothing, of course," the prosecutor said, with a faint smile on his face, and not in the least disturbed. "But your request is so unusual and beside all customary forms——"

"Well, can I get the permission?"

"Permission? Why, yes. I will give you a pass immediately. Please be seated."

He went to the table, sat down and began to write.

"Please be seated."

Nekhludoff stood still.

When he had made out the pass the prosecutor handed it to Nekhludoff and eyed him with curiosity.

"I must also tell you," said Nekhludoff, "that I cannot continue to serve as juror."

"As you know, satisfactory reasons must be given to the court in such cases."

"The reasons are that I consider all courts useless and immoral."

"I see," said the prosecutor, with the same faint smile which seemed to indicate that such statements were familiar to him, and belonged to an amusing class of people well known to him. "I see, but you understand that, as public prosecutor, I cannot agree with you. I therefore advise you to state so to the court, which will either find your reasons satisfactory or unsatisfactory, and in the latter case will impose a fine on you. Apply to the court."

"I have already stated my reasons, and I will not go there," Nekhludoff said angrily.

"I have the honor to salute you," said the prosecutor, bowing, evidently desiring to rid himself of the strange visitor.

"Who was the man that just left your room?" asked one of the judges who entered the prosecutor's cabinet after Nekhludoff had left.

"Nekhludoff. You know, the one who made such strange suggestions in the Krasnopersk town council. Just imagine, he is on the jury, and among the prisoners there was a woman, or girl, who was sentenced to penal servitude, and who, he says, was deceived by him. And now he wishes to marry her."

"It is impossible!"

"That is what he told me. And how strangely excited he was!"

"There is something wrong with our young men."

"He is not so very young."

"What a bore your famous Ivashcukoff is, my dear! He wins his cases by tiring us out—there is no end to his talking."

"They must be curbed, or they become real obstructionists."

CHAPTER XXXVI.

From the public prosecutor Nekhludoff went straight to the detention-house. But no one by the name of Maslova was there. The inspector told him that she might be found in the old temporary prison. Nekhludoff went there and found that Katherine Moslova was one of the inmates.

The distance between the detention-house and the old prison was great, and Nekhludoff did not arrive there until toward evening. He was about to open the door of the huge, gloomy building, when the guard stopped him and rang the bell. The warden responded to the bell. Nekhludoff showed the pass, but the warden told him that he could not be admitted without authority from the inspector. While climbing the stairs to the inspector's dwelling, Nekhludoff heard the sounds of an intricate bravura played on the piano. And when the servant, with a handkerchief tied around one eye, opened the door, a flood of music dazed his senses. It was a tiresome rhapsody by Lizst, well played, but only to a certain place. When that place was reached, the melody repeated itself. Nekhludoff asked the servant if the inspector was in.

The servant said that he was not.

"Will he be in soon?"

The rhapsody again ceased, and with a noisy flourish again repeated itself.

"I will go and inquire." And the servant went away.

The rhapsody again went on at full speed, when suddenly, reaching a certain point, it came to a stand-still and a voice from within was heard.

"Tell him that he is not home, and will not come to-day. He is visiting— why do they bother us?" a woman's voice was heard to say, and the rhapsody continued, then ceased, and the sound of a chair moved back was heard. The angry pianist herself evidently wished to reprimand the importunate visitor who came at such a late hour.

"Papa is not home," angrily said a pale, wretched looking girl with puffed-up hair and blue spots under her eyes, who came to the door. Seeing a young man in a good overcoat, she became calm. "Walk in, please. What do you wish to see him for?"

"I would like to see a prisoner. I hold a pass from the prosecutor."

"Well, I don't know; papa is not in. Why, walk in, please," she again called from the entrance hall. "Or apply to his assistant, who is now in the office. You may talk to him. And what is your name?"

"Thank you," said Nekhludoff, without answering the question, and went away.

Scarcely had the door closed when the same vigorous, merry sound, so inappropriate to the place and so persistently rehearsed by the wretched girl, was heard. In the court-yard Nekhludoff met a young officer with a stiff, dyed mustache, of whom he inquired for the assistant. He himself was the assistant. He took the pass, looked at it, and said that he could not admit any one to the prison on a pass for the detention-house. Besides, it was late.

"At ten o'clock to-morrow the prison is open to all visitors, and the inspector will be here. You could then see her in the common reception-room, or, if the inspector permits it, in the office."

So, without gaining an interview, Nekhludoff returned home. Agitated by the expectation of seeing her, he walked along the streets, thinking not of the court, but of his conversations with the prosecutor and the inspectors. That he was seeking an interview with her, and told the prosecutor of his intention, and visited two prisons preparing for the ordeal, had so excited him that he could not calm down. On returning home he immediately brought forth his unused diary, read some parts and made the following entry: "For two years I have kept no diary, and thought that I should never again return to this childishness. But it was no childishness, but a discourse with myself, with that true, divine I which lives in every man. All this time this I was slumbering and I had no one to discourse with. It was awakened by the extraordinary event of the 28th of April, in court, where I sat as jurymen. I saw her, Katiousha, whom I had deceived, on the prisoners' bench, in a prison coat. Through a strange misunderstanding and my mistake, she was sentenced to penal servitude. I have just returned from the prosecutor and the prison. I was not permitted to see her, but I am determined to do anything to see her, acknowledge my guilt and make reparation even by marrying her. Lord, help me! My soul is rejoicing."

CHAPTER XXXVII.

For a long time that night Maslova lay awake with open eyes, and, looking at the door, mused.

She was thinking that under no circumstances would she marry a convict on the island of Saghalin, but would settle down some other way—with some inspector, or clerk, or even the warden, or an assistant. They are all eager for such a thing. "Only I must not get thin. Otherwise I am done for." And she recalled how she was looked at by her lawyer, the justiciary—in fact, everybody in the court-room. She recalled how Bertha, who visited her in prison, told her that the student, whom she loved while she was an inmate at Kitaeva's, inquired about her and expressed his regrets when told of her condition. She recalled the fight with the red-haired woman, and pitied her. She called to mind the baker who sent her an extra lunch roll, and many others, but not Nekhludoff. Of her childhood and youth, and especially of her love for Nekhludoff, she never thought. That was too painful. These recollections were hidden deeply in her soul. She never saw Nekhludoff even in a dream. She failed to recognize him in court, not so much because when she last saw him he was an army officer, beardless, with small mustache and thick, short hair, while now he was no longer young in appearance, and wore a beard, but more because she never thought of him. She had buried all recollections of her past relations with him in that terrible dark night when, on his return from the army, he visited his aunts.

Up to that night, while she hoped for his return, the child which she bore under her heart was not irksome to her. But from that night forward everything changed, and the coming child was only a hindrance.

The aunts had asked Nekhludoff to stop off at their station and call on them, but he wired that he would not be able to do it, as he had to reach St. Petersburg in time. When Katiousha learned this, she decided to go to the railroad station to see him. The train was to pass at two o'clock in the morning. Katiousha helped the ladies to bed, and, having induced the cook's girl, Mashka, to accompany her, she put on an old pair of shoes, threw a shawl over her head, gathered up her skirts and ran to the station.

It was a dark, rainy, windy, autumn night. The rain now poured down in large, warm drops, now ceased. The road could not be distinguished in the field, and it was pitch dark in the woods. Although Katiousha was familiar with the road she lost her way in the woods, and reached a sub-station, where the train only stopped for three minutes. Running on the platform, she espied Nekhludoff through the window of a first-class car. The car was brightly illuminated. Two officers sat on plush seats playing cards. On the table near the window two thick candles were burning. Nekhludoff sat on the arm of the seat, his elbow resting on the back, laughing. As soon as she recognized him she tapped on the window with her cold hand. But at that moment the third bell rang, and the train began to move, the cars jostling each other forward. One of the players rose with the cards in his hands and began to look through the window. She tapped again, and pressed her face against the window-pane. At that moment the car beside which she stood was tugged forward, and it moved along. She ran alongside, looking in the window. The officer tried to lower the window, but could not. Nekhludoff rose, and, pushing the officer aside, began lowering it. The train went faster, so that Katiousha was obliged to run. The train moved still faster when the window was lowered. At that moment the conductor pushed her aside and jumped on the car. She fell back, but continued to run along the wet boards of the platform, and when she reached the end of the platform and began to descend the steps to the ground, she almost fell exhausted. The first-class car was far ahead of her, and while she was running the second-class cars passed her, then came with greater speed those of the third class. When the last car with the lanterns flew by her she was already beyond the water-tank, unsheltered from the wind which lashed her, blowing the shawl from her head and tangling her feet in her skirt. But still she ran on.

"Aunt Michaelovna!" shouted the little girl, "you have lost your shawl."

Katiousha stopped, threw back her head, and, covering her face with her hands, began to sob.

"He is gone!" she cried.

"While he is in a lighted car, sitting on a plush seat, jesting and drinking, I stand here in the mud, rain and wind, crying," she thought. She sat down on the ground and began to sob aloud. The little girl was frightened, and, embracing her wet clothing, she said:

"Auntie, let's go home."

"I will wait for the next train, throw myself under the wheels, and that will end it all," Katiousha was meanwhile thinking, not heeding the girl.

She made up her mind to carry out her intention. But as it always happens in the first moment of calm after a period of agitation, the child, his child, suddenly shuddered. Immediately all that which so tortured her that she was willing to die, all her wrath and her desire to revenge herself even by death, passed. She became calm, arranged her clothing, put the shawl on her head, and went away.

She returned home exhausted, wet and muddy. From that day began in her that spiritual transformation which ended in her present condition. From that terrible night on she ceased to believe in God and in goodness. Before that night she herself believed in God, and believed that other people believed in Him; but after that night she became convinced that no one believed, and all that was said of God and His law was false and wrong. The one whom she loved, and who loved her—she knew it—abandoned her and made sport of her feelings. And he was the best of all the men she knew. All the others were even worse. This she saw confirmed in all that had happened. His aunts, pious old ladies, drove her out when she was no longer as useful as she used to be. All the women with whom she came in contact tried to make money by her; the men, beginning with the commissary and down to the prison officers, all looked upon her as a means of pleasure. The whole world was after pleasure. Her belief in this was strengthened by the old author whom she met during the second year of her independent life. He had told her frankly that this—he called it poetical and esthetic—is all of life's happiness.

Every one lived for himself only, for his own pleasure, and all the words about God and goodness were deception. And if the questions sometimes occurred to her, Why were the affairs of the world so ill arranged that people harm each other, and all suffer, she thought it best not to dwell on it. If she became lonesome, she took a drink, smoked a cigarette, and the feeling would pass away.

CHAPTER XXXVIII.

When at five o'clock the following morning, which was Sunday, the customary whistle blew, Korableva, who was already awake, roused Maslova.

"A convict," Maslova thought with horror, rubbing her eyes and involuntarily inhaling the foul morning air. She wished to fall asleep again, to transfer herself into a state of unconsciousness, but fear overcame her drowsiness. She raised herself, crossed her legs under her, and looked around. The women were already up, only the children were still sleeping. The moonshining woman with bulging eyes was carefully removing her coat from under them. The rioter was drying near the oven some rags which served for swaddling cloths, while the child, in the hands of the blue-eyed Theodosia, was crying at the top of its lungs, the woman lulling it in a gentle voice. The consumptive, seizing her breast, coughed violently, and, sighing at intervals, almost screamed. The red-headed woman lay prone on her back relating a dream she had had. The old incendiary stood before the image, whispering the same words, crossing herself and bowing. The chanter's daughter sat motionless on her cot, and with dull, half-open eyes was looking into space. Miss Dandy was curling on her finger her oily, rough, black hair.

Presently resounding steps were heard in the corridor, the lock creaked open, and two prisoners in short jackets and gray trousers scarcely reaching their ankles entered, and, raising the ill-smelling vat on a yoke, carried it away. The women went to the faucets in the corridor to wash themselves. The red-headed woman got into a quarrel with a woman from the adjoining cell. Again there were cursing, shouting and complaints.

"You will get into the dark-room yet," shouted the warden, and he slapped the red-headed woman on her fat, bare back, so that it resounded through the entire corridor. "Don't let me hear you again."

"Fooling again, you old man?" she said, treating it as a caress.

"Hurry up! It is time for mass."

Scarcely had Maslova arranged her hair when the inspector entered with his attendants.

"Make ready for inspection!" shouted the warden.

The women of the two cells formed in two rows along the corridor, those of the back row placing their hands on the shoulders of the women in the front row. Then they were counted.

After the count came the woman inspector and led the prisoners to the church. Maslova and Theodosia were in the middle of the column, which consisted of over a hundred women from all the cells. They all had white 'kerchiefs on their heads, and some few wore their own colored dresses. These were the wives and children of convicts. The procession covered the whole stairway. A soft clatter of prison shoes was heard, here and there some conversation, and sometimes laughter. At a turn Maslova noticed the malicious face of her enemy, Bochkova, who was walking in the front row, and pointed her out to Theodosia. At the foot of the stairs the women became silent, and, making the sign of the cross and bowing, they filed into the open door of the empty, gold-bedecked chapel. Their place was on the right, where, crowding each other, they began to arrange themselves in rows, standing. Behind the women came the male convicts who were serving terms or detained for transportation under sentence by the communities. Loudly clearing their throats, they formed a dense crowd on the left and the middle of the chapel. Above, on the gallery, were other convicts with heads half shaven, whose presence was manifested by a clanking of chains.

This prison chapel had been rebuilt and remodeled by a rich merchant, who had spent about thirty thousand rubles on it, and it was all ornamented with gilt and bright colors.

For a few seconds there was silence, which was broken only by the blowing of noses, coughing, and clanking of chains. Suddenly the prisoners who stood in the middle began to press back, making a passage for the inspector, who walked to the middle of the chapel, and the services commenced.

CHAPTER XXXIX.

Nekhludoff left the house early. A peasant was driving along a side alley, shouting in a strange voice: "Milk! milk! milk!"

The first warm, spring rain had fallen the evening before. Wherever there was a patch of unpaved ground the green grass burst forth; the lindens were covered with green nap; the fowl-cherry and poplar unfolded their long, fragrant leaves. In the market-place, through which Nekhludoff had to pass, dense crowds in rags swarmed before the tents, some carrying boots under their arms, others smoothly pressed trousers and vests on their shoulders.

The working people were already crowding near the traktirs (tea-houses), the men in clean, long coats gathered in folds in the back of the waist, and in shining boots; the women in bright-colored silk shawls and cloaks with glass-bead trimmings. Policemen, with pistols attached to yellow cords fastened around their waists, stood at their posts. Children and dogs played on the grass-plots, and gay nurses sat chatting on the benches.

On the streets, the left sides of which were yet cool, moist and shady, heavy carts and light cabs rumbled and jostled, the tram-cars rang their bells. The air was agitated by the pealing of the church-bells summoning the people to mass.

The driver stopped at a turn some distance from the prison. A few men and women stood around, most of them with bundles in their hands. To the right stood a few frame houses; to the left a two-story building over which hung a large sign. The large prison itself was directly in front. An armed soldier walked to and fro challenging every one attempting to pass him.

At the gate of the frame buildings sat the warden in uniform, with an entry booklet in his hand. He made entries of visitors and those whom they wished to see. Nekhludoff approached him, gave his name and that of Moslova, and the officer entered them in his book.

"Why don't they open the door?" asked Nekhludoff.

"The morning service is on. As soon as it is over you will be admitted."

Nekhludoff returned among the waiting crowd.

A man in threadbare clothing, rumpled hat and slippers on his bare feet, and his face full of red lines, pushed his way through the crowd and walked toward the prison door.

"Where are you going?" shouted the soldier.

"What are you bawling about?" answered the man, entirely undisturbed by the soldier's challenge. "If I can't go in, I will wait. No use bawling as if you were a general."

The crowd laughed approvingly. Most of the visitors were poorly dressed, even ragged, but, judging by outward appearance, there were also some decent men and women among them. Beside Nekhludoff stood a well-dressed man, clean shaven, stout and with rosy cheeks, who carried a bundle of what looked like linen. Nekhludoff asked him if that was his first visit. The man answered that he came there every Sunday, and they entered into conversation. He was an employee of a bank, whose brother was under indictment for forgery. This kind-hearted man told Nekhludoff all his story, and was about to ask him about his own when their attention was attracted by a rubber-tired carriage drawn by a blooded chestnut horse. The carriage was occupied by a student and a lady whose face was hidden under a veil. The student alighted, holding in his hand a large bundle. He approached Nekhludoff and asked him where and how he should deliver the loaves of bread he had brought for the prisoners. "I brought them at the request of my bride. That is my bride. Her parents advised us to bring some alms for the prisoners."

"I really don't know, for I am here for the first time, but I think that that officer will tell you," said Nekhludoff, pointing to the warden in the crown-laced uniform.

While Nekhludoff was talking to the student the large iron gate of the prison opened and a uniformed officer with another warden came out. The one with the booklet in his hand announced that the prison was open for visitors. The guard stood aside, and all the visitors, as if fearing to be late, with quick step, and some even running, pressed toward the prison gate. One of the wardens stationed himself at the gate, and in a loud voice counted the passing visitors—16, 17, 18, etc. The other warden, within the gate, touching each with his hand, also counted the visitors as they entered another door. This was to make sure that at their departure no visitor remained in prison, and no prisoner made his way out. The tallying officer, without regard to the person of the visitor, slapped Nekhludoff on the back. This at first offended the latter, but he immediately remembered his mission, and he became ashamed that his feelings should be thus wounded.

The second door opened into a large, vaulted room with small iron-grated windows. In this room, which was called the meeting-room, Nekhludoff saw in a niche a large image of the Crucifixion.

Nekhludoff went on slowly, letting the hurrying visitors pass before, and experienced a mingled feeling of horror at the malefactors imprisoned in this jail, compassion for those innocent people who, like the boy and Katiousha, must be here, and timidity and tenderness before the meeting that was before him. When he reached the end of the room the warden said something, but Nekhludoff, who was absorbed in his thoughts, paid no attention to it, and followed in the direction led by the crowd, that is, to the men's ward instead of the women's.

Letting the hurrying visitors pass, he walked into the next room designated for interviews. On opening the door he was struck by the deafening shouts of a hundred throats turned into a continuous humming noise. Only as he neared the people, who, like flies swarming on sugar pressed their faces against a net which divided the room in two, did Nekhludoff understand the cause of the noise. This room with windows in the rear wall was divided in two not by one, but by two wire nets which stretched from the ceiling to the floor. Two wardens walked between the nets. The prisoners were on the other side of the nets, between which there was a space of about seven feet for visitors, so that not only was it difficult to converse with them but a short-sighted man could not even see the face of the prisoner he was visiting. In order to be heard, it was necessary to shout at the top of one's voice. On both sides, pressing against the nets, were the faces of wives, husbands, fathers, mothers, children, who endeavored to see and speak to each other. But as every one tried to speak so that he could be heard by the person spoken to, and his neighbor did the same, their voices interfered with each other, and each tried to outcry the other. The result was the noise which astonished Nekhludoff when he entered the room. It was absolutely impossible to understand the conversations. Only by the expression of the people's faces could one judge what they were speaking about, and what relation the speakers sustained toward each other. Near Nekhludoff was an old woman with a small 'kerchief on her head, who, with trembling chin, shouted to a pale young man with head half shaven. The prisoner, knitting his brow, was listening to her with raised eyebrows. Beside the old woman stood a young man in a long coat, who was nodding his head while listening to a prisoner with a weary face and beard turning gray, who greatly resembled him. Further on stood a ragamuffin waving his hand, shouting and laughing. On the floor beside this man sat a woman in a good woolen dress, with a child in her arms. She wept bitterly, evidently seeing for the first time that gray-haired man on the other side of the net, manacled, in a prison jacket, and with head half shaven. Over this

170

woman stood the bank employee shouting at the top of his voice to a bald-headed prisoner with shining eyes.

Nekhludoff remained in this room about five minutes, experiencing a strange feeling of anguish, a consciousness of his impotence at the discord in the world, and he was seized with a sensation like a rocking on board of a ship.

"But I must fulfill my mission," he said to himself, taking heart. "What am I to do?"

As he looked around for some officer, he saw a middle-sized man with mustache, wearing epaulets, who was walking behind the crowd.

"Sir, could you not tell me where the women are kept, and where it is permitted to see them?" he asked, making a particular effort to be polite.

"You wish to go to the women's ward?"

"Yes; I would like to see one of the women prisoners," Nekhludoff said, with the same strained politeness.

"You should have said so in the meeting-room. Whom do you wish to see, then?"

"I wish to see Katherine Maslova."

"Has she been sentenced?"

"Yes, she was sentenced the other day," he said humbly, as if fearing to ruffle the temper of the officer, who seemed to be interested in him.

"Then this way, please," said the inspector, who had evidently decided from Nekhludoff's appearance that he deserved attention. "Sidoroff!" he turned to a warrant-officer wearing a mustache, and medals on his breast. "Show this gentleman to the women's ward."

"All right, sir."

At that moment heart-rending cries came from the direction of the grating.

All this seemed strange to Nekhludoff, and strangest of all was that he was obliged to thank and feel himself under obligation to the inspector and warden.

The warden led Nekhludoff from the men's ward into the corridor, and through the open door opposite admitted him to the women's meeting-room.

CHAPTER XL.

This room, like the one in the men's ward, was also divided in three, by two nets, but it was considerably smaller. There were also fewer visitors and fewer prisoners, but the noise was as great as in the men's room. Here, also, the authorities stood guard between the nets. The authorities were here represented by a matron in uniform with crown-laced sleeves and fringed with blue braid and a belt of the same color. Here, too, people pressed against the nets—in the passage—city folks in divers dresses; behind the nets, female prisoners, some in white, others in their own dresses. The whole net was lined with people. Some stood on tip-toe, speaking over the heads of others; others, again, sat on the floor and conversed.

The most remarkable of the women prisoners, both in her shouting and appearance, was a thin, ragged gipsy, with a 'kerchief which had slipped from her head, who stood almost in the middle of the room, near a post, behind the net, gesticulating and shouting to a short and tightly belted gipsy in a blue coat. A soldier sat beside him on the floor, talking to a prisoner. Beyond stood a young peasant with a light beard and in bast shoes, pressing his flushed face to the net, evidently with difficulty suppressing his tears. He was talking to a pretty, light-haired prisoner who gazed at him with her bright, blue eyes. This was Theodosia, with her husband. Beside them stood a tramp, who was talking to a disheveled, broad-faced woman. Further on there were two women, a man, and again a woman, and opposite each was a prisoner. Maslova was not among them. But behind the prisoners stood another woman. Nekhludoff felt the beating of his heart increasing and his breath failing him. The decisive moment was approaching. He neared the net and recognized Katiousha. She stood behind the blue-eyed Theodosia, and, smiling, listened to her conversation. She did not wear the prison coat, but a white waist, tightly belted, and rising high above the breast. As in the court, her black hair hung in curls over her 'kerchiefed forehead.

"It will all be over in a moment," he thought. "Shall I address her, or shall I wait till she addresses me?"

But she did not address him. She was waiting for Clara, and never thought that that man came to see her.

"Whom do you wish to see?" the matron asked Nekhludoff, approaching him.

"Katherine Maslova," he stammered.

"Maslova, you are wanted," shouted the matron.

Maslova turned round, raised her head, and with the familiar expression of submissiveness, came to the net. She did not recognize Nekhludoff, and gazed at him in surprise. However, judging by his dress that he was a rich man, she smiled.

"What are you?" she asked, pressing her smiling face with squinting eyes against the net.

"I wish to see—" He did not know whether to use the respectful "you" or the endearing "thou," and decided on the former. He spoke no louder than usual. "I wish to see you—I——"

"Don't give me any of your song and dance——" the tramp beside him shouted. "Did you take it, or did you not?"

"She is dying; she is very weak," some one shouted on the other side.

Maslova could not hear Nekhludoff, but the expression of his face, as she spoke, suddenly reminded her of that which she did not wish to think of. The smile disappeared from her face, and a wrinkle on her brow evidenced her suffering.

"I cannot hear what you are saying," she shouted, blinking and still more knitting her brows.

"I came——"

"Yes, I am doing my duty; I am repenting," thought Nekhludoff, and immediately tears filled his eyes, and he felt a choking sensation in his throat. His fingers clutched at the net and he made efforts to keep from sobbing.

"I should not have gone if you were well," came from one side.

"I swear by God I know nothing about it!" cried a prisoner from the other side.

Maslova noticed his agitation, and it communicated itself to her. Her eyes sparkled, and her puffy, white cheeks became covered with red spots, but her face retained its severity, and her squinting eyes stared past him.

"You are like him, but I don't know you," she shouted.

"I came here to ask your forgiveness," he said in a loud voice, without intonation, as if repeating a lesson he had learned by heart.

As he said these words he felt ashamed and looked round. But the thought immediately came to his mind that it was well that he was ashamed, for he ought to bear the shame. And in a loud voice he continued:

"I acted meanly, infamously—forgive me."

She stood motionless, her squinting eyes fixed on him.

He could not continue and left the net, making efforts to stifle the sobbing which was convulsing his breast.

The inspector who directed Nekhludoff to the women's ward, evidently becoming interested in him, came into the room, and, seeing him in the middle of the passage, asked him why he was not speaking with the prisoner he had inquired about. Nekhludoff blew his nose, and, endeavoring to assume an air of calmness, said:

"I can't speak through the net; nothing can be heard."

The inspector mused awhile.

"Well, then, she can be brought out for awhile."

"Maria Karlovna!" he turned to the matron. "Lead Maslova out."

CHAPTER XLI.

A moment afterward Maslova came out through a side door. With gentle step she came up to Nekhludoff; stopped and glanced at him from under her lowered eyebrows. Her black hair stood out on her forehead in curly ringlets; her unhealthy, bloated, white face was pretty and very calm, only her shining-black, squinting eyes sparkled from under their swollen lashes.

"You may talk here," said the inspector and went aside.

Nekhludoff moved toward a bench standing beside the wall.

Maslova glanced inquiringly at the inspector, and shrugging her shoulders, as if in wonder, followed Nekhludoff to the bench, and straightening her skirt, sat down beside him.

"I know that it is hard for you to forgive me," began Nekhludoff, but feeling the tears flooding his eyes, again stopped, "but if the past cannot be mended, I will do now everything in my power. Tell me———"

"How did you find me?" she asked without answering his question, her squinting eyes looking and not looking at him.

"Oh, Lord! Help me, teach me what to do!" Nekhludoff said to himself as he looked at her face so completely changed.

"I was on the jury when you were tried," he said. "You did not recognize me?"

"No, I did not. I had no time to recognize you. Besides, I did not look," she answered.

"Wasn't there a child?" he asked, and he felt his face turning red.

"It died at that time, thank God," she said with bitterness, turning away her head.

"How did it happen?"

"I was ill myself—nearly died," she said without raising her eyes.

"How could the aunts let you go?"

"Who would keep a servant with a child? As soon as they noticed it they drove me out. But what is the use of talking! I don't remember anything. It is all over now."

"No, it is not over. I cannot leave it thus. I now wish to atone for my sin."

"There is nothing to atone for; what's gone is gone," she said, and, all unexpected to him, she suddenly looked at him and smiled in an alluring and piteous manner.

His appearance was entirely unexpected to Maslova, especially at this time and place, and therefore the astonishment of the first moment brought to her mind that of which she never thought before. At the first moment she hazily recalled that new, wonderful world of feeling and thought which had been opened to her by that charming young man who loved her, and whom she loved, and then his inexplicable cruelty and the long chain of humiliation and suffering which followed as the direct result of that enchanting bliss, and it pained her. But being unable to account for it all, she did the customary thing for her—banished all these recollections from her mind, and endeavored to obscure them by a life of dissipation. At first she associated this man who sat beside her with that young man whom she had loved once, but as the thought pained her, she drove it from her mind. And now this neatly dressed gentleman, with perfumed beard, was to her not that Nekhludoff whom she had loved, but one of those people who, as opportunity afforded, were taking advantage of such creatures as she, and of whom such creatures as she ought to take advantage as opportunity offers. For this reason she smiled alluringly.

She was silent, thinking how to profit by him.

"All that is over now," she said. "And here I am, sentenced to penal servitude."

Her lips trembled as she spoke the terrible word.

"I knew, I was certain that you were innocent," said Nekhludoff.

"Of course I was innocent. I am no thief or robber. They say here that it all depends on the lawyer; that it is necessary to appeal. Only they say it comes very high——"

"Yes, certainly," said Nekhludoff. "I have already seen a lawyer."

"One must not be sparing, and get a good one," she said.

"I will do everything in my power."

They were silent. She again smiled as before.

"I would like to ask you—for some money, if you have it—not much, say ten rubles," she said suddenly.

"Yes, yes," said Nekhludoff, abashed, and thrust his hand in his pocket.

She quickly glanced at the inspector, who was walking up and down the aisle.

"Don't let him see it, or he will take it away."

Nekhludoff took out his pocketbook as soon as the director turned his back on them, but before he could hand her the ten-ruble bill the inspector turned round, facing them. He crumpled the bill in his hand.

"Why, she is a dead woman," thought Nekhludoff as he looked at her once lovely, but now defiled, bloated face with the unhealthy sparkle in her black, squinting eyes, which looked now at the inspector, now at Nekhludoff's hand with the crumpled bill. And a moment of hesitation came over him.

Again the tempter of the night before whispered in his soul, endeavoring to turn the question, What would be the best thing to do? into, What will be the end of it?

"You can do nothing with that woman," whispered the voice. "She will be like a stone around your neck, which will drag you down, and prevent your being useful to others. Give her all the money you have, bid her good-by and put an end to it for all time."

And immediately he became aware that something important was taking place in his soul; that his inner life was on a wavering scale, which could by

177

the slightest effort be made to overbalance to one side or the other. And he made that effort, calling on that God whom the other day he felt in his soul, and God immediately came to his aid. He resolved to tell her all.

"Katiousha! I came to ask your forgiveness, but you have not answered me whether you have forgiven me, or ever will forgive me," he said suddenly.

She was not listening to him, but looked now at his hand, now at the inspector. When the latter turned away, she quickly stretched forth her hand, seized the money from Nekhludoff's hand and stuck it behind her belt.

"How funny!" she said, smiling contemptuously as it seemed to him.

Nekhludoff saw that there was something inimical to him in her, which stood guard, as it were, over her as she was now, and prevented him from penetrating into her heart.

But—wonderful to relate—so far from repulsing him, this only drew him to her by some new peculiar force. He felt that he ought to awaken her spirit; that it was extremely difficult to do so; but the very difficulty of the undertaking attracted him. He experienced a feeling toward her which he had never experienced before, either toward her or any one else, and in which there was nothing personal. He desired nothing of her for himself, and only wished her to to cease to be what she was now, and become what she had been before.

"Katiousha, why do you speak thus? I know you, I remember you as you were in Panoff——"

But she did not yield—she would not yield.

"Why recall the past!" she said dryly, frowning even more.

"Because I wish to efface, to expiate my sin. Katiousha——" he began, and was about to tell her that he would marry her, but he met her eyes in which he read something so terrible, rude and repulsive that he could not finish.

At that moment the visitors began to take leave. The inspector approached

Nekhludoff and told him that the time for interviewing was ended. Maslova rose and submissively waited to be dismissed.

"Good-by. I have a great deal to tell you yet, but, as you see, I cannot do it now," said Nekhludoff, and extended his hand. "I will call again."

"I think you have said everything——"

She extended her hand, but did not press his.

"No. I will try to see you again, where we can speak together, and then I will tell you something very important," said Nekhludoff.

"Well, all right," she said, smiling as she used to do when she wished to please a man.

"You are more to me than a sister," said Nekhludoff.

"Funny," she repeated, and, shaking her head, she went behind the grating.

CHAPTER XLII.

Nekhludoff expected that at the first meeting Katiousha, learning of his intention to serve her, and of his repentance, would be moved to rejoicing, would become again Katiousha, but to his surprise and horror, he saw that Katiousha was no more; that only Maslova remained.

It surprised him particularly that not only was Maslova not ashamed of her condition, but, on the contrary, she seemed to be content with, and even took pride in it. And yet it could not be different.

It is usually thought that a thief or murderer, acknowledging the harmfulness of his occupation, ought to be ashamed of it. The truth is just the contrary. People, whom fate and their sinful mistakes have placed in a given condition, form such views of life generally that they are enabled to consider their condition useful and morally tenable. In order, however, to maintain such views they instinctively cling to such circles in which the same views are held. We are surprised when we hear thieves boasting of their cleverness, or murderers boasting of their cruelty, but that is only because their circle is

179

limited, and because we are outside of it.

This was the case also with Maslova. She was sentenced to penal servitude, and yet she formed such views of life and her place in it that she could find reasons for self-approval and even boast before people of her condition.

The substance of this view was that the greatest welfare of all men, without exception—young, old, students, generals, educated and uneducated—consisted in associating with attractive women, and that therefore all men, while pretending to occupy themselves with other business, in reality desire nothing else. Now, she is an attractive woman, and can satisfy that desire of theirs, or not, as she wishes, hence she is a necessary and important person. All her life, past and present, attested the justice of this view.

Whomever she met during ten years, beginning with Nekhludoff and the old commissary of police, and ending with the jailers, all wanted her. She had not met any one who did not want her. Hence the world appeared to her as an aggregation of people who watched her from all sides and by all possible means—deceit, violence, gold or craftiness—strewn to possess her.

With such an idea of life, Maslova considered herself a most important person. And she cherished this view above all else in the world, because to change it would be to lose that standing among people which it assured her. And in order not to lose her standing she instinctively clung to that circle which held the same views of life. Seeing, however, that Nekhludoff wished to lead her into another world, she resisted it, feeling that in that other world into which he was luring her she would lose her present standing which gave her confidence and self-respect. For the same reason she drove from her mind all recollection of her first youth and her first relations to Nekhludoff. These recollections clashed with her present views of life, and for that reason were entirely effaced from her memory, or, rather, were preserved somewhere in her memory, but were covered up, as it were, with a thick plastering, to prevent any access to them. Nekhludoff was, therefore, to her not that man whom she had loved with a pure love, but merely a rich gentleman by whom one may and ought to profit, and who was to be treated like any other man.

"I did not tell her the most important thing," thought Nekhludoff, as with the other people he walked toward the door. "I did not tell her that I would marry her, but I will do it."

The inspectors at the doors counted the visitors each with one hand slapping every visitor on the back. But Nekhludoff was not offended by it now; he even took no notice of it.

CHAPTER XLIII.

It was Nekhludoff's intention to alter his manner of living—discharge the servants, let the house and take rooms in a hotel. But Agrippina Petrovna argued that no one would rent the house in the summer, and that as it was necessary to live somewhere and keep the furniture and things, he might as well remain where he was. So that all efforts of Nekhludoff to lead a simple, student life, came to naught. Not only was the old arrangement of things continued, but, as in former times, the house received a general cleaning. First were brought out and hung on a rope uniforms and strange fur garments which were never used by anybody; then carpets, furniture, and the porter, with his assistant, rolling up the sleeves on their muscular arms, began to beat these things, and the odor of camphor rose all over the house. Walking through the court-yard and looking out of the window, Nekhludoff wondered at the great number of unnecessary things kept in the house. The only purpose these things served, he thought, was to afford the servants an opportunity of exercise.

"It isn't worth while to alter my mode of life while Maslova's affair is unsettled," he thought. "Besides, it is too hard. When she is discharged or transported and I follow her, things will change of their own accord."

On the day appointed by the lawyer Fanirin, Nekhludoff called on him. On entering the magnificently appointed apartments of the house owned by the lawyer himself, with its huge plants, remarkable curtains and other evidences of luxury, attesting easily earned wealth, Nekhludoff found in the reception-room a number of people sitting dejectedly around tables on which lay illustrated journals intended for their diversion. The lawyer's clerk, who was sitting in this room at a high desk, recognizing Nekhludoff, greeted him and said that he would announce him. But before the clerk reached the door of the cabinet, the door opened and the animated voices of a thick-set man with a red face and stubby mustache, wearing a new suit, and Fanirin himself were heard. The expression on their faces was such as is seen on people who had just made a profitable, but not very honest, bargain.

"It is your own fault, my dear sir," Fanirin said, smiling.

"I would gladly go to heaven, but my sins prevent me."

"That is all right."

And both laughed unnaturally.

"Ah, Prince Nekhludoff! Pleased to see you," said Fanirin, and bowing again to the departing merchant, he led Nekhludoff into his business-like cabinet. "Please take a cigarette," said the lawyer, seating himself opposite Nekhludoff and suppressing a smile, called forth by the success of the preceding affair.

"Thank you. I came to inquire about Maslova's case."

"Yes, yes, immediately. My, what rogues these moneybags are!" he said. "You have seen that fellow; he is worth twelve millions, and is the meanest skinflint I ever met."

Nekhludoff felt an irresistible loathing toward this ready talker who, by his tone of voice, meant to show that he and Nekhludoff belonged to a different sphere than the other clients.

"He worried me to death. He is an awful rogue. I wanted to ease my mind," said the lawyer, as if justifying his not speaking about Nekhludoff's case. "And now as to your case. I have carefully examined it, 'and could not approve the contents thereof,' as Tourgeniff has it. That is to say, the lawyer was a wretched one, and he let slip all the grounds of appeal."

"What have you decided to do?"

"One moment. Tell him," he turned to his clerk, who had just entered, "that I will not change my terms. He can accept them or not, as he pleases."

"He does not accept them."

"Well, then, let him go," said the lawyer, and his benign and joyful countenance suddenly assumed a gloomy and angry expression.

"They say that lawyers take money for nothing," he said, again assuming a pleasant expression. "I succeeded in obtaining the discharge of an insolent debtor who was incarcerated on flimsy accusations of fraud, and now they all run after me. And every such case requires great labor. We, too, you know, leave some of our flesh in the ink-pot, as some author said."

"Well, now, your case, or rather the case in which you are interested," he continued; "was badly conducted. There are no good grounds for appeal, but, of course, we can make an attempt. This is what I have written."

He took a sheet of paper, and quickly swallowing some uninteresting, formal words, and emphasizing others, he began to read:

"To the Department of Cassation, etc., etc., Katherine, etc. Petition. By the decision, etc., of the etc., rendered, etc., a certain Maslova was found guilty of taking the life, by poisoning, of a certain merchant Smelkoff, and in pursuance of Chapter 1,454 of the Code, was sentenced to etc., with hard labor, etc."

He stopped, evidently listening with pleasure to his own composition, although from constant use he knew the forms by heart.

"'This sentence is the result of grave errors,' he continued with emphasis, 'and ought to be reversed for the following reasons: First, the reading in the indictment of the description of the entrails of Smelkoff was interrupted by the justiciary at the very beginning.'—One."

"But the prosecutor demanded its reading," Nekhludoff said with surprise.

"That is immaterial; the defense could have demanded the same thing."

"But that was entirely unnecessary."

"No matter, it is a ground of appeal. Further: 'Second. Maslova's attorney,' he continued to read, 'was interrupted while addressing the jury, by the justiciary, when, desiring to depict the character of Maslova, he touched upon the inner causes of her fall. The ground for refusing to permit him to continue his address was stated to be irrelevancy to the question at issue. But as has often been pointed out by the Senate, the character and moral features generally of an accused are to be given the greatest weight in determining the question of intent.'—Two."

"But he spoke so badly that we could not understand him," said Nekhludoff with still greater surprise.

"He is a very foolish fellow and, of course, could say nothing sensible," Fanirin said, laughing. "However, it is a ground for appeal. 'Third. In his closing words the justiciary, contrary to the positive requirements of section 1, chapter 801 of the Code of Criminal Procedure, failed to explain to the jury of what legal elements the theory of guilt consisted; nor did he tell them that if they found that Maslova gave the poison to Smelkoff, but without intent to kill, they had the power to discharge her.' This is the principal point."

"We could have known that. That was our mistake."

"And finally: 'Fourth,'" continued the lawyer. "'The answer of the jury to the question of Maslova's guilt was made in a form which was obviously contradictory. Maslova was charged with intentional poisoning of Smelkoff, and with robbery as a motive, while the jury, in their answer, denied her guilt of the robbery, from which it was evident that they intended to acquit her of the intent to kill. Their failure to do so was due to the incomplete charge of the justiciary. Such an answer, therefore, demanded the application of chapters 816 and 808 of the Code. That is to say, it was the duty of the presiding justice to explain to the jury their mistake and refer the question of the guilt of the accused to them for further deliberation.'"

"Why, then, did he not do it?"

"That is just what I would like to know myself," said Fanirin, laughing.

"So the Senate will correct the mistake."

"That will depend on who will be sitting there when the case is heard."

"Well, and then we continue: 'Under these circumstances the court erred in imposing on Maslova punishment, and the application to her of section 3, chapter 771 of the Code was a serious violation of the basic principles of the criminal law. Wherefore applicant demands, etc., etc., be revised in accordance with chs. 909, 910, s. 2, 912 and 928 of the Code, etc., etc., and referring the case back for a new trial to a different part of the same court.' Well, now, everything that could be done was done. But I will be frank with you; the probabilities of success are slight. However, everything depends on who will be sitting in the Senate. If you know any one among them, bestir yourself."

"Yes, I know some."

"Then you must hasten, for they will soon be gone on their vacation, and won't return for three months. In case of failure, the only recourse will be to petition the Czar. I shall be at your service also in that contingency."

"I thank you. And now as to your honorarium?"

"My clerk will hand you the petition and also my bill."

"One more question I would like to ask you. The prosecutor gave me a pass for the prison, but I was told there that it was necessary to obtain the Governor's permission to visit the prison on other than visitors' days. Is it necessary?"

"I think so. But he is away, and the lieutenant is in his place."

"You mean Maslenikoff?"

"Yes."

"I know him," said Nekhludoff, rising to leave.

At that moment the lawyer's wife, an extremely ugly, pug-nosed and bony woman, rushed into the room. Not only was her attire unusually original—she was fairly loaded down with plush and silk things, bright yellow and green—but her oily hair was done up in curls, and she triumphantly rushed into the reception-room, accompanied by a tall, smiling man with an earth-colored face, in a cut-away coat with silk facings and a white tie. This was an author. He knew Nekhludoff by sight.

"Anatal," she said, opening the door, "come here. Semion Ivanovitch promised to read to us his poem, and you must read something from Garshin."

Nekhludoff was preparing to go, but the lawyer's wife whispered something to her husband and turned to him:

"I know you, Prince, and consider an introduction unnecessary. Won't you please attend our literary breakfast? It will be very interesting. Anatal is an excellent reader."

"You see what variety of duties I have," said Anatal, smiling and pointing at his wife, thereby expressing the impossibility of resisting that bewitching person.

With a sad and grave face and with the greatest politeness, Nekhludoff thanked the lawyer's wife for the invitation, pleaded other engagements and went into the reception-room.

"What faces he makes!" the lawyer's wife said of him, when he had left the room.

In the reception-room the clerk handed him the petition, and in answer to Nekhludoff's question about the honorarium, said that Anatal Semionovitch set his fee at a thousand rubles; that he really does not take such cases, but does it for Nekhludoff.

"And who is to sign the petition?" asked Nekhludoff.

"The prisoner may sign it herself, and if that be troublesome, she may empower Anatal Semionovitch."

"No, I will go to the prison and obtain her signature," said Nekhludoff, rejoicing at the opportunity of seeing Katiousha before the appointed day.

CHAPTER XLIV.

At the usual hour the jailers' whistles were heard in the corridors of the prison; with a rattling of irons the doors of the corridors and cells opened,

186

and the patter of bare feet and the clatter of prison shoes resounded through the corridors; the men and women prisoners washed and dressed, and after going through the morning inspection, proceeded to brew their tea.

During the tea-drinking animated conversations were going on among the prisoners in the cells and corridors. Two prisoners were to be flogged that day. One of these was a fairly intelligent young clerk who, in a fit of jealousy, had killed his mistress. He was loved by his fellow-prisoners for his cheerfulness, liberality and firmness in dealing with the authorities. He knew the laws and demanded compliance with them. Three weeks ago the warden struck one of the chambermen for spilling some soup on his new uniform. The clerk, Vasilieff, took the chamberman's part, saying that there was no law permitting an official to beat prisoners. "I will show you the law," said the warden, reviling Vasilieff. The latter answered in kind. The warden was about to strike him, but Vasilieff caught hold of his hands and held him fast for about three minutes and then pushed him out of the door. The warden complained and the inspector ordered Vasilieff placed in solitary confinement.

These cells for solitary confinement were dark closets iron-bolted from the outside. In these cold, damp cells, devoid of bed, table or chair, the prisoners were obliged to sit or lie on the dirty floor. The rats, of which there was a large number, crawled all over them, and were so bold that they devoured the prisoner's bread and often attacked the prisoners themselves when they remained motionless. Vasilieff resisted, and with the aid of two other prisoners, tore himself loose from the jailers, but they were finally overcome and all three were thrust into cells. It was reported to the Governor that something like a mutiny occurred, and in answer came a document ordering that the two chief culprits, Vasilieff and the tramp Don'tremember (an application given to some tramps and jail birds who, to conceal the identity, with characteristic ingenuity and stupidity make that answer to all questions relating to their names), be given thirty lashes each.

The flogging was to take place in the women's reception-room.

This was known to all the inmates of the prison since the previous evening, and every one was talking of the coming flogging.

Korableva, Miss Dandy, Theodosia and Maslova, flushed and animated, for they had already partaken of vodka which Maslova now had in abundance, were sitting in their corner, talking of the same thing.

"Why, he has not misbehaved," Korableva said of Vasilieff, biting off a piece of sugar with her strong teeth. "He only sided with a comrade. Fighting, you know, is not allowed nowadays."

"They say he is a fine fellow," added Theodosia, who was sitting on a log on which stood a tea-pot.

"If you were to tell him, Michaelovna," the watch-woman said to Maslova, meaning Nekhludoff.

"I will. He will do anything for me," Maslova answered, smiling and shaking her head.

"It will be too late; they are going to fetch him now," said Theodosia. "It is awful," she added, sighing.

"I have seen once a peasant flogged in the town hall. My father-in-law had sent me to the Mayor of the borough, and when I came there I was surprised to see him——" The watch-woman began a long story.

Her story was interrupted by voices and steps on the upper corridor.

The women became silent, listening.

"They are bringing him, the fiends," said Miss Dandy. "Won't he get it now! The jailers are very angry, for he gave them no rest."

It became quiet in the upper corridor, and the watch-woman finished her story, how she was frightened when she saw the peasant flogged, and how it turned her stomach. Miss Dandy told how Schezloff was flogged with a lash while he never uttered a word. Theodosia then removed the pots and bowls; Korableva and the watch-woman took to their sewing, while Maslova, hugging her knees, became sad from ennui. She was about to lay down to sleep when the matron called her into the office, where a visitor was waiting for her.

188

"Don't fail to tell him about us," said the old Menshova, while Maslova was arranging her headgear before a looking-glass half void of mercury. "It was not me who set the fire, but he, the villain, himself did it, and the laborer saw it. He would not kill a man. Tell him to call Dmitry. Dmitry will explain to him everything. They locked us up here for nothing, while the villain is living with another man's wife and sits around in dram-shops."

"That's wrong!" affirmed Korableva.

"I will tell him—yes, I will," answered Maslova. "Suppose we have a drink, for courage?" she added, winking one eye.

Korableva poured out half a cup for her. Maslova drank it and wiped her mouth. Her spirits rose, and repeating the words "for courage," shaking her head and smiling, she followed the matron.

CHAPTER XLV.

Nekhludoff had been waiting for a long time in the vestibule.

Arriving at the prison he rang the front-door bell and handed his pass to the warden on duty.

"What do you want?"

"I wish to see the prisoner Maslova."

"Can't see her now; the inspector is busy."

"In the office?" asked Nekhludoff.

"No, here in the visitors' room," the warden answered, somewhat embarrassed, as it seemed to Nekhludoff.

"Why, are visitors admitted to-day?"

"No—special business," he answered.

"Where can I see him, then?"

"He will come out presently. Wait."

At that moment a sergeant-major in bright crown-laced uniform, his

189

face radiant, and his mustache impregnated with smoke, appeared from a side door.

"Why did you admit him here? What is the office for?" he said sternly, turning to the warden.

"I was told that the inspector was here," said Nekhludoff, surprised at the embarrassment noticeable on the officer's face.

At that moment the inner door opened and Petroff, flushed and perspiring, came out.

"He will remember it," he said, turning to the sergeant-major.

The latter pointed with his eyes to Nekhludoff, and Petroff became silent, frowned and walked out through the rear door.

"Who will remember? What? Why are they all so embarrassed? Why did the sergeant make that sign?" thought Nekhludoff.

"You cannot wait here; please walk into the office," the sergeant-major turned to Nekhludoff, who was about to go out when the inspector came in through the inner door, more embarrassed even than his assistants. He was sighing incessantly. Seeing Nekhludoff, he turned to the warden:

"Fedotoff, call Maslova."

"Follow me, please," he said to Nekhludoff. They passed up a winding stairway leading into a small room with one window and containing a writing table and a few chairs. The inspector sat down.

"Mine are disagreeable duties," he said, turning to Nekhludoff and lighting a thick cigarette.

"You seem tired," said Nekhludoff.

"I am very tired of all this business; my duties are very onerous. I am trying my best to alleviate the condition of the prisoners and things are getting only worse. I am very anxious to get away from here; the duties are very, very unpleasant."

Nekhludoff could not understand what it was that made it so unpleasant for the inspector, but to-day he noticed on the inspector's face an expression of despondency and hopelessness which was pitiful to behold.

"Yes, I think they are very trying," he said. "But why do you not resign?"

"I have a family and am without means."

"But if it is difficult——"

"Well, you see, I manage to improve somewhat their lot after all. Another one in my place would hardly exert himself as I do. It is no easy matter to handle two thousand people. They are also human and one feels pity for them, and yet they can't be allowed to have all their own way."

And the inspector related the case of a recent fight among the prisoners which ended in murder.

His story was interrupted by the entrance of Maslova, who was preceded by the warden.

Nekhludoff got sight of her when she appeared on the threshold and before she saw the inspector. Her face was red, and she walked briskly behind the warden, smiling and shaking her head. Noticing the inspector she gazed at him with frightened face, but immediately recovered herself and boldly and cheerfully turned to Nekhludoff.

"How do you do?" she said, drawlingly, smiling and vigorously shaking his hand, not as on the former occasion.

"Here I have brought you the petition to sign," said Nekhludoff, somewhat surprised at the forward manner in which she accosted him. "The lawyer wrote it. It must be signed and sent to St. Petersburg."

"Why, certainly. I will do anything," she said, winking one eye and smiling.

"May she sign it here?" Nekhludoff asked of the inspector.

"Come here and sit down," said the inspector. "Here is a pen for you.

Can you write?"

"I could write once," she said, smiling, and, arranging her skirt and waist-sleeve, sat down, clumsily took the pen into her small, energetic hand, began to laugh and looked round at Nekhludoff.

He pointed out to her where to sign.

Diligently dipping and shaking the pen she signed her name.

"Do you wish anything else?" she asked, looking now at Nekhludoff, now at the inspector, and depositing the pen now on the ink-stand, now on the paper.

"I wish to tell you something," said Nekhludoff, taking the pen from her hand.

"Very well; go on," she uttered, and suddenly, as though meditating or growing sleepy, her face became grave.

The inspector rose and walked out, leaving Nekhludoff with her alone.

CHAPTER XLVI.

The warden who brought Maslova to the office seated himself on the window-sill, away from the table. This was a decisive moment for Nekhludoff. He had been constantly reproaching himself for not telling her at their first meeting of his intention to marry her, and was now determined to do so. She was sitting on one side of the table, and Nekhludoff seated himself on the other side, opposite her. The room was well lighted, and for the first time Nekhludoff clearly saw her face from a short distance, and noticed wrinkles around the eyes and lips and a slight swelling under her eyes, and he pitied her even more than before.

Resting his elbows on the table so that he should not be heard by the warden, whose face was of a Jewish type, with grayish side-whiskers, he said:

"If this petition fails we will appeal to His Majesty. Nothing will be left undone."

"If it had been done before—if I had had a good lawyer"—she

192

interrupted him. "That lawyer of mine was such a little fool. He was only making me compliments," she said, and began to laugh. "If they had only known that I was your acquaintance, it would have been different. They think that everybody is a thief."

"How strange she is to-day," thought Nekhludoff, and was about to tell her what he had on his mind when she again began to speak.

"I wanted to tell you. There is an old woman here—we are even surprised—such a good little woman, but there she is—she and her son, both in prison, and everybody knows that they are innocent. They are accused of setting fire, so they are in prison. She learned, you know, that I am acquainted with you," said Maslova, turning her head and casting glances at him, "and she says to me: 'Tell him,' she says, 'to call my son; he will tell him the whole story.' Menshoff is his name. Well, will you do it? Such a good little woman. You can see for yourself that she is not guilty. You will help them, dear, won't you?" she said, glancing at him; then she lowered her eyes and smiled.

"Very well; I will do it," said Nekhludoff, his surprise at her easy manner growing, "but I would like to talk to you about my own affair. Do you remember what I told you that time?"

"You have spoken so much. What did you say that time?" she said, continuing to smile and turning her head now to one side, now to the other.

"I said that I came to ask your forgiveness," he said.

"Oh! Forgiveness, forgiveness! That is all nonsense. You had better——"

"That I wish to atone for my sin," continued Nekhludoff, "and to atone not by words but by deed. I have decided to marry you."

Her face suddenly showed fright. Her squinting eyes became fixed, and they looked and did not look at him.

"What is that for?" And she frowned maliciously.

"I feel that before God I must do it."

"What God, now, are you talking about? You are not talking to the point. God? What God? Why didn't you think of God then?" she said, and opening her mouth, stopped short.

Nekhludoff only now smelled a strong odor of liquor and understood the cause of her excitement.

"Be calm," he said.

"I have nothing to be calm about. You think I am drunk? Yes, I am drunk, but I know what I am talking about," she said quickly, and her face became purple. "I am a convict, while you are a lord, a prince, and needn't stay here to soil your hands. Go to your princesses——"

"You cannot be too cruel to me; you do not know how I feel," he said in a low voice, his whole body trembling. "You cannot imagine how strongly I feel my guilt before you!"

"Feel my guilt," she mocked him maliciously. "You did not feel it then, but thrust a hundred rubles in my hands. 'That's your price——'"

"I know, I know, but what am I to do now? I have decided not to leave you," he repeated; "and what I say I will do."

"And I say that you will not!" she said, and laughed aloud.

"Katinsha!" he began.

"Leave me. I am a convict, and you are a prince; and you have no business here," she shrieked, violently releasing her hand from his, her wrath knowing no limit.

"You wish to save yourself through me," she continued, hastening to pour out all that had accumulated in her soul. "You have made me the means of your enjoyment in life, and now you wish to make me the means of saving you after death! You disgust me, as do your eye-glasses and that fat, dirty face of yours. Go, go away!" she shrieked, energetically springing to her feet.

The warden approached them.

"Don't you make so much noise! You know whom——"

194

"Please desist," said Nekhludoff.

"She must not forget herself," said the warden.

"Please wait a while," said Nekhludoff.

The warden returned to his seat on the window-sill.

Maslova again seated herself, her eyes downcast and her little hands clutching each other.

Nekhludoff stood over her, not knowing what to do.

"You do not believe me," he said.

"That you wish to marry me? That will never happen. I will sooner hang myself."

"But I will serve you anyway."

"That is your business. Only I don't want anything from you. Now, that is certain," she said. "Oh, why did I not die then!" she added, and began to cry piteously.

Nekhludoff could not speak; her tears called forth tears in his own eyes.

She raised her eyes, looked at him, as if surprised, and with her 'kerchief began to wipe the tears streaming down her cheeks.

The warden again approached them and reminded them that it was time to part. Maslova rose.

"You are excited now. If possible I will call to-morrow. Meantime, think it over," said Nekhludoff.

She made no answer, and without looking at him left the room, preceded by the warden.

"Well, girl, good times are coming," said Korableva to Maslova when the latter returned to the cell. "He seems to be stuck on you, so make the most of it while he is calling. He will get you released. The rich can do anything."

"That's so," drawled the watch-woman. "The poor man will think ten times before he will marry, while the rich man can satisfy his every whim. Yes, my dear; there was a respectable man in our village, and he——"

"Have you spoken to him of my case?" asked the old woman.

But Maslova was silent. She lay down on her bunk, gazing with her squinting eyes into the corner, and remained in that position till evening. Her soul was in torment. That which Nekhludoff told her opened to her that world in which she had suffered and which she had left, hating without understanding it. She had now lost that forgetfulness in which she had lived, and to live with a clear recollection of the past was painful. In the evening she again bought wine, which she drank with her fellow-prisoners.

CHAPTER XLVII.

"So, that is how it is!" thought Nekhludoff as he made his way out of the prison, and he only now realized the extent of his guilt. Had he not attempted to efface and atone for his conduct, he should never have felt all the infamy of it, nor she all the wrong perpetrated against her. Only now it all came out in all its horror. He now for the first time perceived how her soul had been debased, and she finally understood it. At first Nekhludoff had played with his feelings and delighted in his own contrition; now he was simply horrified. He now felt that to abandon her was impossible. And yet he could not see the result of these relations.

At the prison gate some one handed Nekhludoff a note. He read it when on the street. The note was written in a bold hand, with pencil, and contained the following:

"Having learned that you are visiting the prison I thought it would be well to see you. You can see me by asking the authorities for an interview with me. I will tell you something very important to your protege as well as to the politicals. Thankfully, Vera Bogodukhovskaia"

"Bogodukhovskaia! Who is Bogodukhovskaia?" thought Nekhludoff, entirely absorbed in the impression of his meeting with Maslova, and failing at the first moment to recall either the name or the handwriting. "Oh, yes!" he suddenly recalled. "The deacon's daughter at the bear-hunt."

Vera Bogodukhovskaia was a teacher in the obscure district of Novgorod, whither Nekhludoff, on one occasion, went bear hunting with his friends. This teacher had asked Nekhludoff to give her some money to enable her to study. He gave it to her, and the incident dropped from his memory. And now it seemed that this lady was a political prisoner, had probably learned his history in prison, and was now offering her services. At that time everything was easy and simple; now everything was difficult and complex. Nekhludoff readily and joyfully recalled that time and his acquaintance with Bogodukhovskaia. It was on the eve of Shrovetide, in the wilds about sixty versts from the railroad. The hunt was successful; two bears were bagged, and they were dining before their journey home, when the woodsman, in whose hut they were stopping, came to tell them that the deacon's daughter had come and wished to see Prince Nekhludoff.

"Is she good looking?" some one asked.

"Come, come!" said Nekhludoff, rising, and wondering why the deacon's daughter should want him, assumed a grave expression and went to the woodsman's hut.

In the hut there was a girl in a felt hat and short fur coat, sinewy, and with an ugly and unpleasant face, relieved, however, by her pleasant eyes and raised eyebrows.

"This is the Prince, Vera Efremovna," said the old hostess. "I will leave you."

"What can I do for you?" asked Nekhludoff.

"I—I—You see, you are rich and throw away your money on trifles, on a chase. I know," began the girl, becoming confused, "but I wish but one thing; I wish to be useful to people, and can do nothing because I know nothing."

"What, then, can I do for you?"

"I am a teacher, and would like to enter college, but they don't let me. It is not exactly that they don't let me, but we have no means. Let me have some money; when I am through with my studies I shall return it to you."

Her eyes were truthful and kindly, and the expression of resolution and timidity on her face was so touching that Nekhludoff, as it was usual with him, suddenly mentally placed himself in her position, understood and pitied her.

"I think it is wrong for rich people to kill bears and get the peasants drunk. Why don't they make themselves useful? I only need eighty rubles. Oh, if you don't wish to, it is all the same to me," she said, angrily, interpreting the grave expression on Nekhludoff's face to her disadvantage.

"On the contrary, I am very thankful to you for the opportunity——"

When she understood that he consented her face turned a purple color and she became silent.

"I will fetch it immediately," said Nekhludoff.

He went into the entrance hall where he found an eavesdropping friend. Without taking notice of his comrade's jests, he took the money from his hand-bag and brought it to her.

"Please don't be thanking me. It is I who ought to be thankful to you."

It was pleasant to Nekhludoff to recall all that; it was pleasant to recall how he came near quarreling with the army officer who attempted to make a bad joke of it; how another comrade sided with him, which drew them more closely together; how merry and successful was the hunt, and how happy he felt that night returning to the railroad station. A long file of sleighs moved noiselessly in pairs at a gentle trot along the narrow fir-lined path of the forests, which were covered with a heavy layer of snowflakes. Some one struck a red light in the dark, and the pleasant aroma of a good cigarette was wafted toward him. Osip, the sleigh-tender, ran from sleigh to sleigh, knee-deep in snow, telling of the elks that were roaming in the deep snow, nibbling the bark of aspen trees, and of the bears emitting their warm breath through the airholes of their wild haunts.

Nekhludoff remembered all that, and above all the happy consciousness of his own health, strength and freedom from care. His lungs, straining his tight-fitting fur coat, inhaled the frosty air; the trees, grazed by the shaft, sent showers of white flakes into his face; his body was warm, his face ruddy; his soul was without a care or blemish, or fear or desire. How happy he was! But now? My God! How painful and unbearable it all was!

CHAPTER XLVIII.

Rising the next morning Nekhludoff recalled the events of the previous day and was seized with fear.

But, notwithstanding this fear, he was even more determined than before to carry out his plan already begun.

With this consciousness of the duty that lay upon him he drove to Maslenikoff for permission to visit in jail, besides Maslova, the old woman Menshova and her son, of whom Maslova had spoken to him. Besides, he also wished to see Bogodukhovskaia, who might be useful to Maslova.

Nekhludoff had known Maslenikoff since they together served in the army. Maslenikoff was the treasurer of the regiment. He was the most kind-hearted officer, and possessed executive ability. Nothing in society was of any interest to him, and he was entirely absorbed in the affairs of the regiment. Nekhludoff now found him an administrator in the civil government. He was married to a rich and energetic woman to whom was due his change of occupation.

She laughed at him and patted him as she would a tamed animal. Nekhludoff had visited them once the previous winter, but the couple seemed so uninteresting to him that he never called again.

Maslenikoff's face became radiant when he saw Nekhludoff. His face was as fat and red, his dress as excellent as when he served in the army. As an army officer he was always neat, dressed in a tight uniform made according to the latest style; now his dress fitted his well-fed body as perfectly. He wore a uniform. Notwithstanding the difference in their age—Maslenikoff was about forty—they familiarly "thoued" each other.

"Very glad you remembered me. Come to my wife. I have just ten minutes to spare, and then I must to the session. My chief, you know, is away.

I am directing the affairs of the district," he said, with joy which he could not conceal.

"I came to you on business."

"What's that?" Maslenikoff said in a frightened and somewhat stern voice, suddenly pricking his ears.

"There is a person in jail in whom I am very much interested;" at the word "jail" Maslenikoff's face became even more stern, "and I would like to have the right of interview in the office instead of the common reception room, and oftener than on the appointed days. I was told that it depended on you."

"Of course, mon cher, I am always ready to do anything for you," Maslenikoff said, touching his knees with both hands, as if desiring to soften his own greatness. "I can do it, but you know I am caliph only for an hour."

"So you can give me a pass that will enable me to see her?"

"It is a woman?"

"Yes."

"What is the charge against her?"

"Poisoning. But she was irregularly convicted."

"Yes, there is justice for you! Ils n'en font point d'autres," he said, for some reason in French. "I know that you do not agree with me, but c'est mon opinion bien arretee," he added, repeating the opinion that had been reiterated during the past year by a retrograde, conservative newspaper. "I know you are a liberal."

"I don't know whether I am a liberal or something else," smilingly said Nekhludoff, who always wondered at being joined to some party, or called a liberal only because he held that a man must not be judged without being heard; that all are equal before the law; that it is wrong to torture and beat people generally, especially those that are not convicted. "I don't know whether I am a liberal or not, but I do know that our present courts, bad as they are, are nevertheless better than those that preceded them."

"And what lawyer have you retained?"

"I have retained Fanarin."

"Ah, Fanarin!" Maslenikoff said, frowning as he recalled how Fanarin, examining him as a witness the year before, in the most polite manner made him the butt of ridicule.

"I would not advise you to have anything to do with him. Fanarin est un homme tare."

"I have another request to make of you," Nekhludoff said, without answering him. "A long time ago I made the acquaintance of a girl teacher, a very wretched creature. She is now in jail and desires to see me. Can you give me a pass to her?"

Maslenikoff leaned his head to one side and began to reflect.

"She is a political."

"Yes, I was told so."

"You know politicals can only be seen by their relatives, but I will give you a general pass. Je sais que vous n'abuserez pas——"

"What is the name of this your protege? Bogodukhovskaia? Elle est jolie?"

"Hideuse."

Maslenikoff disapprovingly shook his head, went to the table and on a sheet of paper with a printed letter-head wrote in a bold hand: "The bearer, Prince Dmitri Ivanovich Nekhludoff, is hereby permitted to visit the prisoners, Maslova and Bogodukhovskaia, now detained in the prison," and signed his name to it with a broad flourish.

"You will see now what order there is in prison. And to keep order there is very difficult, because it is overcrowded, especially by those to be transported. But I watch over them, and like the occupation. You will see there are very many there, but they are content, and are faring well. It is necessary to know how to deal with them. Some unpleasantness occurred there a few days ago—disobedience. Another man in my place would have treated it as a riot and made many people miserable, but we arranged it all pleasantly. What is necessary is solicitude on the one hand, and prompt and vigorous dealing on the other," he said, clenching his soft, white fist projecting from under a white, starched cuff and adorned with a turquoise ring—"solicitude and vigorous dealing."

"Well, I don't know about that," said Nekhludoff. "I was there twice, and I was very much distressed by the sight."

"You know what I will tell you? You ought to get acquainted with Princess Passek," continued Maslenikoff, who had become talkative; "she has entirely devoted herself to this cause. Elle fait beaucoup de bien. Thanks to her and, without false modesty, to myself, everything has been changed, and changed so that none of the old horrors can be found there, and they are decidedly well off there. You will see it. There is Fanarin. I am not personally acquainted with him; besides, our roads do not meet because of my position in society, but he is decidedly a bad man, and allows himself to state in court such things, such things!"

"Well, thank you," said Nekhludoff, taking the document, and took leave of his old comrade.

"Would you not like to see my wife?"

"No, thank you; I have no time now."

"Well, now, she will never forgive me," said Maslenikoff, conducting his old comrade to the first landing, as he did with people of secondary importance, among whom he reckoned Nekhludoff. "Do come but for a moment."

But Nekhludoff was firm, and while the footman and porter sprang toward him, handing him his overcoat and cane, and opening the door, before which a policeman stood, he excused himself, pleading want of time.

"Well, then, Thursday, please. That is her reception day. I will tell her!" Maslenikoff shouted from the top of the stairs.

202

CHAPTER XLIX.

From Maslenikoff, Nekhludoff went directly to the prison and approached the familiar apartments of the inspector. The sounds of a tuneless piano again assailed his ears, but this time it was not a rhapsody that was played, but a study by Clementi, and, as before, with unusual force, precision and rapidity. The servant with a handkerchief around one eye said that the captain was in, and showed Nekhludoff into the small reception-room, in which was a lounge, a table and a lamp, one side of the rose-colored shade of which was scorched, standing on a knitted woolen napkin. The inspector appeared with an expression of sadness and torment on his face.

"Glad to see you. What can I do for you?" he said, buttoning up the middle button of his uniform.

"I went to the vice-governor, and here is my pass," said Nekhludoff, handing him the document. "I would like to see Maslova."

"Markova?" asked the inspector, who could not hear him on account of the music.

"Maslova."

"O, yes! O, yes!"

The inspector rose and approached the door through which Clementi's roulade was heard.

"Marusia; if you would only stop for a little while," he said in a voice which showed that this music was the cross of his life; "I cannot hear anything."

The music ceased; discontented steps were heard, and some one looked through the door.

The inspector, as if relieved by the cessation of the music, lit a thick cigarette of light tobacco and offered one to Nekhludoff, which he refused.

"Can Maslova——"

"It is not convenient to see Maslova to-day," said the inspector.

"Why?"

"It is your own fault," slightly smiling, said the inspector. "Prince, you must not give her any money. If you wish to give her money, leave it with me; I will keep it for her. You see, you must have given her money yesterday, for she bought wine—it is hard to eradicate that evil—and is intoxicated to-day. In fact, she became unruly."

"Is it possible?"

"Why, I even had to employ strict measures, had her transferred to another cell. She is very tractable, but, please do not give her money. That is their failing."

Nekhludoff quickly recalled the incident of yesterday, and he was seized with fear.

"And may I see Bogodukhovskaia, the political?" Nekhludoff asked, after some silence.

"Well, yes," said the inspector. "What are you doing here?" he turned to a five-year-old girl who came into the room, walking toward her father, her eyes riveted on Nekhludoff. "Look out, or you will fall," he said, smiling, as the little girl, walking with her head turned toward Nekhludoff, tripped on the carpet and ran to her father.

"If she may be seen, I would go now."

"Oh yes; she may be seen, of course," said the inspector, embracing the little girl, who was still looking at Nekhludoff. "All right——"

The inspector rose and gently turning the girl aside, walked into the vestibule.

He had scarcely donned the overcoat handed him by the girl with the bandaged eye and crossed the threshold when the distinct sounds of Clementi's roulade broke out.

"She was at the Conservatory, but there is disorder in that institution. But she is very gifted," said the inspector, walking down the stairs. "She intends to appear at concerts."

The inspector and Nekhludoff neared the prison. The wicket immediately opened at the approach of the inspector. The wardens standing to attention followed him with their eyes. Four men with heads half shaved, carrying large vessels, met him in the vestibule, and as they spied him slunk back. One of them, in a particularly gloomy way, knit his brow, his black eyes flashing fire.

"Of course, her talent must be perfected; it cannot be neglected. But in a small apartment it is hard, you know," the inspector continued the conversation without paying any attention to the prisoners, and dragging his tired legs passed into the meeting-room, followed by Nekhludoff.

"Whom do you wish to see?" asked the inspector.

"Bogodukhovskaia."

"That is from the tower. You will have to wait a little," he turned to Nekhludoff.

"Couldn't you let me see, meantime, the prisoners Menshov—mother and son—who are charged with incendiarism?"

"That is from cell 21. Why, yes; they may be called out."

"Would you allow me to see the son in his cell?"

"It is quieter in the meeting-room."

"But it is interesting to see him there."

"Interesting!"

At that moment a dashing officer, the inspector's assistant, appeared at a side door.

"Conduct the Prince to Menshov's cell—No. 21," said the inspector to his assistant. "Then show him to the office. And I will call—what is her name?"

"Vera Bogodukhovskaia," said Nekhludoff.

The inspector's assistant was a light-haired young officer with dyed mustache, who spread around him the odor of perfume.

"Follow me, please." He turned to Nekhludoff with a pleasant smile. "Does our institution interest you?"

"Yes. And I am also interested in that man who, I was told, is innocent." The assistant shrugged his shoulders.

"Yes, that may be," he said calmly, courteously admitting the guest into the ill-smelling corridor. "But they also lie often. Walk in, please."

The doors of the cells were open, and some prisoners stood in the corridor. Slightly nodding to the wardens and looking askance at the prisoners, who either pressed against the walls, entered their cells, or, stopping at the doors, stood erect like soldiers, the assistant escorted Nekhludoff through one corridor into another, on the left, which was iron-bolted.

This corridor was darker and more ill-smelling than the first. There was a row of cells on each side, the doors of which were locked. There was a hole in each door—eyelet, so called—of about an inch in diameter. There was no one in this corridor except an old warden with a wrinkled, sad face.

"Where is Menshov's cell?" asked the assistant.

"The eighth one on the left."

"Are these occupied?" asked Nekhludoff.

"All but one."

CHAPTER L.

"May I look in?" asked Nekhludoff.

"If you please," the assistant said with a pleasant smile, and began to make inquiries of the warden. Nekhludoff looked through one of the openings. A tall young man with a small black beard, clad only in his linen, walked rapidly up and down the floor of his cell. Hearing a rustle at the door, he looked up, frowned, and continued to walk.

Nekhludoff looked into the second opening. His eye met another large, frightened eye. He hastily moved away. Looking into the third, he saw a small-sized man sleeping curled up on a cot, his head covered with his prison coat. In the fourth cell a broad-faced, pale-looking man sat with lowered head, his elbows resting on his knees. Hearing steps, this man raised his head and looked up. In his face and eyes was an expression of hopeless anguish. He was apparently unconcerned about who it was that looked into his cell. Whoever it might be, he evidently hoped for no good from any one. Nekhludoff was seized with fear, and he hastened to Number 21—Menshov's cell. The warden unlocked and opened the door. A young, muscular man with a long neck, kindly, round eyes and small beard, stood beside his cot, hastily donning his prison coat and, with frightened face, looking at the two men who had entered. Nekhludoff was particularly struck by the kindly, round eyes whose wondering and startled look ran from him to the warden and back.

"This gentleman wishes to ask you about your case."

"Thank you."

"Yes, I was told about your case," said Nekhludoff, going into the depth of the cell and stopping at the barred, dirty window, "and would like to hear it from yourself."

Menshov also drew near the window and immediately began to relate the particulars of his case—at first timidly, from time to time glancing at the warden, then growing bolder and bolder. And when the warden had left the cell to give some orders, his timidity left him entirely. Judging by his speech and manner, his was a story of a simple, honest peasant, and it seemed very strange to Nekhludoff to hear it from the lips of a prisoner in the garb of disgrace and in prison. While listening to him, Nekhludoff examined the low cot, with its straw mattress, the window, with its thick iron bars, the damp, plastered walls, the pitiful face and the figure of the unfortunate, mutilated peasant in bast shoes and prison coat, and he became sad; he would not believe that what this kind-hearted man told him was true. And it was still harder to think that this truthful story should be false, and that kindly face should deceive him. His story, in short, was that soon after his wedding a tapster enticed away his wife. He had recourse to the law everywhere, and the tapster was everywhere acquitted. Once he took her away by force, but she ran away the following day. He went to the seducer, demanding his wife. The tapster told him that she was not there, although he saw her when coming in, and ordered him to depart. He would not go. Then the tapster and another workman beat him until he bled, and the following day the tapster's house took fire. He and his mother were charged with incendiarism, although at the time the fire broke out he was visiting a friend.

"And you really did not set the fire?"

"I never even thought of such a thing, master. The villain must have done it himself. They say that he had just insured his house. And he said that I and my mother came and threatened him. It is true, I abused him at that time—couldn't help it—but I did not set the fire, and was not even in the neighborhood when the fire started. He set the fire purposely on the day I was there with my mother. He did it for the insurance money, and threw it on us."

"Is it possible?"

"As true as there is a living God, master. Do help us!" He was about to bow to the ground, but Nekhludoff forcibly prevented him. "Release me. I am suffering here innocently," he continued. His face suddenly began to twitch; tears welled up in his eyes, and, rolling up the sleeve of his coat, he began to wipe his eyes with the dirty sleeve of his shirt.

"Have you finished?" asked the warden.

"Yes. Cheer up; I will do what I can for you," Nekhludoff said, and walked out. Menshov stood in the door, so that when the warden closed it he pushed him in. While the warden was locking the door, Menshov looked through the hole.

CHAPTER LI.

It was dinner time when Nekhludoff retraced his steps through the wide corridor, and the cells were open. The prisoners, in light yellow coats, short, wide trousers and prison shoes, eyed him greedily. Nekhludoff experienced strange feelings and commiseration for the prisoners, and, for some reason, shame that he should so calmly view it.

208

In one of the corridors a man, clattering with his prison shoes, ran into one of the cells, and immediately a crowd of people came out, placed themselves in his way, and bowed.

"Your Excellency—I don't know what to call you—please order that our case be decided."

"I am not the commander. I do not know anything."

"No matter. Tell them, the authorities, or somebody," said an indignant voice, "to look into our case. We are guilty of no offense, and have been in prison the second month now."

"How so? Why?" asked Nekhludoff.

"We don't know ourselves why, but we have been here the second month."

"That is true," said the assistant inspector. "They were taken because they had no passports, and they were to be transported to their district, but the prison had burned down there, and the authorities asked us to keep them here. Those belonging to other districts were transported, but these we keep here."

"Is that the only reason?" asked Nekhludoff, stopping in the doorway.

The crowd, consisting of about forty men, all in prison garb, surrounded Nekhludoff and the assistant. Several voices began talking at once. The assistant stopped them.

"Let one of you speak."

A tall old man of good mien came forward. He told Nekhludoff that they were all imprisoned on the ground that they had no passports, but that, as a matter of fact, they had passports which had expired and were not renewed for about two weeks. It happened every year, but they were never even fined. And now they were imprisoned like criminals.

"We are all masons and belong to the same association. They say that the prison has burned down, but that isn't our fault. For God's sake, help us!"

Nekhludoff listened, but scarcely understood what the old man was saying.

"How is that? Can it be possible that they are kept in prison for that sole reason?" said Nekhludoff, turning to the assistant.

"Yes, they ought to be sent to their homes," said the assistant.

At that moment a small-sized man, also in prison attire, pushed his way through the crowd and began to complain excitedly that they were being tortured without any cause.

"Worse than dogs——" he began.

"Tut, tut! do not talk too much, or else you know——"

"Know what?" said the little man desperately. "Are we guilty of anything?"

"Silence!" shouted the assistant, and the little man subsided.

"What a peculiar state of things!" Nekhludoff said to himself as he ran the gauntlet, as it were, of a hundred eyes that followed him through the corridor.

"Is it possible that innocent people are held in durance here?" Nekhludoff said, when they emerged from the corridor.

"What can we do? However, many of them are lying. If you ask them, they all claim to be innocent," said the assistant inspector; "although some are there really without any cause whatever."

"But these masons don't seem to be guilty of any offense."

"That is true so far as the masons are concerned. But those people are spoiled. Some measure of severity is necessary. They are not all as innocent as they look. Only yesterday we were obliged to punish two of them."

"Punish, how?" asked Nekhludoff.

"By flogging. It was ordered——"

"But corporal punishment has been abolished."

"Not for those that have been deprived of civil rights."

Nekhludoff recalled what he had seen the other day while waiting in the vestibule, and understood that the punishment had then been taking place, and with peculiar force came upon him that mingled feeling of curiosity, sadness, doubt, and moral, almost passing over into physical, nausea which he had felt before, but never with such force.

Without listening to the assistant or looking around him, he hastily passed through the corridor and ascended to the office. The inspector was in the corridor, and, busying himself with some affair, had forgot to send for Bogodukhovskaia. He only called it to mind when Nekhludoff entered the office.

"I will send for her immediately. Take a seat," he said.

CHAPTER LII.

The office consisted of two rooms. In the first room, which had two dirty windows and the plastering on the walls peeled off, a black measuring rod, for determining the height of prisoners, stood in one corner, while in another hung a picture of Christ. A few wardens stood around in this room. In the second room, in groups and pairs, about twenty men and women were sitting along the walls, talking in low voices. A writing table stood near one of the windows.

The inspector seated himself at the writing table and offered Nekhludoff a chair standing near by. Nekhludoff seated himself and began to examine the people in the room.

His attention was first of all attracted by a young man with a pleasant face, wearing a short jacket, who was standing before a man prisoner and a girl, gesticulating and talking to them in a heated manner. Beside them sat an old man in blue eye-glasses, immovably holding the hand of a woman in prison garb and listening to her. A boy in high-school uniform, with an expression of fright on his face, stood gazing on the old man. Not far from them, in the corner, a pair of lovers were sitting. She was a very young, pretty, stylishly-dressed girl with short-cropped, flaxen hair and an energetic face;

he was a fine-featured, handsome youth, with wavy hair, and in a prison coat. They occupied the corner, whispering to each other, apparently wrapped in their love. Nearest of all to the table was a gray-haired woman in black, evidently the mother of a consumptive young man in a rubber jacket, who stood before her. Her eyes were fixed on him, and her tears prevented her speaking, which she several times attempted to do, but was forced to desist. The young man held a piece of paper in his hand, and, evidently not knowing what to do, with an angry expression on his face was folding and crumpling it. Sitting beside the weeping mother, and patting her on the shoulder, was a stout, pretty girl with red cheeks, in a gray dress and cape. Everything in this girl was beautiful—the white hands, the wavy, short hair, the strong nose and lips; but the principal charm of her face were her hazel, kindly, truthful, sheep eyes. Her beautiful eyes turned on Nekhludoff at the moment he entered, and met his. But she immediately turned them again on her mother, and whispered to her something. Not far from the lovers a dark man with gloomy face sat talking angrily to a clean-shaven visitor resembling a Skopetz (a sect of castrates). At the very door stood a young man in a rubber jacket, evidently more concerned about the impression he was making on the visitors than what he was saying. Nekhludoff sat down beside the inspector and looked around him with intense curiosity. He was amused by a short-haired boy coming near him and asking him in a shrill voice:

"And whom are you waiting for?"

The question surprised Nekhludoff, but, seeing the boy's serious, intelligent face, with bright, attentive eyes, gravely answered that he was awaiting a woman acquaintance.

"Well, is she your sister?" asked the boy.

"No, she is not my sister," Nekhludoff answered with surprise. "And with whom are you?"

"I am with mamma. She is a political," said the boy.

"Maria Pavlovna, take away Kolia!" said the inspector, evidently finding Nekhludoff's conversation with the boy contrary to the law.

Maria Pavlovna, the same beautiful woman who had attracted Nekhludoff's attention, rose and with heavy, long strides approached him.

"What is he asking you? Who you are?" she asked, slightly smiling with her beautifully curved lips, and confidingly looking at him with her prominent, kindly eyes, as though expecting Nekhludoff to know that her relations to everybody always have been, are and ought to be simple, affable, and brotherly. "He must know everything," she said, and smiled into the face of the boy with such a kindly, charming smile that both the boy and Nekhludoff involuntarily also smiled.

"Yes, he asked me whom I came to see."

"Maria Pavlovna, you know that it is not permitted to speak to strangers," said the inspector.

"All right," she said, and, taking the little hand of the boy into her own white hand, she returned to the consumptive's mother.

"Whose boy is that?" Nekhludoff asked the inspector.

"He is the son of a political prisoner, and was born in prison."

"Is it possible?"

"Yes, and now he is following his mother to Siberia."

"And that girl?"

"I cannot answer it," said the inspector, shrugging his shoulders. "Ah, there is Bogodukhovskaia."

CHAPTER LIII.

The short-haired, lean, yellow-faced Vera Efremovna, with her large, kindly eyes, entered timidly through the rear door.

"Well, I thank you for coming here," she said, pressing Nekhludoff's hand. "You remember me? Let us sit down."

"I did not expect to find you here."

"Oh, I am doing excellently—so well, indeed, that I desire nothing better," said Vera Efremovna, looking frightened, as usual, with her kindly, round eyes at Nekhludoff, and turning her very thin, sinewy neck, which projected from under the crumpled, dirty collar of her waist.

Nekhludoff asked her how she came to be in prison. She related her case to him with great animation. Her discourse was interspersed with foreign scientific terms about propaganda, disorganization, groups, sections and sub-sections, which, she was perfectly certain, everybody knew, but of which Nekhludoff had never even heard.

She was evidently sure that it was both interesting and pleasant to him to know all that she was relating. Nekhludoff, however, looked at her pitiful neck, her thin, tangled hair, and wondered why she was telling him all that. He pitied her, but not as he pitied the peasant Menshov with his hands and face white as potato sprouts, and innocently languishing in an ill-smelling prison. He pitied her on account of the evident confusion that reigned in her head. She seemed to consider herself a heroine, and showed off before him. And this made her particularly pitiful. This trait Nekhludoff noticed in other people then in the room. His arrival attracted their attention, and he felt that they changed their demeanor because of his presence. This trait was also present in the young man in the rubber jacket, in the woman in prison clothes, and even in the actions of the two lovers. The only people who did not possess this trait were the consumptive young man, the beautiful girl with sheep eyes, and the dark-featured man who was talking to the beardless man who resembled a Skopetz.

The affair of which Vera Efremovna wished to speak to Nekhludoff consisted of the following: A chum of hers, Shustova, who did not even belong to her sub-section, was arrested because in her dwelling were found books and papers which had been left with her for safe keeping. Vera Efremovna thought that it was partly her fault that Shustova was imprisoned, and implored Nekhludoff, who was well connected, to do everything in his power to effect her release.

Of herself, she related that, after having graduated as midwife, she joined some party. At first everything went on smoothly, but afterward one of the party was caught, the papers were seized, and then all were taken in a police drag-net.

"They also took me, and now I am going to be transported," she wound up her story. "But that is nothing. I feel excellently," and she smiled piteously.

Nekhludoff asked her about the girl with the sheep eyes, and Vera Efremovna told him that she was the daughter of a general, that she had assumed the guilt of another person, and was now going to serve at hard labor in Siberia.

"An altruistic, honest person," said Vera Efremovna.

The other case of which Vera Efremovna wished to speak concerned Maslova. As the history of every prisoner was known to everyone in prison, she knew Maslova's history, and advised him to procure her removal to the ward for politicals, or, at least, to the hospital, which was just now crowded, requiring a larger staff of nurses.

Nekhludoff said that he could hardly do anything, but promised to make an attempt when he reached St. Petersburg.

CHAPTER LIV.

Their conversation was interrupted by the inspector, who announced that it was time to depart. Nekhludoff rose, took leave of Vera Efremovna, and strode to the door, where he stopped to observe what was taking place before him.

"Ladies and gentlemen, the time is up," said the inspector as he was going out. But neither visitors nor prisoners stirred.

The inspector's demand only called forth greater animation, but no one thought of departing. Some got up and talked standing; some continued to talk sitting; others began to cry and take leave. The young man continued to crumple the bit of paper, and he made such a good effort to remain calm that his face seemed to bear an angry expression. His mother, hearing that the visit was over, fell on his shoulder and began to sob. The girl with the sheep eyes—Nekhludoff involuntarily followed her movements—stood before the sobbing mother, pouring words of consolation into her ear. The old man with the blue eye-glasses held his daughter by the hand and nodded affirmatively to her words. The young lovers rose, holding each other's hands and silently looking into each other's eyes.

"Those are the only happy people here," said the young man in the rubber jacket who stood near Nekhludoff, pointing to the young lovers.

Seeing the glances of Nekhludoff and the young man, the lovers—the convict and the flaxen-haired girl—stretched their clasping hands, threw back their heads, and began to dance in a circle.

"They will be married this evening in the prison, and she will go with him to Siberia," said the young man.

"Who is he, then?"

"He is a penal convict. Although they are making merry, it is very painful to listen," added the young man, listening to the sobbing of the old man with the blue eye-glasses.

"Please, please don't compel me to take severe measures," said the inspector, several times repeating the same thing. "Please, please," he said, weakly and irresolutely. "Well, now, this cannot go on. Please, now come. For the last time I repeat it," he said, in a sad voice, seating himself and rising again; lighting and then extinguishing his cigarette.

Finally the prisoners and visitors began to depart—the former passing through the inner, the latter through the outer, door. First the man in the rubber coat passed out; then the consumptive and the dark-featured convict; next Vera Efremovna and Maria Pavlovna, and the boy who was born in the prison.

The visitors also filed out. The old man with the blue eye-glasses started with a heavy gait, and after him came Nekhludoff.

"What a peculiar state of things!" said the talkative young man to Nekhludoff on the stairs, as though continuing the interrupted conversation. "It is fortunate that the captain is a kind-hearted man, and does not enforce

216

the rules. But for him it would be tantalizing. As it is, they talk together and relieve their feelings."

When Nekhludoff, talking to this man, who gave his name as Medyntzev, reached the entrance-hall, the inspector, with weary countenance, approached him.

"So, if you wish to see Maslova, then please call to-morrow," he said, evidently desiring to be pleasant.

"Very well," said Nekhludoff, and hastened away. As on the former occasion, besides pity he was seized with a feeling of doubt and a sort of moral nausea.

"What is all that for?" he asked himself, but found no answer.

CHAPTER LV.

On the following day Nekhludoff drove to the lawyer and told him of the Menshovs' case, asking him to take up their defense. The lawyer listened to him attentively, and said that if the facts were really as told to Nekhludoff, he would undertake their defense without compensation. Nekhludoff also told him of the hundred and thirty men kept in prison through some misunderstanding, and asked him whose fault he thought it was. The lawyer was silent for a short while, evidently desiring to give an accurate answer.

"Whose fault it is? No one's," he said decisively. "If you ask the prosecutor, he will tell you that it is Maslenikoff's fault, and if you ask Maslenikoff, he will tell you that it is the prosecutor's fault. It is no one's fault."

"I will go to Maslenikoff and tell him."

"That is useless," the lawyer retorted, smiling. "He is—he is not your friend or relative, is he? He is such a blockhead, and, saving your presence, at the same time such a sly beast!"

Nekhludoff recalled what Maslenikoff had said about the lawyer, made no answer, and, taking leave, directed his steps toward Maslenikoff's residence.

Two things Nekhludoff wanted of Maslenikoff. First, to obtain Maslova's transfer to the hospital, and to help, if possible, the hundred and thirty unfortunates. Although it was hard for him to be dealing with this man, and especially to ask favors of him, yet it was the only way of gaining his end, and he had to go through it.

As Nekhludoff approached Maslenikoff's house, he saw a number of carriages, cabs and traps standing in front of it, and he recalled that this was the reception day to which he had been invited. While Nekhludoff was approaching the house a carriage was standing near the curb, opposite the door, and a lackey in a cockaded silk hat and cape, was seating a lady, who, raising the long train of her skirt, displayed the sharp joints of her toes through the thin slippers. Among the carriages he recognized the covered landau of the Korchagins. The gray-haired, rosy-cheeked driver deferentially raised his hat. Nekhludoff had scarcely asked the porter where Michael Ivanovich (Maslenikoff) was, when the latter appeared on the carpeted stairway, escorting a very important guest, such as he usually escorted not to the upper landing, but to the vestibule. This very important military guest, while descending the stairs, was conversing in French about a lottery for the benefit of orphan asylums, giving his opinion that it was a good occupation for ladies. "They enjoy themselves while they are raising money."

"Qu'elles s'amusent et que le bon Dieu les bénisse. Ah, Nekhludoff, how do you do? You haven't shown yourself for a long time," he greeted Nekhludoff. "Allez présenter vos devoirs à madame. The Korchagins are here, too. Toutes les jolies femmes de la ville," he said, holding out and somewhat raising his military shoulders for his overcoat, which was being placed on him by his own magnificent lackey in gold-braided uniform. "Au revoir, mon cher." Then he shook Maslenikoff's hand.

"Well, now let us go upstairs. How glad I am," Maslenikoff began excitedly, seizing Nekhludoff by the arm, and, notwithstanding his corpulence, nimbly leading him up the stairs. Maslenikoff was in a particularly happy mood, which Nekhludoff could not help ascribing to the attention shown him by the important person. Every attention shown him by an important person put him into such an ecstasy as may be observed in a fawning little dog when its master pats it, strokes it, and scratches under its ears. It wags its tail, shrinks, wriggles, and, straightening its ears, madly runs in a circle.

Maslenikoff was ready to do the same thing. He did not notice the grave expression on Nekhludoff's face, nor hear what he was saying, but irresistibly dragged him into the reception-room. Nekhludoff involuntarily followed.

"Business afterward. I will do anything you wish," said Maslenikoff, leading him through the parlor. "Announce Prince Nekhludoff to Her Excellency," he said on the way to a lackey. The lackey, in an ambling gait, ran ahead of them. "Vous n'avez qu'à ordonner. But you must see my wife without fail. She would not forgive my failure to present you last time you were here."

The lackey had already announced him when they entered, and Anna Ignatievna, the vice-governess—Mrs. General, as she called herself—sat on a couch surrounded by ladies. As Nekhludoff approached she was already leaning forward with a radiant smile on her face. At the other end of the reception-room women sat around a table, while men in military uniforms and civil attire stood over them. An incessant cackle came from that direction.

"Enfin! Why do you estrange yourself? Have we offended you in any way?"

With these words, presupposing an intimacy between her and Nekhludoff, which never existed, Anna Ignatievna greeted him.

"Are you acquainted? Madam Beliavskaia—Michael Ivanovich Chernoff. Take a seat here."

"Missy, venez donc à notre table. On vous opportera votre thé. And you," she turned to the officer who was conversing with Missy, evidently forgetting his name, "come here, please. Will you have some tea, Prince?"

"No, no; I will never agree with you. She simply did not love him," said a woman's voice.

"But she loved pie."

"Eternally those stupid jests," laughingly interfered another lady in a high hat and dazzling with gold and diamonds.

"C'est excellent, these waffles, and so light! Let us have some more."

"Well, how soon are you going to leave us?"

"Yes, this is the last day. That is why we came here."

"Such a beautiful spring! How pleasant it is in the country!"

Missy in her hat and some dark, striped dress which clasped her waist without a wrinkle, was very pretty. She blushed when she saw Nekhludoff.

"I thought you had left the city," she said to him.

"Almost. Business keeps me here. I come here also for business."

"Call on mamma. She is very anxious to see you," she said, and, feeling that she was lying, and that he understood it, her face turned a still deeper purple.

"I shall hardly have the time," gloomily answered Nekhludoff, pretending not to see that she was blushing.

Missy frowned angrily, shrugged her shoulders, and turned to an elegant officer, who took from her hands the empty teacup and valiantly carried it to another table, his sword striking every object it encountered.

"You must also contribute toward the asylum."

"I am not refusing, only I wish to keep my contribution for the lottery. There I will show all my liberality."

"Don't forget, now," a plainly dissimulating laugh was heard.

The reception day was brilliant, and Anna Ignatievna was delighted.

"Mika told me that you busy yourself in the prisons. I understand it very well," she said to Nekhludoff. "Mika"—she meant her stout husband, Maslenikoff—"may have his faults, but you know that he is kind. All these unfortunate prisoners are his children. He does not look on them in any other light. Il est d'une bonté——"

She stopped, not finding words to express bonté of a husband, and immediately, smiling, turned to an old, wrinkled woman in lilac-colored bows who had just entered.

Having talked as much and as meaninglessly as it was necessary to preserve the decorum, Nekhludoff arose and went over to Maslenikoff.

"Will you please hear me now?"

"Ah! yes. Well, what is it?"

"Come in here."

They entered a small Japanese cabinet and seated themselves near the window.

CHAPTER LVI.

"Well, je suis à vous. Will you smoke a cigarette? But wait; we must not soil the things here," and he brought an ash-holder. "Well?"

"I want two things of you."

"Is that so?"

Maslenikoff's face became gloomy and despondent. All traces of that animation of the little dog whom its master had scratched under the ears entirely disappeared. Voices came from the reception-room. One, a woman's voice, said: "Jamais, jamais je ne croirais;" another, a man's voice from the other corner, was telling something, constantly repeating: "La Comtesse Vorouzoff" and "Victor Apraksine." From the third side only a humming noise mingled with laughter was heard. Maslenikoff listened to the voices; so did Nekhludoff.

"I want to talk to you again about that woman."

"Yes; who was innocently condemned. I know, I know."

"I would like her to be transferred to the hospital. I was told that it can be done."

Maslenikoff pursed up his lips and began to meditate.

"It can hardly be done," he said. "However, I will consult about it, and will wire you to-morrow."

"I was told that there are many sick people in the hospital, and they need assistants."

"Well, yes. But I will let you know, as I said."

"Please do," said Nekhludoff.

There was a burst of general and even natural laughter in the reception-room.

"That is caused by Victor," said Maslenikoff, smiling. "He is remarkably witty when in high spirits."

"Another thing," said Nekhludoff. "There are a hundred and thirty men languishing in prison for the only reason that their passports were not renewed in time. They have been in prison now for a month."

And he related the causes that kept them there.

"How did you come to know it?" asked Nekhludoff, and his face showed disquietude and displeasure.

"I was visiting a prisoner, and these people surrounded me and asked——"

"What prisoner were you visiting?"

"The peasant who is innocently accused, and for whom I have obtained counsel. But that is not to the point. Is it possible that these innocent people are kept in prison only because they failed to renew their passports?"

"That is the prosecutor's business," interrupted Maslenikoff, somewhat vexed. "Now, you say that trials must be speedy and just. It is the duty of the assistant prosecutor to visit the prisons and see that no one is innocently kept there. But these assistants do nothing but play cards."

"So you can do nothing for them?" Nekhludoff asked gloomily, recalling the words of the lawyer, that the governor would shift the responsibility.

"I will see to it. I will make inquiries immediately."

"So much the worse for her. C'est un souffre-douleur," came from the reception-room, the voice of a woman apparently entirely indifferent to what she was saying.

"So much the better; I will take this," from the other side was heard a man's playful voice, and the merry laughter of a woman who refused him something.

"No, no, for no consideration," said a woman's voice.

"Well, then, I will do everything," repeated Maslenikoff, extinguishing the cigarette with his white hand, on which was a turquoise ring. "Now, let us go to the ladies."

"And yet another question," said Nekhludoff, without going into the reception-room, and stopping at the door. "I was told that some people in the prison were subjected to corporal punishment. Is it true?"

Maslenikoff's face flushed.

"Ah! you have reference to that affair? No, mon cher, you must positively not be admitted there—you want to know everything. Come, come; Annette is calling us," he said, seizing Nekhludoff's arm with the same excitement he evinced after the attention shown him by the important person, but this time alarming, and not joyful.

Nekhludoff tore himself loose, and, without bowing or saying anything, gloomily passed through the reception-room, the parlor and by the lackeys, who sprang to their feet in the ante-chamber, to the street.

"What is the matter with him? What did you do to him?" Annette asked her husband.

"That is à la française," said some one.

"Rather à la zoulon."

"Oh, he has always been queer."

Some one arose, some one arrived, and the chirping continued.

The following morning Nekhludoff received from Maslenikoff a letter on heavy, glossy paper, bearing a coat-of-arms and seals, written in a fine, firm hand, in which he said that he had written to the prison physician asking that Maslova be transferred, and that he hoped his request would be acceded to. It was signed, "Your loving senior comrade," followed by a remarkably skillful flourish.

"Fool!" Nekhludoff could not help exclaiming, especially because he felt that by the word "comrade" Maslenikoff was condescending, i. e., although he considered himself a very important personage, he nevertheless was not too proud of his greatness, and called himself his comrade.

CHAPTER LVII.

One of the most popular superstitions consists in the belief that every man is endowed with definite qualities—that some men are kind, some wicked; some wise, some foolish; some energetic, some apathetic, etc. This is not true. We may say of a man that he is oftener kind than wicked; oftener wise than foolish; oftener energetic than apathetic, and vice versa. But it would not be true to say of one man that he is always kind or wise, and of another that he is always wicked or foolish. And yet we thus divide people. This is erroneous. Men are like rivers—the water in all of them, and at every point, is the same, but every one of them is now narrow, now swift, now wide, now calm, now clear, now cold, now muddy, now warm. So it is with men. Every man bears within him the germs of all human qualities, sometimes manifesting one quality, sometimes another; and often does not resemble himself at all, manifesting no change. With some people these changes are particularly sharp. And to this class Nekhludoff belonged. These changes in him had both physical and spiritual causes; and one of these changes he was now undergoing.

That feeling of solemnity and joy of rejuvenation which he had experienced after the trial and after his first meeting with Katiousha had passed away, and, after the last meeting, fear and even disgust toward her had taken its place. He was also conscious that his duty was burdensome to him. He had decided not to leave her, to carry out his intention of marrying her, if she so desired; but this was painful and tormenting to him.

224

On the day following his visit to Maslenikoff he again went to the prison to see her.

The inspector permitted him to see her; not in the office, however, nor in the lawyer's room, but in the women's visiting-room. Notwithstanding his kind-heartedness, the inspector was more reserved than formerly. Evidently Nekhludoff's conversations with Maslenikoff had resulted in instructions being given to be more careful with this visitor.

"You may see her," he said, "only please remember what I told you as to giving her money. And as to her transfer to the hospital, about which His Excellency has written, there is no objection to it, and the physician also consented. But she herself does not wish it. 'I don't care to be chambermaid to that scurvy lot,' she said. That is the kind of people they are, Prince," he added.

Nekhludoff made no answer and asked to be admitted to her. The inspector sent the warden, and Nekhludoff followed him into the empty visiting-room.

Maslova was already there, quietly and timidly emerging from behind the grating. She approached close to Nekhludoff, and, looking past him, quietly said:

"Forgive me, Dmitri Ivanovich; I have spoken improperly the other day."

"It is not for me to forgive you——" Nekhludoff began.

"But you must leave me," she added, and in the fearfully squinting eyes with which she glanced at him Nekhludoff again saw a strained and spiteful expression.

"But why should I leave you?"

"So."

"Why so?"

She again looked at him with that spiteful glance, as it seemed to him.

"Well, then, I will tell you," she said. "You leave me—I tell you that truly. I cannot. You must drop that entirely," she said, with quivering lips, and became silent. "That is true. I would rather hang myself."

Nekhludoff felt that in this answer lurked a hatred for him, an unforgiven wrong, but also something else—something good and important. This reiteration of her refusal in a perfectly calm state destroyed in Nekhludoff's soul all his doubts, and brought him back to his former grave, solemn and benign state of mind.

"Katiousha, I repeat what I said," he said, with particular gravity. "I ask you to marry me. If, however, you do not wish to, and so long as you do not wish to, I will be wherever you will be, and follow you wherever you may be sent."

"That is your business. I will speak no more," she said, and again her lips quivered.

He was also silent, feeling that he had no strength to speak.

"I am now going to the country, and from there to St. Petersburg," he said finally. "I will press your—our case, and with God's help the sentence will be set aside."

"I don't care if they don't. I deserved it, if not for that, for something else," she said, and he saw what great effort she had to make to repress her tears.

"Well, have you seen Menshova?" she asked suddenly, in order to hide her agitation. "They are innocent, are they not?"

"Yes, I think so."

"Such a wonderful little woman!" she said.

He related everything he had learned from Menshova, and asked her if she needed anything. She said she needed nothing.

They were silent again.

"Well, and as to the hospital," she said suddenly, casting on him her

226

squinting glance, "if you wish me to go, I will go; and I will stop wine drinking, too."

Nekhludoff silently looked in her eyes. They were smiling.

"That is very good," was all he could say.

"Yes, yes; she is an entirely different person," thought Nekhludoff, for the first time experiencing, after his former doubts, the to him entirely new feeling of confidence in the invincibility of love.

Returning to her ill-smelling cell, Maslova removed her coat and sat down on her cot, her hands resting on her knees. In the cell were only the consumptive with her babe, the old woman, Menshova, and the watch-woman with her two children. The deacon's daughter had been removed to the hospital; the others were washing. The old woman lay on the cot sleeping; the children were in the corridor, the door to which was open. The consumptive with the child in her arms and the watch-woman, who did not cease knitting a stocking with her nimble fingers, approached Maslova.

"Well, have you seen him?" they asked.

Maslova dangled her feet, which did not reach the floor, and made no answer.

"What are you whimpering about?" said the watch-woman. "Above all, keep up your spirits. Oh, Katiousha! Well?" she said, rapidly moving her fingers.

Maslova made no answer.

"The women went washing. They say that to-day's alms were larger. Many things have been brought, they say," said the consumptive.

"Finashka!" shouted the watch-woman. "Where are you, you little rogue?" She drew out one of the knitting needles, stuck it into the ball of thread and stocking, and went out into the corridor.

At this moment the inmates of the cell, with bare feet in their prison shoes, entered, each bearing a loaf of twisted bread, some even two. Theodosia immediately approached Maslova.

"Why, anything wrong?" she asked, lovingly, looking with her bright, blue eyes at Maslova. "And here is something for our tea," and she placed the leaves on the shelf.

"Well, has he changed his mind about marrying you?" asked Korableva.

"No, he has not, but I do not wish to," answered Maslova, "and I told him so."

"What a fool!" said Korableva, in her basso voice.

"What is the good of marrying if they cannot live together?" asked Theodosia.

"Is not your husband going with you?" answered the watch-woman.

"We are legally married," said Theodosia. "But why should he marry her legally if he cannot live with her?"

"What a fool! Why, if he marries her he will make her rich!"

"He said: 'Wherever you may be, I will be with you,'" said Maslova.

"He may go if he likes; he needn't if he don't. I will not ask him. He is now going to St. Petersburg to try to get me out. All the ministers there are his relatives," she continued, "but I don't care for them."

"Sure enough," Korableva suddenly assented, reaching down into her bag, and evidently thinking of something else. "What do you say—shall we have some wine?"

"Not I," answered Maslova. "Drink yourselves."

PART SECOND.

CHAPTER I.

The Senate could hear the case in two weeks, and by that time Nekhludoff intended to be in St. Petersburg, and, in case of an adverse decision, to petition the Emperor, as the lawyer had advised. In case the appeal failed, for which, his lawyer had told him, he must be prepared, as the grounds of appeal were very weak, the party of convicts to which Maslova belonged would be transported in May. It was therefore necessary, in order to be prepared to follow Maslova to Siberia, upon which Nekhludoff was firmly resolved, to go to the villages and arrange his affairs there.

First of all, he went to the Kusminskoie estate, the nearest, largest black-earth estate, which brought the greatest income. He had lived on the estate in his childhood and youth, and had also twice visited it in his manhood, once when, upon the request of his mother, he brought a German manager with whom he went over the affairs of the estate. So that he knew its condition and the relations the peasants sustained toward the office, i. e., the landowner. Their relations toward the office were such that they have always been in absolute dependence upon it. Nekhludoff had already known it when as a student he professed and preached the doctrines of Henry George, and in carrying out which he had distributed his father's estate among the peasants. True, after his military career, when he was spending twenty thousand rubles a year, those doctrines ceased to be necessary to the life he was leading, were forgotten, and not only did he not ask himself where the money came from, but tried not to think of it. But the death of his mother, the inheritance, and the necessity of taking care of his property, i. e., his lands, again raised the question in his mind of his relation to private ownership of land. A month before Nekhludoff would have argued that he was powerless to change the existing order of things; that he was not managing the estate, and living and receiving his income far away from the estate, would feel more or less at ease. But now he resolved that, although there was before him a trip to Siberia and complex and difficult relations to the prison world, for which social standing, and especially money, were necessary, he could not, nevertheless, leave his affairs in their former condition, but must, to his own detriment, change them. For this purpose he had decided not to work the land himself, but, by renting it at a low price to the peasants, to make it possible for them to live independent of the landlord. Often, while comparing the position of the landlord with that of the owner of serfs, Nekhludoff found a parallel in the renting of the land to the peasants, instead of working it by hired labor, to what the slave-owners did when they substituted tenancy for serfdom. That did not solve the question, but it was a step toward its solution; it was a transition from a grosser to a less gross form of ownership of man. He also intended to act thus.

Nekhludoff arrived at Kusminskoie about noon. In everything simplifying his life, he did not wire from the station of his arrival, but hired a two-horse country coach. The driver was a young fellow in a nankeen regulation coat, belted below the waist, sitting sidewise on the box. He was the more willing to carry on a conversation because the broken-down, lame, emaciated, foaming shaft-horse could then walk, which these horses always preferred.

The driver spoke about the manager of the Kusminskoie estate, not knowing that he was carrying its master, Nekhludoff purposely refrained from enlightening him.

"A dandy German," he said, turning half around, cracking his long whip now over the heads, now under the horses. "There is nothing here to compare with his fine team of three bay horses. You ought to see him driving out with his wife! I took some guests to his house last Christmas—he had a fine tree. You couldn't find the like of it in the whole district! He robbed everybody, right and left. But what does he care? He is bossing everybody. They say he bought a fine estate."

Nekhludoff thought that he was indifferent to the manner of the

German's management, and to the way he was profiting by it. But the story of the driver with the long waist was unpleasant to him. He was enchanted with the fine weather; the darkening clouds, sometimes obscuring the sun; the fields over which the larks soared; the woods, just covering up the top and bottom with green; the meadows on which the flocks and horses browsed, and the fields on which plowmen were already seen—but a feeling of dissatisfaction crept over him. And when he asked himself the reason for it, he recalled the driver's account of the German's management.

But by the time he was busying himself with the affairs of Kusminskoie he had forgotten it.

After an examination of the books and his conversation with the clerk, who artlessly set forth the advantages of the peasants having small holdings and the fact that they were hemmed in by the master's land, Nekhludoff grew only more determined to put an end to his ownership, and give the land to the peasants. From the books and his conversations with the clerk he learned that, as before, two-thirds of the best arable land was cultivated by his own men, and the rest by peasants who were paid five rubles per acre—that is to say, for five rubles the peasant undertook to plow, harrow and sow an acre of land three times, then mow it, bind or press it, and carry it to the barn. In other words, he was paid five rubles for what hired, cheap labor would cost at least ten rubles. Again, the prices paid by the peasants to the office for necessaries were enormous. They worked for meadow, for wood, for potatoe seed, and they were almost all in debt to the office. Thus, the rent charged the peasants for lands beyond the fields was four times as great as it could bring on a five per cent. basis.

Nekhludoff knew all that before, but he was now learning it as something new, and only wondered why he and all those who stood in a similar position could fail to see the enormity of such relations. The arguments of the clerk that not one-fourth of the value of the stock could be realized on a sale, that the peasants would permit the land to run to waste, only strengthened his determination and confirmed him in his belief that he was doing a good deed by giving the land to the peasants, and depriving himself of the greater part of his income. Desiring to dispose of the land forthwith, he asked the manager to call together the peasants of the three villages surrounded by his lands the very next day, for the purpose of declaring to them his intention and agreeing with them as to the price.

With a joyful consciousness of his firmness, in spite of the arguments of the manager, and his readiness to make sacrifices for the peasants, Nekhludoff left the office, and, reflecting on the coming arrangement, he strolled around the house, through the flower-garden, which lay opposite the manager's house, and was neglected this year; over the lawn-tennis ground, overgrown with chicory, and through the alleys lined with lindens, where it had been his wont to smoke his cigar, and where, three years before, the pretty visitor, Kirimova, flirted with him. Having made an outline of a speech, which he was to deliver to the peasants the following day, Nekhludoff went to the manager's house, and after further deliberating upon the proper disposition of the stock, he calmly and contentedly retired to a room prepared for him in the large building.

In this clean room, the walls of which were covered with views of Venice, and with a mirror hung between two windows, there was placed a clean spring bedstead and a small table with water and matches. On a large table near the mirror lay his open traveling-bag with toilet articles and books which he brought with him; one Russian book on criminology, one in German, and a third in English treating of the same subject. He intended to read them in spare moments while traveling through the villages, but as he looked on them now he felt that his mind was far from these subjects. Something entirely different occupied him.

In one corner of the room there stood an ancient arm-chair with incrustations, and the sight of this chair standing in his mother's bed-room suddenly raised in his soul an unexpected feeling. He suddenly felt sorry for the house that would decay, the gardens which would be neglected, the woods which would be cut down, and all the cattle-houses, courts, stables, sheds, machinery, horses, cows which had been accumulated with such effort, although not by him. At first it seemed to him easy to abandon all that, but now he was loth to part with it, as well as the land and one-half of the income which would be so useful now. And immediately serviceable arguments come

232

to his aid, by which it appeared that it was not wise to give the land to the peasants and destroy his estate.

"I have no right to own the land. And if I do not own the land, I cannot keep the property intact. Besides, I will now go to Siberia, and for that reason I need neither the house nor the estate," whispered one voice. "All that is true," whispered another voice, "but you will not pass all your life in Siberia. If you should marry, you may have children. And you must hand over the estate to them in the same condition in which you found it. There are duties toward the land. It is easy to give away the land, to destroy everything; but it is very hard to accumulate it. Above all, you must mark out a plan of your life, and dispose of your property accordingly. And, then, are you acting as you do in order to satisfy conscientious scruples, or for the praise you expect of people?" Nekhludoff asked himself, and could not help acknowledging that the talk that it would occasion influenced his decision. And the more he thought the more questions raised themselves, and the more perplexing they appeared. To rid himself of these thoughts he lay down on the fresh-made bed, intending to go over them again the next day with a clearer mind. But he could not fall asleep for a long time. Along with the fresh air, through the open window, came the croaking of frogs, interrupted by the whistling of nightingales, one of which was in a lilac bush under the window. Listening to the nightingales and the frogs, Nekhludoff recalled the music of the inspector's daughter; and, thinking of that music, he recalled Maslova—how, like the croaking of a frog, her lips trembled when she said, "You must drop that." Then the German manager descended to the frogs. He should have been held back, but not only did he come down, but he was transformed into Maslova and started to taunt him: "I am a convict, and you are a Prince." "No, I shall not yield," thought Nekhludoff, and came to. "Am I acting properly or improperly?" he asked himself. "I don't know; I will know to-morrow." And he began to descend to where the manager and Maslova were. And there everything ended.

CHAPTER II.

With a feeling of timidity and shame Nekhludoff the following morning, walked out to meet the peasants who had gathered at a small square in front of the house. As he approached them the peasants removed their caps, and for a long time Nekhludoff could not say anything. Although he was going to do something for the peasants which they never dared even to think of, his conscience was troubled. The peasants stood in a fine, drizzling rain, waiting to hear what their master had to say, and Nekhludoff was so confused that he could not open his mouth. The calm, self-confident German came to his relief. This strong, overfed man, like Nekhludoff himself, made a striking contrast to the emaciated, wrinkled faces of the peasants, and the bare shoulder-bones sticking out from under their caftans.

"The Prince came to befriend you—to give you the land, but you are not worthy of it," said the German.

"Why not worthy, Vasily Karlych? Have we not labored for you? We are much satisfied with our late mistress—may she enjoy eternal life!—and we are grateful to the young Prince for thinking of us," began a red-haired peasant with a gift of gab.

"We are not complaining of our masters," said a broad-faced peasant with a long beard. "Only we are too crowded here."

"That is what I called you here for—to give you the land, if you wish it," said Nekhludoff.

The peasants were silent, as if misunderstanding him, or incredulous.

"In what sense do you mean to give us the land?" asked a middle-aged peasant in a caftan.

"To rent it to you, that you might use it at a low price."

"That is the loveliest thing," said an old man.

"If the payment is not above our means," said another.

"Of course we will take the land."

"It is our business—we get our sustenance from the land."

"So much the better for you. All you have to do is to take the money. And what sins you will spare yourself——"

234

"The sin is on you," said the German. "If you would only work and keep things in order——"

"We cannot, Vasily Karlych," said a lean old man with a pointed nose. "You ask, Who let the horse feed in the field? But who did it? Day in and day out—and every day is as long as a year—I worked with the scythe, and as I fell asleep the horse went among the oats. And now you are fleecing me."

"You should keep order."

"It is easy for you to say keep order. But we have no strength," retorted a middle-aged peasant, all covered with hair.

"I told you to fence it in."

"You give us the timber," said an unsightly little peasant. "When I cut a joist last summer, intending to make a fence, you locked me up for three months in the castle to feed the insects. There was a fence for you!"

"Is that true?" asked Nekhludoff of the manager.

"Der erste dich im dorfe," said the manager in German. "He was caught every year in the woods. You must learn to respect other people's property."

"Do we not respect you?" said an old man. "We cannot help respecting you, because you have us in your hands, and you are twisting us into rope."

"If you would only abstain from doing wrong," said the manager. "It is pretty hard to wrong you."

"And who battered my face last summer? Of course, there is no use going to law with a rich man."

"You only keep within bounds of the law."

This was evidently a wordy tourney of which the participants hardly knew the purpose. Nekhludoff tried to get back to business.

"Well, what do you say? Do you wish the land, and what price do you set on it?"

"It is your goods; you name the price."

Nekhludoff set the price, and though much lower than the prevailing price, the peasants began to bargain, finding it high. He expected that his offer would be accepted with pleasure, but there was no sign of satisfaction. Only when the question was raised whether the whole community would take the land, or have individual arrangements did he know that it was profitable for them. For there resulted fierce quarrels between those who wished to exclude the weak ones and bad payers from participating in the land, and those whom it was sought to exclude. But the German finally arranged the price and time of payment, and the peasants, noisily talking, returned to the village.

The price was about thirty per cent. lower than the one prevailing in the district, and Nekhludoff's income was reduced to almost one-half, but, with money realized from the sale of the timber and yet to be realized from the sale of the stock, it was amply sufficient for him. Everything seemed to be satisfactory, and yet Nekhludoff felt sad and lonesome, but, above all, his conscience troubled him. He saw that although the peasants spoke words of thanks, they were not satisfied and expected something more. The result was that while he deprived himself of much, he failed to do that which the peasants expected.

On the following day, after the contract was signed, Nekhludoff, with an unpleasant feeling of having left something undone, seated himself in the "dandy" three-horse team and took leave of the peasants, who were shaking their heads in doubt and dissatisfaction. Nekhludoff was dissatisfied with himself—he could not tell why, but he felt sad, and was ashamed of something.

CHAPTER III.

From Kusminskoie Nekhludoff went to Panovo, the estate left him by his aunts, and where he had first seen Katiousha. He intended to dispose of this land in the same manner as he disposed of the other, and also desired to learn all there was known about Katiousha, and to find out if it was true that their child had died.

As he sat at the window observing the familiar scenery of the now somewhat neglected estate, he not only recalled, but felt himself as he was fourteen years ago; fresh, pure and filled with the hope of endless possibilities. But as it happens in a dream, he knew that that was gone, and he became very sad.

Before breakfast he made his way to the hut of Matrena Kharina, Katiousha's aunt, who was selling liquor surreptitiously, for information about the child, but all he could learn from her was that the child had died on the way to a Moskow asylum; in proof of which the midwife had brought a certificate.

On his way back he entered the huts of some peasants, and inquired about their mode of living. The same complaints of the paucity of land, hunger and degradation he heard everywhere. He saw the same pinched faces, threadbare homespuns, bare feet and bent shoulders.

In front of a particularly dilapidated hut stood a number of women with children in their arms, and among them he noticed a lean, pale-faced woman, easily holding a bloodless child in a short garment made of pieces of stuff. This child was incessantly smiling. Nekhludoff knew that it was the smile of suffering. He asked who that woman was.

It transpired that the woman's husband had been in prison for the past six months—"feeding the insects"—as they termed it, for cutting down two lindens.

Nekhludoff turned to the woman, Anisia.

"How do you fare?" he asked. "What do you live on?"

"How do I live? I sometimes get some food," and she began to sob.

The grave face of the child, however, spread into a broad smile, and its thin legs began to wriggle.

Nekhludoff produced his pocketbook and gave the woman ten rubles. He had scarcely made ten steps when he was overtaken by another woman with a child; then an old woman, and again another woman. They all spoke of their poverty and implored his help. Nekhludoff distributed the sixty rubles that were in his pocketbook and returned home, i. e., to the wing inhabited by the clerk. The clerk, smiling, met Nekhludoff with the information that the peasants would gather in the evening, as he had ordered. Nekhludoff thanked him and strolled about the garden, meditating on what he had seen. "The people are dying in large numbers, and are used to it; they have acquired modes of living natural to a people who are becoming extinct—the death of children, exhausting toil for women, insufficiency of food for all, especially for the aged—all comes and is received naturally. They were reduced to this condition gradually, so that they cannot see the horror of it, and bear it uncomplainingly. Afterward, we, too, come to consider this condition natural; that it ought to be so."

All this was so clear to him now that he could not cease wondering how it was that people could not see it; that he himself could not see that which is so patent. It was perfectly clear that children and old people were dying for want of milk, and they had no milk because they had not land enough to feed the cattle and also raise bread and hay. And he devised a scheme by which he was to give the land to the people, and they were to pay an annual rent which was to go to the community, to be used for common utilities and taxes. This was not the single-tax, but it was the nearest approach to it under present conditions. The important part consisted in that he renounced his right to own land.

When he returned to the house, the clerk, with a particularly happy smile on his face, offered him dinner, expressing his fear that it might spoil.

The table was covered with a gloomy cloth, an embroidered towel serving as a napkin, and on the table, in vieux-saxe, stood a soup-bowl with a broken handle, filled with potato soup and containing the same rooster that he had seen carried into the house on his arrival. After the soup came the same rooster, fried with feathers, and cakes made of cheese-curds, bountifully covered with butter and sugar. Although the taste of it all was poor, Nekhludoff kept on eating, being absorbed in the thoughts which relieved him of the sadness that oppressed him on his return from the village.

After dinner Nekhludoff with difficulty seated the superserviceable clerk, and in order to make sure of himself and at the same time to confide

238

to some one the thoughts uppermost in his mind, told him of his project and asked his opinion. The clerk smiled, as though he had been thinking of the same thing, and was very glad to hear it, but in reality did not understand it, not because Nekhludoff did not express himself plainly enough, but because, according to this project, Nekhludoff deprived himself of advantages for the benefit of others, whereas the truth that every man strives to obtain advantages at the expense of others, was so firmly rooted in the clerk's mind, that he thought that he misunderstood Nekhludoff when the latter said that the entire income of the land was to go into the community's treasury.

"I understand. So you will draw the interest on the capital?" he said, becoming radiant.

"No, no. I transfer the land to them entirely."

"In that case you will get no income?" asked the clerk and he ceased to smile.

"I relinquish that."

The clerk sighed deeply, then began to smile again. Now he understood. He understood that Nekhludoff's mind was not entirely sound, and he immediately tried to find a way of profiting by Nekhludoff's project, and endeavored to so construe it that he might turn it to his own advantage.

When, however, he understood that there was no such opportunity, he ceased to take interest in the projects, and continued to smile only to please his master. Seeing that the clerk could not understand him, Nekhludoff dismissed him from his presence, seated himself at the ink-stained table and proceeded to commit his project to paper.

The sun was already descending behind the unfolding lindens, and the mosquitos filled the room, stinging him. While he was finishing his notes, Nekhludoff heard the lowing of cattle in the village, the creaking of the opening gates and the voices of the peasants who were coming to meet their master. Nekhludoff told the clerk not to call them before the office, that he would go and meet them at any place in the village, and gulping down a glass of tea offered him by the clerk, he went to the village.

CHAPTER IV.

The crowd stood talking in front of the house of the bailiff, and as Nekhludoff approached, the conversation ceased and the peasants, like those of Kusminskoie, removed their caps. It was a coarser crowd than the peasants of Kusminskoie, and almost all the peasants wore bast shoes and homespun shirts and caftans. Some of them were bare-footed and only in their shirts.

With some effort Nekhludoff began his speech by declaring that he intended to surrender the land to them. The peasants were silent, and there was no change in the expression of their faces.

"Because I consider," said Nekhludoff, blushing, "that every man ought to have the right to use the land."

"Why, certainly." "That is quite right," voices of peasants were heard.

Nekhludoff continued, saying that the income from the land should be distributed among all, and he therefore proposed that they take the land and pay into the common treasury such rent as they may decide upon, such money to be used for their own benefit. Exclamations of consent and approbation continued to be heard, but the faces of the peasants became more and more grave, and the eyes that at first were fixed on the master were lowered, as if desiring not to shame him with the fact that his cunning was understood by all, and that he could not fool anybody.

Nekhludoff spoke very clearly, and the peasants were sensible folks; but he was not understood, and could not be understood by them for the same reason which prevented the clerk from understanding him for a long time. They were convinced that it was natural for every man to look out for his own interest. And as to the land owners, the experience of several generations had taught them long ago that these were always serving their own interests.

"Well, what rate do you intend to assess," asked Nekhludoff.

"Why assess? We cannot do that? The land is yours; it is for you to say," some in the crowd said.

"But understand that you are to use the money for the common wants."

"We cannot do it. The community is one thing, and this is another thing."

"You must understand," said the smiling clerk, wishing to explain the offer, "that the Prince is giving you the land for money which is to go into the community's treasury."

"We understand it very well," said a toothless old man without raising his eyes. "Something like a bank, only we must pay in time. We cannot do it; it is hard enough as it is. That will ruin us entirely."

"That is to no purpose. We would rather continue as before," said several dissatisfied and even rough voices.

The resistance was particularly hot when Nekhludoff mentioned that he would draw a contract which he himself and they would have to sign.

"What is the good of a contract? We will keep on working as we did before. We don't care for it. We are ignorant people."

"We cannot consent, because that is an uncustomary thing. Let it be as it was before. If you would only do away with the seed," several voices were heard.

"Doing away with the seed" meant that under the present regime the sowing-seed was chargeable to the peasants, and they asked that it be furnished by the master.

"So you refuse to take the land?" asked Nekhludoff, turning to a middle-aged, bare-footed peasant in tattered caftan and with a radiant face who held his cap straight in front of him, like a soldier hearing "Hats off!"

"Yes, sir," said this peasant.

"Then you have enough land?" asked Nekhludoff.

"No, sir," said the ex-soldier, with artificial cheerfulness, holding his torn cap before him, as though offering it to anyone deserving to take it.

"Think it over at your leisure," said the surprised Nekhludoff, again repeating his offer.

"There is nothing to think over; as we said, so it will be," the toothless, gloomy old man said angrily.

"I will stay here all day to-morrow. If you alter your decision, let me know."

The peasants made no answer.

On their return to the office the clerk explained to Nekhludoff that it was not a want of good sense that prevented their acceptance of the offer; that when gathered in assembly they always acted in that stubborn manner.

Nekhludoff then asked him to summon for the following day several of the most intelligent peasants to whom he would explain his project at greater length.

Immediately after the departure of the smiling clerk, Nekhludoff heard angry women's voices interrupted by the voice of the clerk. He listened.

"I have no more strength. You want the cross on my breast," said an exasperated voice.

"She only ran in," said another voice. "Give her up, I say. Why do you torture the beast, and keep the milk from the children?"

Nekhludoff walked around the house where he saw two disheveled women, one of whom was evidently pregnant, standing near the staircase. On the stairs, with his hands in the pockets of his crash overcoat, stood the clerk. Seeing their master, the women became silent and began to arrange their 'kerchiefs, which had fallen from their heads, while the clerk took his hands out of his pockets and began to smile.

The clerk explained that the peasants purposely permitted their calves, and even cows, to roam over the master's meadows. That two cows belonging to these women had been caught on the meadow and driven into an inclosure. The clerk demanded from the women thirty copecks per cow, or two days' work.

"Time and again I told them," said the smiling clerk, looking around at Nekhludoff, as if calling him to witness, "to look out for cows when driving them to feed."

"I just went to see to the child, and they walked away."

"Don't leave them when you undertake to look after them."

"And who would feed my child?"

"If they had only grazed, at least, they would have no pains in their stomachs. But they only walked in."

"All the meadows are spoiled," the clerk turned to Nekhludoff. "If they are not made to pay there will be no hay left."

"Don't be sinning," cried the pregnant woman. "My cow was never caught."

"But now that she was caught, pay for her, or work."

"Well, then, I will work. But return me the cow; don't torture her," she cried angrily. "It is bad enough as it is; I get no rest, either day or night. Mother-in-law is sick; my husband is drunk. Single-handed I have to do all the work, and I have no strength. May you choke yourself!" she shouted and began to weep.

Nekhludoff asked the clerk to release the cows and returned to the house, wondering why people do not see what is so plain.

CHAPTER V.

Whether it was because there were fewer peasants present, or because he was not occupied with himself, but with the matter in hand, Nekhludoff felt no agitation when the seven peasants chosen from the villagers responded to the summons.

He first of all expressed his views on private ownership of land.

"As I look upon it," he said, "land ought not to be the subject of purchase and sale, for if land can be sold, then those who have money will buy it all in and charge the landless what they please for the use of it. People will then be compelled to pay for the right to stand on the earth," he added, quoting Spencer's argument.

"There remains to put on wings and fly," said an old man with smiling eyes and gray beard.

"That's so," said a long-nosed peasant in a deep basso.

"Yes, sir," said the ex-soldier.

"The old woman took some grass for the cow. They caught her, and to jail she went," said a good-natured, lame peasant.

"There is land for five miles around, but the rent is higher than the land can produce," said the toothless, angry old man.

"I am of the same opinion as you," said Nekhludoff, "and that is the reason I want to give you the land."

"Well, that would be a kind deed," said a broad-shouldered old peasant with a curly, grayish beard like that of Michael Angelo's Moses, evidently thinking that Nekhludoff intended to rent out the land.

"That is why I came here. I do not wish to own the land any longer, but it is necessary to consider how to dispose of it."

"You give it to the peasants—that's all," said the toothless, angry peasant.

For a moment Nekhludoff was confused, seeing in these words doubt of the sincerity of his purpose. But he shook it off, and took advantage of the remark to say what he intended.

"I would be only too glad to give it," he said, "but to whom and how shall I give it? Why should I give it to your community rather than to the Deminsky community?" Deminsky was a neighboring village with very little land.

They were all silent. Only the ex-soldier said, "Yes, sir."

"And now tell me how would you distribute the land?"

"How? We would give each an equal share," said an oven-builder, rapidly raising and lowering his eyebrows.

"How else? Of course divide it equally," said a good-natured, lame peasant, whose feet, instead of socks, were wound in a white strip of linen.

This decision was acquiesced in by all as being satisfactory.

"But how?" asked Nekhludoff, "are the domestics also to receive equal shares?"

"No, sir," said the ex-soldier, assuming a cheerful mood. But the sober-minded tall peasant disagreed with him.

"If it is to be divided, everybody is to get an equal share," after considering awhile, he said in a deep basso.

"That is impossible," said Nekhludoff, who was already prepared with his objection. "If everyone was to get an equal share, then those who do not themselves work would sell their shares to the rich. Thus the land would again get into the hands of the rich. Again, the people that worked their own shares would multiply, and the landlords would again get the landless into their power."

"Yes, sir," the ex-soldier hastily assented.

"The selling of land should be prohibited; only those that cultivate it themselves should be allowed to own it," said the oven-builder, angrily interrupting the soldier.

To this Nekhludoff answered that it would be difficult to determine whether one cultivated the land for himself or for others.

Then the sober-minded old man suggested that the land should be given to them as an association, and that only those that took part in cultivating it should get their share.

Nekhludoff was ready with arguments against this communistic scheme, and he retorted that in such case it would be necessary that all should have plows, that each should have the same number of horses, and that none should lag behind, or that everything should belong to society, for which the consent of every one was necessary.

"Our people will never agree," said the angry old man.

"There will be incessant fighting among them," said the white-bearded peasant with the shining eyes. "The women will scratch each other's eyes out."

"The next important question is," said Nekhludoff, "how to divide the land according to quality. You cannot give black soil to some and clay and sand to others."

"Let each have a part of both," said the oven-builder.

To this Nekhludoff answered that it was not a question of dividing the land in one community, but of the division of land generally among all the communities. If the land is to be given gratis to the peasants, then why should some get good land, and others poor land? There would be a rush for the good land.

"Yes, sir," said the ex-soldier.

The others were silent.

"You see, it is not as simple as it appears at first sight," said Nekhludoff. "We are not the only ones, there are other people thinking of the same thing. And now, there is an American, named George, who devised the following scheme, and I agree with him."

"What is that to you? You are the master; you distribute the land, and there is an end to it," said the angry peasant.

This interruption somewhat confused Nekhludoff, but he was glad to see that others were also dissatisfied with this interruption.

"Hold on, Uncle Semen; let him finish," said the old man in an impressive basso.

This encouraged Nekhludoff, and he proceeded to explain the single-tax theory of Henry George.

"The land belongs to no one—it belongs to the Creator."

"That's so!"

"Yes, sir."

"The land belongs to all in common. Every one has an equal right to it. But there is good land, and there is poor land. And the question is, how to divide the land equally. The answer to this is, that those who own the better land should pay to those who own the poorer the value of the better land. But as it is difficult to determine how much anyone should pay, and to whom, and as society needs money for common utilities, let every land owner pay to society the full value of his land—less, if it is poorer; more, if it is better. And those who do not wish to own land will have their taxes paid by the land owners."

"That's correct," said the oven-builder. "Let the owner of the better land pay more."

"What a head that Jhorga had on him!" said the portly old peasant with the curls.

"If only the payments were reasonable," said the tall peasant, evidently understanding what it was leading to.

"The payments should be such that it would be neither too cheap nor too dear. If too dear, it would be unprofitable; if too cheap, people would begin to deal in land. This is the arrangement I would like you to make."

Voices of approval showed that the peasants understood him perfectly.

"What a head!" repeated the broad-shouldered peasant with the curls, meaning "Jhorga."

"And what if I should choose to take land?" said the clerk, smiling.

"If there is an unoccupied section, take and cultivate it," said Nekhludoff.

"What do you want land for? You are not hungering without land," said the old man with the smiling eyes.

Here the conference ended.

Nekhludoff repeated his offer, telling the peasants to consult the wish of the community, before giving their answer.

The peasants said that they would do so, took leave of Nekhludoff and departed in a state of excitement. For a long time their loud voices were heard, and finally died away about midnight.

The peasants did not work the following day, but discussed their master's proposition. The community was divided into two factions. One declared the proposition profitable and safe; the other saw in the proposition a plot which it feared the more because it could not understand it. On the third day, however, the proposition was accepted, the fears of the peasants having been allayed by an old woman who explained the master's action by the suggestion that he began to think of saving his soul. This explanation was confirmed by the large amount of money Nekhludoff had distributed while he remained in Panov. These money gifts were called forth by the fact that here, for the first time, he learned to what poverty the peasants had been reduced and though he knew that it was unwise, he could not help distributing such money as he had, which was considerable.

As soon as it became known that the master was distributing money, large crowds of people from the entire surrounding country came to him asking to be helped. He had no means of determining the respective needs of the individuals, and yet he could not help giving these evidently poor people money. Again, to distribute money indiscriminately was absurd. His only way out of the difficulty was to depart, which he hastened to do.

On the third day of his visit to Panov, Nekhludoff, while looking over the things in the house, in one of the drawers of his aunt's chiffonnier, found a picture representing a group of Sophia Ivanovna, Catherine Ivanovna, himself, as student, and Katiousha—neat, fresh, beautiful and full of life. Of all the things in the house Nekhludoff removed this picture and the letters. The rest he sold to the miller for a tenth part of its value.

Recalling now the feeling of pity over the loss of his property which he had experienced in Kusminskoie, Nekhludoff wondered how he could have done so. Now he experienced the gladness of release and the feeling of novelty akin to that experienced by an explorer who discovers new lands.

CHAPTER VI.

It was evening when Nekhludoff arrived in the city, and as he drove through the gas-lit streets to his house, it looked to him like a new city. The odor of camphor still hung in the air through all the rooms, and Agrippina, Petrovna and Kornei seemed tired out and dissatisfied, and even quarreled about the packing of the things, the use of which seemed to consist chiefly in being hung out, dried and packed away again. His room was not occupied, but was not arranged for his coming, and the trunks blocked all the passages, so that his coming interfered with those affairs which, by some strange inertia, were taking place in this house. This evident foolishness, to which he had once been a party, seemed so unpleasant to Nekhludoff, after the impressions he had gained of the want in the villages, that he decided to move to a hotel the very next day, leaving the packing to Agrippina until the arrival of his sister.

He left the house in the morning, hired two modest and not over-clean furnished rooms near the prison, and went to his lawyer.

After the storms and rains came those cold, piercing winds that usually occur in the fall. Protected only by a light overcoat, Nekhludoff was chilled to the bone. He walked quickly in order to warm himself.

The village scenes came to his mind—the women, children and old men, whose poverty and exhaustion he had noticed as if for the first time, especially that oldish child which twisted its little calfless legs—and he involuntarily compared them with the city folks. Passing by the butcher, fish and clothing shops, he was struck, as if it was the first time he looked upon them—by the physical evidences of the well-being of such a large number of clean, well-fed shopkeepers which was not to be seen anywhere in the villages. Equally well fed were the drivers in quilted coats and buttons on their backs, porters, servant girls, etc. In all these people he now involuntarily saw those same village folks whom privation had driven to the city. Some of them were able to take advantage of the conditions in the city and became happy proprietors themselves; others were reduced to even greater straits and became even more wretched. Such wretchedness Nekhludoff saw in a number of shoemakers that he saw working near the window of a basement; in the lean, pale, disheveled washerwomen ironing with bare hands before open windows from which soap-laden steam poured out; in two painters, aproned and bare-footed, who were covered with paint from temple to heel. In their sunburnt, sinewy, weak hands, bared above the elbows, they carried a bucket of paint and incessantly cursed each other. Their faces were wearied and angry. The same expression of weariness and anger he saw in the dusty faces of the truck drivers; on the swollen and tattered men, women and children who stood begging on the street corners. Similar faces were seen in the windows of the tea-houses which Nekhludoff passed. Around the dirty tables, loaded with bottles and tea services, perspiring men with red, stupefied faces sat shouting and singing, and white-aproned servants flitted to and fro.

"Why have they all gathered here?" thought Nekhludoff, involuntarily inhaling, together with the dust, the odor of rancid oil spread by the fresh paint.

On one of the streets he suddenly heard his name called above the rattling of the trucks. It was Shenbok, with curled and stiffened mustache and radiant face. Nekhludoff had lost sight of him long ago, but heard that on leaving his regiment and joining the cavalry, notwithstanding his debts he managed to hold his own in rich society.

"I am glad I met you. There is not a soul in the city. How old you have grown, my boy! I only recognized you by your walk. Well, shall we have dinner together? Where can we get a good meal here?"

"I hardly think I will have the time," answered Nekhludoff, who wished to get rid of his friend without offending him. "What brings you here?" he asked.

"Business, my boy. Guardianship affairs. I am a guardian, you know. I have charge of Samanoff's business—the rich Samanoff, you know. He is a spendthrift, and there are fifty-four thousand acres of land!" he said with particular pride, as if he had himself made all these acres. "The affairs were fearfully neglected. The land was rented to the peasants, who did not pay anything and were eighty thousand rubles in arrears. In one year I changed everything, and realized seventy per cent. more for the estate. Eh?" he asked, with pride.

Nekhludoff recalled a rumor that for the very reason that Shenbok squandered his own wealth and was inextricably in debt, he was appointed guardian over a rich old spendthrift, and was now evidently obtaining an income from the guardianship.

Nekhludoff refused to take dinner with Shenbok, or accompany him to the horse races, to which the latter invited him, and after an exchange of commonplaces the two parted.

"Is it possible that I was like him?" thought Nekhludoff. "Not exactly, but I sought to be like him, and thought that I would thus pass my life."

The lawyer received him immediately on his arrival, although it was not his turn. The lawyer expressed himself strongly on the detention of the Menshovs, declaring that there was not a particle of evidence against them on record.

"If the case is tried here, and not in the district, I will stake anything on their discharge. And the petition in behalf of Theodosia Brinkova is ready. You had better take it with you to St. Petersburg and present it there. Otherwise there will begin an inquiry which will have no end. Try to reach some people who have influence with the commission on petitions. Well, that's all, isn't it?"

"No. Here they write me——"

"You seem to be the funnel into which all the prison complaints are poured. I fear you will not hold them all."

"But this case is simply shocking," said Nekhludoff, and related the substance of it.

"What is it that surprises you?"

"Everything. I can understand the orderly who acted under orders, but the assistant prosecutor who drew the indictment is an educated man——"

"That is the mistake. We are used to think that the prosecuting officers—the court officers generally—are a kind of new, liberal men. And so they were at one time, but not now. The only thing that concerns these officers is to draw their salaries on the 20th of every month. Their principles begin and end with their desire to get more. They will arrest, try and convict anybody——. I am always telling these court officers that I never look upon them without gratitude," continued the lawyer, "because it is due to their kindness that I, you and all of us are not in jail. To deprive any one of us of all civil rights and send him to Siberia is the easiest thing imaginable."

"But if everything depends on the pleasure of the prosecutor, who can enforce the law or not, then what is the use of the courts?"

The lawyer laughed merrily.

"That is the question you are raising. Well, my dear sir, that is philosophy. However, we can discuss that. Come to my house next Saturday. You will find there scholars, litterateurs, artists. We will have a talk on social questions," said the lawyer, pronouncing the words "social questions" with ironical pathos. "Are you acquainted with my wife? Call on Saturday."

"I will try," answered Nekhludoff, feeling that he was saying an untruth; that if there was anything he would try hard to do it was not to be present at the lawyer's amid the scholars, litterateurs and artists.

The laughter with which the lawyer met Nekhludoff's remark concerning the uselessness of courts if the prosecutors can do what they please, and the intonation with which he pronounced the words "philosophy" and "social questions," showed how utterly unlike himself were the lawyer and the people of his circle, both in character and in views of life.

CHAPTER VII.

It was late and the distance to the prison was long, so Nekhludoff hired a trap. On one of the streets the driver, who was a middle-aged man with an intelligent and good-natured face, turned to Nekhludoff and pointed to an immense building going up.

252

"What a huge building there is going up!" he said with pride, as if he had a part in the building of it.

It was really a huge structure, built in a complex, unusual style. A scaffolding of heavy pine logs surrounded the structure, which was fenced in by deal boards. It was as busy a scene as an ant hill.

Nekhludoff wondered that these people, while their wives were killing themselves with work at home, and their children starving, should think it necessary to build that foolish and unnecessary house for some foolish and unnecessary man.

"Yes, a foolish building," he spoke his thought aloud.

"How foolish?" retorted the offended driver. "Thanks to them, the people get work. It is not foolish."

"But the work is unnecessary."

"It must be necessary if they are building it," said the driver. "It gives the people food."

Nekhludoff became silent, the more so because it was too noisy to be heard. When they had reached the macadamized road near the prison the driver again turned to Nekhludoff.

"And what a lot of people are coming to the city—awful," he said, turning around on the box and pointing to a party of laborers with saws, axes, coats and sacks thrown over their shoulders, and coming from the opposite direction.

"More than in former years?" asked Nekhludoff.

"No comparison. The masters are kicking them about like shavings. The market places are glutted with them."

"What is the reason?"

"They have multiplied. They have no homes."

"And what if they have multiplied! Why do they not remain in the villages?"

"There is nothing to do there. There is no land."

Nekhludoff experienced that which happens with a sore place—it is struck oftener than any other part of the body. But it only seems so because it is more noticeable.

"Can it be possible that it is everywhere the same?" he thought, and asked the driver how much land there was in his village; how much he himself owned, and why he lived in the city.

"There is but an acre to every person. We are renting three acres. There is my father and brother. Another brother is in the army. They are managing it. But there is really nothing to manage, and my brother intended to go to Moskow."

"Is there no land for rent?"

"Where could one get land nowadays? The masters' children have squandered theirs. The merchants have it all in their hands. One cannot rent it from them; they cultivate it themselves. Our lands are held by a Frenchman who bought them of the former landlord. He won't rent any of it, and that is all."

"What Frenchman?"

"Dufar, the Frenchman—you may have heard. He is making wigs for the actors. He is now our master, and does what he pleases with us. He is a good man himself, but his wife is Russian—and what a cur! She is robbing the people—simply awful! But here is the prison. Shall I drive up to the front? I think they don't admit through the front."

CHAPTER VIII.

With a faint heart and with horror at the thought that he might find Maslova in an inebriate condition and persistently antagonistic, and at the mystery which she was to him, Nekhludoff rang the bell and inquired of the inspector about Maslova. She was in the hospital.

A young physician, impregnated with carbolic acid, came out into the corridor and sternly asked Nekhludoff what he wanted. The physician indulged the prisoners' shortcomings and often relaxed the rules in their favor, for which he often ran afoul of the prison officials and even the head physician. Fearing that Nekhludoff might ask something not permitted by the rules, and, moreover, desiring to show that he made no exceptions in favor of anybody, he feigned anger.

"There are no women here; this is the children's ward," he said.

"I know it, but there is a nurse here who had been transferred from the prison."

"Yes, there are two. What do you wish, then?"

"I am closely related to one of them, Maslova," said Nekhludoff, "and would like to see her. I am going to St. Petersburg to enter an appeal in her case. I would like to hand her this; it is only a photograph," and he produced an envelope from his pocket.

"Yes, you may do that," said the softened physician, and turning to an old nurse in a white apron, told her to call Maslova. "Won't you take a seat, or come into the reception-room?"

"Thank you," said Nekhludoff, and taking advantage of the favorable change in the physician's demeanor, asked him what they thought of Maslova in the hospital.

"Her work is fair, considering the conditions amid which she had lived," answered the physician. "But there she comes."

The old nurse appeared at one of the doors, and behind her came Maslova. She wore a white apron over a striped skirt; a white cap on her head hid her hair. Seeing Nekhludoff she flushed, stopped waveringly, then frowned, and with downcast eyes approached him with quick step. Coming near him she stood for a moment without offering her hand, then she did offer her hand and became even more flushed. Nekhludoff had not seen her since the conversation in which she excused herself for her impetuosity, and he expected to find her in a similar mood. But she was entirely different to-day; there was something new in the expression of her face; something timid and reserved, and, as it seemed to him, malevolent toward him. He repeated the words he had said to the physician and handed her the envelope with the photograph which he had brought from Panov.

"It is an old picture which I came across in Panov. It may please you to have it. Take it."

Raising her black eyebrows she looked at him with her squinting eyes, as though asking, "What is that for?" Then she silently took the envelope and tucked it under her apron.

"I saw your aunt there," said Nekhludoff.

"Did you?" she said, with indifference.

"How do you fare here?" asked Nekhludoff.

"Fairly well," she said.

"It is not very hard?"

"Not very. I am not used to it yet."

"I am very glad. At any rate, it is better than there."

"Than where?" she said, and her face became purple.

"There, in the prison," Nekhludoff hastened to say.

"Why better?" she asked.

"I think the people here are better. There are no such people here as there."

"There are many good people there."

"I did what I could for the Menshovs and hope they will be freed," said Nekhludoff.

"May God grant it. Such a wonderful little woman," she said, repeating her description of the old woman, and slightly smiled.

"I am going to-day to St. Petersburg. Your case will be heard soon, and, I hope, will be reversed."

"It is all the same now, whether they reverse it or not," she said.

"Why now?"

"So," she answered, and stealthily glanced at him inquiringly.

Nekhludoff understood this answer and this glance as a desire on her part to know if he were still holding to his decision, or had changed it since her refusal.

"I don't know why it is all the same to you," he said, "but to me it really is all the same whether you are acquitted or not. In either case, I am ready to do what I said," he said, with determination.

She raised her head, and her black, squinting eyes fixed themselves on his face and past it, and her whole face became radiant with joy. But her words were in an entirely different strain.

"Oh, you needn't talk that way," she said.

"I say it that you may know."

"Everything has been already said, and there is no use talking any more," she said, with difficulty repressing a smile.

There was some noise in the ward. A child was heard crying.

"I think I am called," she said, looking around with anxiety.

"Well, then, good-by," he said.

She pretended not to see his extended hand, turned round, and endeavoring to hide her elation, she walked away with quick step.

"What is taking place in her? What is she thinking? What are her feelings? Is she putting me to a test, or is she really unable to forgive me? Can she not say what she thinks and feels, or simply will not? Is she pacified or angered?" Nekhludoff asked himself, but could give no answer. One thing he knew, however, and that was that she had changed; that a spiritual transformation was taking place in her, and this transformation united him not only to her, but to Him in whose name it was taking place. And this union caused him joyful agitation.

Returning to the ward where eight children lay in their beds, Maslova began to remake one of the beds, by order of the Sister, and, leaning over too far with the sheet, slipped and nearly fell. The convalescing boy, wound in bandages to his neck, began to laugh. Maslova could restrain herself no longer, and seating herself on the bedstead she burst into loud laughter, infecting several children, who also began to laugh. The Sister angrily shouted:

"What are you roaring about? Think you this is like the place you came from? Go fetch the rations."

Maslova stopped laughing, and taking a dish went on her errand, but exchanging looks with the bandaged boy, who giggled again.

Several times during the day, when Maslova remained alone, she drew out a corner of the picture and looked at it with admiration, but in the evening, when she and another nurse retired for the night, she removed the picture from the envelope and immovably looked with admiration at the faces; her own, his and the aunt's, their dresses, the stairs of the balcony, the bushes in the background, her eyes feasting especially on herself, her young, beautiful face with the hair hanging over her forehead. She was so absorbed that she failed to notice that the other nurse had entered.

"What is that? Did he give it you?" asked the stout, good-natured nurse, leaning over the photograph.

"Is it possible that that is you?"

"Who else?" Maslova said, smiling and looking into her companion's face.

"And who is that? He himself? And that is his mother?"

"His aunt. Couldn't you recognize me?" asked Maslova.

"Why, no. I could never recognize you. The face is entirely different.

That must have been taken about ten years ago."

"Not years, but a lifetime," said Maslova, and suddenly her face became sullen and a wrinkle formed between her eyebrows.

"Yours was an easy life, wasn't it?"

"Yes, easy," Maslova repeated, closing her eyes and shaking her head. "Worse than penal servitude."

"Why so?"

"Because. From eight in the evening to four in the morning—every day the same."

"Then why don't they get out?"

"They like to, but cannot. But what is the use of talking!" cried Maslova, and she sprang to her feet, threw the photograph into the drawer of the table, and suppressing her angry tears, ran into the corridor, slamming the door. Looking on the photograph she imagined herself as she had been at the time the photograph was made, and dreamed how happy she had been and might still be with him. The words of her companion reminded her what she was now—reminded her of all the horror of that life which she then felt but confusedly, and would not allow herself to admit. Only now she vividly recalled all those terrible nights, particularly one Shrovetide night. She recalled how she, in a low-cut, wine-bespattered, red silk dress, with a red bow in her dishevelled hair, weak, jaded and tipsy, after dancing attendance upon the guest, had seated herself, at two in the morning, near the thin, bony, pimpled girl-pianist and complained of her hard life. The girl said that her life was also disagreeable to her, and that she wished to change her occupation. Afterward their friend Clara joined them, and all three suddenly decided to change their life. They were about to leave the place when the drunken guests became noisy, the fiddler struck up a lively song of the first figure of a Russian quadrille, the pianist began to thump in unison, a little drunken man in a white necktie and dress coat caught her up. Another man, stout and bearded, and also in a dress coat, seized Clara, and for a long time they whirled, danced, shouted and drank. Thus a year passed, a second and a third. How could she help changing! And the cause of it all was he. And suddenly her former wrath against him rose in her; and she felt like chiding and reproving him. She was sorry that she had missed the opportunity of telling him again that she knew him, and would not yield to him; that she would not allow him to take advantage of her spiritually as he had done corporeally; that she would not allow him to make her the subject of his magnanimity. And in order to deaden the painful feeling of pity for herself and the useless reprobation of him, she yearned for wine. And she would have broken her word and drunk some wine had she been in the prison. But here wine could only be obtained from the assistant surgeon, and she was afraid of him, because he pursued her with his attentions, and all relations with men were disgusting to her. For some time she sat on a bench in the corridor, and returning to her closet, without heeding her companion's questions, she wept for a long time over her ruined life.

CHAPTER IX.

Nekhludoff had four cases in hand: Maslova's appeal, the petition of Theodosia Birukova, the case of Shustova's release, by request of Vera Bogodukhovskaia, and the obtaining of permission for a mother to visit her son kept in a fortress, also by Bogodukhovskaia's request.

Since his visit to Maslenikoff, especially since his trip to the country, Nekhludoff felt an aversion for that sphere in which he had been living heretofore, and in which the sufferings borne by millions of people in order to secure the comforts and pleasures of a few, were so carefully concealed that the people of that sphere did not and could not see these sufferings, and consequently the cruelty and criminality of their own lives.

Nekhludoff could no longer keep up relations with these people without reproving himself. And yet the habits of his past life, the ties of friendship and kinship, and especially his one great aim of helping Maslova and the other unfortunates, drew him into that sphere against his will; and he was compelled to ask the aid and services of people whom he had not only ceased to respect but who called forth his indignation and contempt.

Arriving at St. Petersburg, and stopping at his aunt's, the wife of an ex-Minister of State, he found himself in the very heart of the aristocratic circle. It was unpleasant to him, but he could do no different. Not to stop at his aunt's was to offend her. Besides, through her connections she could be of great service to him in those affairs for the sake of which he came to St. Petersburg.

"What wonders I hear about you!" said Countess Catherine Ivanovna Charskaia, while Nekhludoff was drinking the coffee brought him immediately after his arrival. "Vous posez pour un Howard. You are helping the convicts; making the rounds of the prisons; reforming them."

"You are mistaken; I never had such intentions."

"Why, that is not bad. Only, I understand, there is some love affair— come, tell me."

Nekhludoff related the story of Maslova, exactly as it happened.

"Yes, yes, I remember. Poor Hellen told me at the time you lived at the old maids' house that, I believe, they wished you to marry their ward." Countess Catherine Ivanovna always hated Nekhludoff's aunts on his father's side. "So, that is she? Elle est encore jolie?"

Aunt Catherine Ivanovna was a sixty-year-old, healthy, jolly, energetic, talkative woman. She was tall, very stout, with a black, downy mustache on her upper lip. Nekhludoff loved her, and since childhood had been accustomed to get infected with her energy and cheerfulness.

"No, ma tante, all that belongs to the past. I only wish to help her, because she is innocent, and it is my fault that she was condemned, her whole wrecked life is upon my conscience. I feel it to be my duty to do for her what I can."

"But how is it? I was told that you wish to marry her."

"I do wish it, it is true; but she doesn't."

Catherine Ivanovna raised her eyebrows and silently looked at Nekhludoff in surprise. Suddenly her face changed and assumed a pleased expression.

"Well, she is wiser than you are. Ah! what a fool you are! And you would marry her?"

"Certainly."

"After what she has been?"

"The more so—is it not all my fault?"

"Well, you are simply a crank," said the aunt, suppressing a smile. "You are an awful crank, but I love you for the very reason that you are such an awful crank," she repeated, the word evidently well describing, according to her view, the mental and moral condition of her nephew. "And how opportune. You know, Aline has organized a wonderful asylum for Magdalens. I visited it once. How disgusting they are! I afterward washed myself from head to foot. But Aline is corps et ame in this affair. So we will send her, your Magdalen, to her. If any one will reform her, it is Aline."

"But she was sentenced to penal servitude. I came here for the express purpose of obtaining a reversal of her sentence. That is my first business to you."

"Is that so? Where is the case now?"

"In the Senate."

"In the Senate? Why, my dear cousin Levoushka is in the Senate. However, he is in the Heraldry Department. Let me see. No, of the real ones I do not know any. Heaven knows what a mixture they are: either Germans, such as Ge, Fe, De—tout l'alphabet—or all sorts of Ivanvas, Semenovs, Nikitins, or Ivaneukos, Semeneukos, Nikitenkas pour varier. Des gens de l'autre monde. However, I will tell my husband. He knows all sorts of people. I will tell him. You explain it to him, for he never understands me. No matter what I may say, he always says that he cannot understand me. C'est un parti pris. Everybody understands, only he does not understand."

At that moment a servant in knee-breeches entered with a letter on a silver tray.

"Ah, that is from Aline. Now you will have an opportunity to hear Kisiweather."

"Who is that Kisiweather?"

"Kisiweather? Come around to-day and you will find out who he is. He speaks so that the most hardened criminals fall on their knees and weep, and repent."

Countess Catherine Ivanovna, however strange it might be, and how so little it agreed with her character, was a follower of that teaching which held that essence of Christianity consisted in a belief in redemption. She visited the meetings where sermons were delivered on this teaching then in vogue, and invited the adherents to her own house. Although this teaching rejected all rites, images and even the sacraments, the Princess had images hanging in all her rooms, even over her bedstead, and she complied with all the ritual requirements of the church, seeing nothing contradictory in that.

"Your Magdalen ought to hear him; she would become converted," said the Countess. "Don't fail to come to-night. You will hear him then. He is a remarkable man."

"It is not interesting to me, ma tante."

"I tell you it is interesting. You must come to-night. Now, what else do you want me to do? Videz votre sac."

"There is the man in the fortress."

"In the fortress? Well, I can give you a note to Baron Kriegmuth. C'est un très-brave homme. But you know him yourself. He was your father's comrade. Il donne dans le spiritisme. But that is nothing. He is a kind man. What do you want there?"

"It is necessary to obtain permission for a mother to visit her son who is incarcerated there. But I was told that Cherviansky and not Kriegmuth is the person to be applied to."

"I do not like Cherviansky, but he is Mariette's husband. I will ask her; she will do it for me. Elle est tres gentille."

"There is another woman I wish you would speak to her about. She has been in prison for several months, and no one knows for what."

"Oh, no; she herself surely knows for what. They know very well. And it serves them right, those short-haired ones."

"I do not know whether it serves them right or not. But they are suffering. You are a Christian, and believe in the Gospel, and yet are so pitiless."

"That has nothing to do with it. The Gospel is one thing; what I dislike is another thing. It would be worse if I pretended to like the Nihilists, especially the female Nihilists, when as a matter of fact I hate them."

"Why do you hate them?"

"Why do they meddle in other people's affairs? It is not a woman's business."

"But you have nothing against Mariette occupying herself with business," said Nekhludoff.

"Mariette? Mariette is Mariette, but who is she? A conceited ignoramus who wants to teach everybody."

"They do not wish to teach; they only wish to help the people."

"We know without them who should and who should not be helped."

"But the people are impoverished. I have just been in the country. Is it proper that peasants should overwork themselves without getting enough to eat, while we are living in such wasteful luxury?"

"What do you wish me to do? You would like to see me work and not eat anything?"

"No, I do not wish you not to eat," smiling involuntarily, answered Nekhludoff. "I only wish that we should all work, and all have enough to eat."

The aunt again raised her eyebrows and gazed at him with curiosity.

"Mon cher, vous finirez mal," she said.

At that moment a tall, broad-shouldered general entered the room. It was Countess Charskaia's husband, a retired Minister of State.

"Ah, Dmitri, how do you do?" he said, putting out his clean-shaven cheek. "When did you get here?"

He silently kissed his wife on the forehead.

"Non, il est impayable." Countess Catherine Ivanovna turned to her husband. "He wants me to do washing on the river and feast on potatoes. He is an awful fool, but, nevertheless, do for him what he asks. An awful crank," she corrected herself. "By the way, they say that Kamenskaia is in a desperate condition; her life is despaired of," she turned to her husband. "You ought to visit her."

"Yes, it is awful," said the husband.

"Go, now, and have a talk together; I must write some letters."

Nekhludoff had just reached the room next to the reception-room when she shouted after him:

"Shall I write then to Mariette?"

"If you please, ma tante."

"I will learn that which you want to say about the short-haired en blanc, and she will have her husband attend to it. Don't think that I am angry. They are hateful, your protegees, but—je ne leur veux pas de mal. But God forgive them. Now, go, and don't forget to come in the evening; you will hear Kisiweather. We will also pray. And if you do not resist, ca vous fera beaucoup de bien. I know that Hellen and all of you are very backward in that respect. Now, au revoir."

CHAPTER X.

The man in whose power it was to lighten the condition of the prisoners in St. Petersburg had earned a great number of medals, which, except for a white cross in his button-hole, he did not wear, however. The old general was of the German barons, and, as it was said of him, had become childish. He had served in the Caucasus, where he had received this cross; then in Poland and in some other place, and now he held the office which gave him good quarters, maintenance and honor. He always strictly carried out the orders of his superiors, and considered their execution of great importance and significance, so much so that while everything in the world could be changed, these orders, according to him, were above the possibility of any alteration.

As Nekhludoff was approaching the old general's house the tower clock struck two. The general was at the time sitting with a young artist in the darkened reception-room, at a table, the top of which was of inlaid work, both of them turning a saucer on a sheet of paper. Holding each others fingers over the saucer, placed face downward, they pulled in different directions over the paper on which were printed all the letters of the alphabet. The saucer was answering the general's question. How would souls recognize each other after death?

At the moment one of the servants entered with Nekhludoff's card, the soul of Jeanne D'Arc was speaking through the saucer. The soul had already said, "They will recognize each other," which was duly entered on a sheet of paper. When the servant entered, the saucer, stopping first on the letter p, then on the letter o, reached the letter s and began to jerk one way and another. That was because, as the general thought, the next letter was to be l, that is to say, Jeanne D'Arc, according to his idea, intended to say that souls would recognize each other only after they had been purged of everything mundane, or something to that effect, and that therefore the next letter ought to be l (posl, i. e., after); the artist, on the other hand, thought that the next letter would be v; that the soul intended to say that souls would recognize each other by the light—posv (ietu) that would issue from the ethereal body of the souls. The general, gloomily knitting his brow, gazed fixedly on the hands, and imagining that the saucer moved itself, pulled it toward the letter l. The young, anaemic artist, with his oily hair brushed behind his ears, looked into the dark corner of the room, with his blue, dull eyes, and nervously twitching his lips, pulled toward the letter v. The general frowned at the interruption, and, after a moment's silence, took the card, put on his

266

pince-nez and, groaning from pain in his loins, rose to his full height, rubbing his benumbed fingers.

"Show him into the cabinet."

"Permit me, Your Excellency, to finish it myself," said the artist, rising. "I feel a presence."

"Very well; finish it," said the general with austerity, and went, with firm, long strides, into the cabinet.

"Glad to see you," said the general in a rough voice to Nekhludoff, pointing to an arm-chair near the desk. "How long have you been in St. Petersburg?"

Nekhludoff said that he had but lately arrived.

"Is your mother, the Princess, well?"

"My mother is dead."

"Beg pardon; I was very sorry. My son told me that he had met you."

The general's son was making the same career as his father, and was very proud of the business with which he was entrusted.

"Why, I served with your father. We were friends, comrades. Are you in service?"

"No, I am not."

The general disapprovingly shook his head.

"I have a request to make of you, general," said Nekhludoff.

"Very glad. What can I do for you?"

"If my request be out of season, please forgive me. But I must state it."

"What is it?"

"There is a man, Gurkevitch, kept in prison under your jurisdiction. His mother asks to be permitted to visit him, or, at least to send him books."

The general expressed neither satisfaction nor dissatisfaction at Nekhludoff's request, but, inclining his head to one side, seemed to reflect. As a matter of fact he was not reflecting; Nekhludoff's question did not even interest him, knowing very well that his answer would be as the law requires. He was simply resting mentally without thinking of anything.

"That is not in my discretion, you know," he said, having rested awhile. "There is a law relating to visits, and whatever that law permits, that is permitted. And as to books, there is a library, and they are given such books as are allowed."

"Yes, but he wants scientific books; he wishes to study."

"Don't believe that." The general paused. "It is not for study that they want them, but so, it is simply unrest."

"But their time must be occupied somehow?"

"They are always complaining," retorted the general. "We know them."

He spoke of them in general as of some peculiar race of people.

"They have such conveniences here as is seldom seen in a prison," he continued.

And as though justifying himself, he began to recount all the conveniences enjoyed by the prisoners in a manner to make one believe that the chief aim of the institution consisted in making it a pleasant place of abode.

"Formerly, it is true, the regulations were very harsh, but now their condition is excellent. They get three dishes, one of which is always of meat—chopped meat or cutlet. Sundays they get a fourth dish—dessert. May God grant that every Russian could feed so well."

The general, like all old men, evidently having committed to memory the oft-repeated words, proceeded to prove how exacting and ungrateful the prisoners were by repeating what he had told many times before.

"They are furnished books on spiritual topics, also old journals. We have a library of suitable books, but they seldom read them. At first they appear to be interested, and then it is found that the pages of all the new books are barely half cut, and of the old ones there is no evidence of any thumb-marks at all. We even tried," with a remote semblance of a smile the general continued, "to put a piece of paper between the pages, and it remained untouched. Writing, too, is allowed. A slate is given them, also a slate-pencil, so that they may write for diversion. They can wipe it out and write again. And yet they don't write. No, they become quiet very soon. At first they are uneasy, but afterward they even grow stout and become very quiet."

Nekhludoff listened to the hoarse, feeble voice; looked on that fleshless body, those faded eyes under the gray eyebrows, those sunken, shaved cheeks, supported by a military collar, that white cross, and understood that to argue and explain to him the meaning of those words were futile. But, making another effort, he asked him about the prisoner, Shustova, whose release, he had received information, had been ordered, through the efforts of Mariette.

"Shustova? Shustova—I don't remember them all by name. There are so many of them," he said, evidently reproving them for being so numerous. He rang the bell and called for the secretary.

While a servant was going after the secretary he admonished Nekhludoff to go into service, saying that the country was in need of honest, noble men.

"I am old, and yet I am serving to the extent of my ability."

The secretary came and reported that there were no papers received relating to Shustova, who was still in prison.

"As soon as we receive an order we release them the very same day. We do not keep them; we do not particularly value their presence," said the general, again with a waggish smile, which had the effect only of making his face wry.

"Good-by, my dear," he continued. "Don't be offended for advising you, for I do so only because I love you. Have nothing to do with the prisoners. You will never find innocent people among them. They are the most immoral set. We know them," he said, in a tone of voice which did not permit the possibility of doubt. "You had better take an office. The Emperor and the country need honest people. What if I and such as you refused to serve? Who would be left? We are complaining of conditions, but refuse to aid the government."

Nekhludoff sighed deeply, made a low bow, pressed the bony hand condescendingly extended, and departed.

The general disapprovingly shook his head, and, rubbing his loins, went to the reception-room, where the artist awaited him with the answer of Jeanne D'Arc. The general put on his pince-nez and read: "They will recognize each other by the light issuing from the ethereal bodies."

"Ah!" said the general, approvingly, closing his eyes. "But how will one recognize another when all have the same light?" he asked, and again crossing his fingers with those of the artist, seated himself at the table.

Nekhludoff's driver drove up to the gate.

"It is very dull here, sir," he said, turning to Nekhludoff. "It was very tiresome, and I was about to drive away."

"Yes, tiresome," assented Nekhludoff with a deep sigh, resting his eyes on the clouds and the Neva, dotted with variegated boats and steamers.

CHAPTER XI.

With a note from Prince Ivan Michaelovitch, Nekhludoff went to Senator Wolf—un homme très comme il faut, as the Prince had described him.

Wolf had just breakfasted and, as usual, was smoking a cigar, to aid his digestion, when Nekhludoff arrived. Vladimir Vasilievtch Wolf was really un homme très comme il faut, and this quality he placed above all else; from the height of it he looked upon all other people, and could not help valuing this quality, because, thanks to it, he had gained a brilliant career—the same career he strove for; that is to say, through marriage he obtained a fortune, which brought him a yearly income of eighteen thousand rubles, and by his own efforts he obtained a senatorship. He considered himself not only un homme très comme il faut, but a man of chivalric honesty. By honesty he understood

270

the refusal to take bribes from private people. But to do everything in his power to obtain all sorts of traveling expenses, rents and disbursements he did not consider dishonest. Nor did he consider it dishonest to rob his wife and sister-in-law of their fortunes. On the contrary, he considered that a wise arrangement of his family affairs.

The home circle of Vladimir Vasilievitch consisted of his characterless wife, her sister, whose fortune he managed to get into his own hands by selling her property and depositing the money in his own name, and his gentle, scared, homely daughter, who was leading a solitary, hard life, and whose only diversion consisted in visiting the religious meetings at Aline's and Countess Catherine Ivanovna's.

The son of Vladimir Vasilievitch, a good-natured, bearded boy of fifteen, who at that age had already commenced to drink and lead a depraved life which lasted till he was twenty years old, was driven from the house for the reason that he did not pass examinations in any school, and keeping bad company, and, running into debt, he had compromised his father. The father paid once for his son two hundred and thirty rubles, and paid six hundred rubles a second time, but declared that that was the last time, and if the son did not reform he would drive him from the house and have nothing to do with him. Not only did the son not reform, but contracted another debt of a thousand rubles, and told his father that he did not care if he was driven from the house, since life at home was torture to him. Then Vladimir Vasilievitch told his son that he could go where he pleased; that he was no longer his son. Since then no one in the house dared to speak of his son to him. And Vladimir Vasilievitch was quite certain that he had arranged his family affairs in the best possible manner.

Wolf, with a flattering and somewhat derisive smile—it was an involuntary expression of his consciousness of his comme il faut superiority—halted in his exercise long enough to greet Nekhludoff and read the note.

"Please take a seat, but you must excuse me. If you have no objection I will walk," he said, putting his hands in the pockets of his jacket, and treading lightly up and down the diagonal of the large cabinet, furnished in an austere

271

style. "Very glad to make your acquaintance, and, of course, to please the Count Ivan Michaelovitch," emitting the fragrant, blue smoke, and carefully removing the cigar from his mouth so as not to lose the ashes.

"I would like to ask you to hasten the hearing of the appeal, because if the prisoner is to go to Siberia, it would be desirable that she go as soon as possible," said Nekhludoff.

"Yes, yes, with the first steamer from Nijhni; I know," said Wolf, with his condescending smile, who always knew everything in advance, whatever the subject mentioned to him. "What is the name of the prisoner?"

"Maslova."

Wolf walked to the table and looked into the papers.

"That's right—Maslova. Very well; I will ask my associates. We will hear the case Wednesday."

"May I wire my lawyer?"

"So you have a lawyer? What for? But if you wish it, all right."

"The grounds of appeal may be insufficient," said Nekhludoff, "but I think it may be seen from the case that the sentence was the result of a misunderstanding."

"Yes, yes; that may be so, but the Senate cannot enter into the merits of the case," said Vladimir Vasilievitch, sternly, glancing at the ashes of his cigar. "The Senate only looks after the proper interpretation and application of the law."

"This, I think, is an exceptional case."

"I know; I know. All cases are exceptional. We will do what the law requires. That is all." The ashes were still intact, but had already cracked and were in danger of collapse. "And do you often visit St. Petersburg?" asked Wolf, holding the cigar so that the ashes would not fall. The ashes were unstable, however, and Wolf carefully carried them to the ash-holder, into which they were finally precipitated.

"What an awful catastrophe Kamensky met with," said Wolf. "A fine young man, and an only son. Especially the condition of the mother"—he went on repeating almost word for word the story of a duel of which all St. Petersburg was talking at the time. After a few more words about Countess Catherine Ivanovna and her passion for the new religious tendency which Vladimir Vasilievitch neither praised nor condemned, but which, for un homme très comme il faut, was evidently superfluous, he rang the bell.

Nekhludoff bowed himself out.

"If it is convenient for you, come to dinner," said Wolf, extending his hand, "say on Wednesday. I will then give you a definite answer."

It was already late, and Nekhludoff drove home, that is, to his aunt's.

CHAPTER XII.

Maslova's case was to be heard the following day, and Nekhludoff went to the Senate. He met Fanirin at the entrance to the magnificent Senate building, where several carriages were already waiting. Walking up the grand, solemn staircase to the second floor, the lawyer, who was familiar with all the passages, turned into a room to the left, on the door of which was carved the year of the institution of the Code. The lawyer removed his overcoat, remaining in his dress-coat and black tie on a white bosom, and with cheerful self-confidence walked into the next room. There were about fifteen spectators present, among whom were a young woman in a pince-nez, and a gray-haired lady. A gray-haired old man of patriarchal mien, wearing a box-coat and gray trousers, and attended by two men, attracted particular attention. He crossed the room and entered a wardrobe.

An usher, a handsome man with red cheeks and in a pompous uniform, approached Fanirin with a piece of paper in his hand and asked him in what case he appeared. Being told that in Maslova's case, the usher made a note of something and went away. At that time the door of the wardrobe opened and the patriarchal looking old man came forth, no longer in the coat, but in a brilliant uniform which made him resemble a bird. His uniform evidently embarrassed the old man, and he walked into the room opposite the entrance with quicker than his ordinary step.

Fanirin pointed him out to Nekhludoff as Bé, "a most honorable gentleman." The spectators, including Fanirin, went into the next room and seated themselves behind the grating on benches reserved for spectators. Only the St. Petersburg lawyer took a seat behind a desk on the other side of the grating.

The session room of the Senate was smaller than the room of the Circuit Court, was furnished in simpler style, only the table behind which the Senators sat was of crimson plush instead of green cloth, bordered with gold lace.

There were four Senators. The President, Nikitin, with a closely shaved, narrow face and steel-gray eyes; Wolf, with thin lips and small white hands, with which he was turning over the papers before him; then Skovorodnikoff, stout, massive and pock-marked, and a very learned jurist, and finally, Bé, the same partriarchal old man, who was the last to arrive. Immediately behind the Senators came the Chief Secretary and Associate Attorney General. He was a young man of medium height, shaved, lean, with a very dark face and black, sad eyes. Nekhludoff recognized him, notwithstanding his strange uniform and the fact that he had not seen him for about six years, as one of his best friends during his student life.

"Is the associate's name Selenin?" he asked the lawyer.

"Yes, why?"

"I know him very well; he is an excellent man——"

"And a good associate of the Attorney General—very sensible. It would have been well to see him," said Fanirin.

"At all events, he will follow the dictates of his conscience," said Nekhludoff, remembering his close relations with and friendship for Selenin, and the latter's charming qualities of purity, honesty and good breeding, in the best sense of the word.

The first case before the Senate was an appeal from the decision of the Circuit Court of Appeals affirming a judgment in favor of the publisher of a newspaper in a libel suit brought against him.

Nekhludoff listened and tried to understand the arguments in the case, but as in the Circuit Court, the chief difficulty in understanding what was going on was found in the fact that the discussion centered not on what appeared naturally to be the main point, but on side issues.

The libel consisted in an article accusing the president of a stock company of swindling. It seemed, then, that the main point to consider was, whether or not the president was guilty of swindling the stockholders, and what was to be done to stop his swindling. But this was never mentioned. The questions discussed were: Had the publisher the legal right to print the article of its reporter? What crime has he committed by printing it—defamation or libel? And does defamation include libel, or libel defamation? And a number of other things unintelligible to ordinary people, including various laws and decisions of some "General Department."

The only thing Nekhludoff did understand was that, though Wolf had sternly suggested but yesterday that the Senate could not consider the substance of a case, in the case at bar he argued with evident partiality in favor of reversing the judgment, and that Selenin, in spite of his characteristic reserve, argued in favor of affirming the judgment with unexpected fervor. The cause of Selenin's ardor lay in the fact that he knew the president of the stock company to be dishonest in money affairs, while he accidentally learned that Wolf, almost on the eve of the hearing of the case, had attended a sumptuous dinner at the president's house. And now, when Wolf, though with great caution, showed undoubted partiality, Selenin became excited and expressed his opinion with more nervousness than an ordinary case would justify. Wolf was evidently offended by the speech; he twitched nervously, changed color, made silent gestures of wonder, and with an haughty air of being offended he departed with the other Senators into the deliberation-room.

"What case are you interested in?" the usher again asked Fanirin, as soon as the Senators had left the room.

"I have already told you that I am here in behalf of Maslova."

"That is so. The case will be heard to-day. But——"

"What is that?" asked the lawyer.

"You see, the case was to be argued without counsel, so that the Senators would hardly consider it in open session. But—I will announce——" and he made a note on the piece of paper.

The Senators really intended, after announcing their decision in the libel case, to consider the other cases, including Maslova's, while drinking their tea and smoking cigarettes in the consultation-room.

CHAPTER XIII.

As soon as the Senators seated themselves at the table in the consultation-room, Wolf began to set forth in an animated manner the grounds upon which he thought the case ought to be reversed.

The President, always an ill-natured man, was in a particularly bad humor to-day. While listening to the case during the session he formed his opinion, and sat, absorbed in his thoughts, without listening to Wolf. These thoughts consisted in a recollection of what note he had made the other day in his memoirs anent the appointment of Velianoff to an important post which he desired for himself. The President, Nikitin, quite sincerely thought that the officials with whom his duties brought him in contact were worthy of a place in history. Having written an article the other day in which some of these officials were vehemently denounced for interfering with his plan to save Russia from ruin, as he put it, but in reality for interfering with his getting a larger salary than he was now getting, he was now thinking that posterity would give an entirely new interpretation to that incident.

"Why, certainly," he said to Wolf, who was addressing him, although he did not hear what Wolf said.

Bé listened to Wolf with a sad face, drawing garlands on a piece of paper which lay before him. Bé was a liberal of the deepest dye. He scarcely held to the traditions of the sixties, and if he ever deviated from strict impartiality, it was invariably in favor of liberality. Thus, in this case, besides the consideration that the complaining president of the stock company was an unclean man,

276

Bé was in favor of affirming the judgment, also because this charge of libel against a journalist was a restriction on the freedom of the press. When Wolf had finished his argument, Bé, leaving the garland unfinished, in a sad—it was sad for him to be obliged to prove such truisms—soft, pleasant voice, convincingly proved in a few simple words that the charge had no foundation, and, again drooping his hoary head, continued to complete the garland.

Skovorodnikoff, who was sitting opposite Wolf, continually gathering with his thick fingers his beard and mustache into his mouth, as soon as Bé was through with his argument, stopped chewing his beard, and, in a loud, rasping voice, said that although the president of the stock company was a villain, he should favor a reversal if there were legal grounds to sustain it, but as there were none, he joined in the opinion of Ivan Semenovitch (Bé), and he invariably rejoiced at this shot aimed at Wolf. The President supported Skovorodnikoff's opinion, and the judgment was confirmed.

Wolf was dissatisfied, especially because by this judgment he seemed to stand convicted of arguing in bad faith; but, feigning indifference, he opened his papers in the next case, Maslova's, and began to peruse it attentively. The other Senators in the meantime called for tea, and began a talk about Kamensky's duel and his death, which was then the subject of conversation throughout the city.

The usher entered and announced the desire of the lawyer and Nekhludoff to be present at the hearing of the case.

"This case here," said Wolf, "is a whole romantic story," and he related what he knew of Nekhludoff's relations to Maslova.

After talking awhile of the story, smoking cigarettes and finishing their tea, the Senators returned to the session-room, announced their decision in the preceding case, and began to consider Maslova's case.

Wolf very circumstantially set forth Maslova's appeal from the sentence, and again not without partiality, but with the evident desire to reverse the judgment.

"Have you anything to add?" the President asked Fanirin.

Fanirin rose, and, projecting his broad, starched front, with remarkable precision of expression began to discuss the errors of the court below in the application of the law on the six points raised, and permitted himself, though briefly, to touch upon the merits of the case and the crying injustice of the decision. By the tone of his short but strong speech, he seemed to excuse himself, to insist that the honorable Senators with their power of penetration and judicial wisdom saw and understood better than he, but that he was speaking only because his duties demanded it. After Fanirin's speech there seemed to be no doubt left that the Senate had to reverse the judgment. When he was through, Fanirin smiled triumphantly. Looking at his lawyer and seeing that smile, Nekhludoff was convinced that the case was won. But as he looked at the Senators Nekhludoff saw that Fanirin alone was smiling and triumphant. The Senators and Associate Attorney General were neither smiling nor triumphant, but wore the air of people suffering from ennui and saying: "Oh, we know these cases! You are wasting your time." They were all evidently relieved only when the lawyer had finished, and they were no longer unnecessarily detained. After the speech the President turned to Selenin, who plainly, briefly and accurately expressed himself against a reversal. Then the Senators arose and went to consult.

The Senators were divided. Wolf favored a reversal. Bé, who thoroughly understood the case, warmly argued also in favor of a reversal, and in glowing terms pictured the court scene and the misunderstanding of the jury. Nikitin, who, as usual, stood for severity and for strict formality, was against it. The whole case, then, depended on Skovorodnikoff's vote. And his vote was thrown against a reversal, principally for the reason that Nekhludoff's determination to marry the girl on moral grounds was extremely repugnant to him.

Skovorodnikoff was a materialist, a Darwinist, and considered every manifestation of abstract morality, or, worse still, piety, not only as contemptible and absurd but as an affront to his person. All this bustle about a fallen girl, and the presence there in the Senate of her famous counsel and Nekhludoff himself, was to him simply disgusting. And, stuffing his mouth with his beard, and making grimaces, he in a very natural manner pretended to know nothing of the entire affair, except that the grounds of appeal were insufficient, and therefore agreed with the President to affirm the judgment.

The appeal was denied.

CHAPTER XIV.

"It is awful!" said Nekhludoff to the lawyer, as they entered the waiting-room. "In the plainest possible case they cavil at idle forms. It is awful!"

"The case was spoiled at the trial," said Fanirin.

"Selenin, too, was against reversal. It is awful, awful!" Nekhludoff continued to repeat. "What is to be done now?"

"We will petition the Emperor. Head it yourself while you are here. I will prepare the petition."

At that moment Wolf in his uniform and stars hung on his breast entered the waiting-room and approached Nekhludoff.

"I am sorry, my dear Prince, but the grounds were insufficient," he said, shrugging his narrow shoulders; and, closing his eyes, he proceeded on his way.

After Wolf came Selenin, who had learned from the Senators that Nekhludoff, his former friend, was present.

"I did not expect to meet you here," he said, approaching Nekhludoff and smiling with his lips, while his eyes remained sad.

"And I did not know that you were the Attorney General."

"Associate," Selenin corrected him. "But what brought you to the Senate?"

"I came here hoping to find justice, and to save an innocent woman."

"What woman?"

"The case that has just been decided."

"Oh, the Maslova case!" said Selenin. "An entirely groundless appeal."

"The question is not of the appeal, but of the woman, who is innocent and undergoing punishment."

Selenin sighed.

"Quite possible, but——"

"It is not merely possible, but certain."

"How do you know?"

"I know because I was on the jury. I know wherein we made the mistake."

Selenin became thoughtful.

"It should have been declared on the trial," he said.

"I did so."

"It should have been made part of the record. If that had appeared in the appeal——"

Selenin, who was always busy, and did not mingle in society, had evidently not heard of Nekhludoff's romance. Nekhludoff, however, decided not to speak to him of his relations to Maslova.

"But it is evident even now that the verdict was preposterous," he said.

"The Senate has no right to say so. If the Senate attempted to interfere with the verdicts of the courts upon its own view of the justness of the verdicts themselves, there would be greater risks of justice being miscarried than established," he said, recalling the preceding case. "Besides, the verdicts of juries would lose their significance."

"I only know one thing, and that is that the woman is entirely innocent, and the last hope of saving her from an undeserved punishment is gone. The highest judicial institution has affirmed what was absolutely unjust."

"It has not affirmed because it has not and could not consider the merits of the case," said Selenin, blinking his eyes. "You have probably stopped at your aunts," he added, evidently wishing to change the subject of conversation. "I learned yesterday that you were in St. Petersburg. Countess Catherine Ivanovna had invited me and you to be present at the meeting of the English preacher," said Selenin, smiling only with his lips.

"Yes, I was present, but left with disgust," Nekhludoff said angrily, vexed at Selenin's leading away from the conversation.

"Why should you be disgusted? At all events it is a manifestation of religious feeling, although one-sided and sectarian," said Selenin.

"It is such strange nonsense," said Nekhludoff.

"Well, no. The only strange thing here is that we know so little of the teachings of our church that we receive an exposition of its fundamental dogmas as a new revelation," said Selenin, as though hastening to tell his former friends his new views.

Nekhludoff gazed at Selenin with wonder. Selenin did not lower his eyes, in which there was an expression not only of sadness, but of ill-will.

"But we will discuss it later," said Selenin. "I am coming," he turned to the usher who approached him deferentially. "We must meet again," he added, sighing; "but you can never be found. You will always find me at home at seven. I live on Nadeghinskaia," and he mentioned the number. "It is a long time since we met," he added, again smiling with his lips.

"I will come if I have the time," said Nekhludoff, feeling that the man whom he had once loved was made strange and incomprehensible to him, if not hostile, by this short conversation.

As student Nekhludoff knew Selenin as a dutiful son, a true friend, and, for his years, an educated, worldly man, with great tact, always elegant and handsome, and uncommonly truthful and honest withal. He studied diligently, without any difficulty and without the slightest ostentation, receiving gold medals for his compositions.

He had made it the aim of his young life, not merely by word, but in reality, to serve others, and thought he saw his chance of doing so in government service. Systematically looking over the various activities to which he might devote his energies, he decided that he could be most useful in the legislative department, and entered it. But notwithstanding his most accurate and conscientious attention to his duties, he found nothing in them to satisfy his desire to be useful. His discontent, due to the pettiness and vanity of his immediate superiors, grew until an opportunity offered to enter the Senate. He was better off in the Senate, but the same feeling of dissatisfaction pursued him. He constantly felt that things were not what he expected them to be, and what they should be. During his service in the Senate, his relations obtained for him the post of gentleman of the Emperor's bed-chamber, and he was obliged to drive around in gorgeous uniform to thank various people. In this post he felt even more than before out of place. At the same time, on the one hand, he could not refuse the appointment, because he would not disappoint those who thought they were pleasing him by it, and, on the other hand, the appointment flattered his vanity. It pleased him to see himself in a looking-glass in a gold embroidered uniform, and to receive the tokens of respect shown him by some people on his appointment.

The same thing happened with respect to his marriage. A brilliant match was arranged for him, as it is regarded from the world's standpoint. And he married principally because to refuse would have been to offend and cause pain to the bride and those who had arranged the match. Hence the marriage to a young, pretty, distinguished girl flattered his vanity and gave him pleasure. But the marriage soon turned out to be "not the thing, you know," more so even than Court service. After her first child, his wife did not wish to have any more, and plunged into luxurious social life, in which he was obliged to participate nolens volens. Although this poisoned the life of her husband, and brought her only exertion and fatigue, she nevertheless diligently pursued it. All his efforts to change her mode of life could not alter her confidence, supported by all her relatives and acquaintances, that it was quite proper.

The child, a girl with long, golden curls, was an entire stranger to her father, mainly because she was brought up not in accord with his desires. The result was the customary misunderstanding between the husband and wife, and even in a want of desire to understand each other, and a quiet, silent struggle, hidden from strangers and tempered by propriety, which made Selenin's life at home very burdensome. So that his family life turned out to be "not the thing, you know," in still greater degree than his service or the Court appointment.

These were the reasons why his eyes were always sad. And this was why, seeing Nekhludoff, whom he had known before all these lies had fastened themselves upon him, he thought of himself as he had been then, and more than ever felt the discord between his character and his surroundings, and he became painfully sad. The same feeling came over Nekhludoff, after the first impression of joy at meeting an old friend.

That was why, having promised that they would meet each other, neither sought that meeting, nor had they seen each other on this visit of Nekhludoff to St. Petersburg.

CHAPTER XV.

On leaving the Senate, Nekhludoff and his lawyer walked along the sidewalk. Fanirin told his driver to follow him, and he began to relate to Nekhludoff how the mistress of so-and-so had made millions on 'Change, how so-and-so had sold, and another had bought, his wife. He also related some stories of swindling and all sorts of crimes committed by well-known people who were not occupying cells in prison, but presidents' chairs in various institutions. These stories, of which he seemed to possess an inexhaustible source, afforded the lawyer great pleasure, as showing most conclusively that the means employed by him as a lawyer to make money were perfectly innocent in comparison with those used by the more noted public men of St. Petersburg. And the lawyer was greatly surprised when Nekhludoff, in the middle of one of these stories, hailed a trap, took leave and drove home. Nekhludoff was very sad. He was sad because the Senate's judgment continued the unreasonable suffering of the innocent Maslova, and also because it made it more difficult for him to carry out his unalterable intention of joining his fate to hers. His sadness increased as the lawyer related with so much pleasure the frightful stories of the prevailing wickedness. Besides, the unkind, cold, repelling gaze of the once charming, open-hearted and noble Selenin constantly recurred to his mind. Nekhludoff, after the impressions of his stay in St. Petersburg, was almost in despair of ever reaching any results. All the plans he had laid out in Moskow seemed to him like those youthful dreams which usually end in disappointment. However, he considered it his duty, while in St. Petersburg, to exhaust his resources in endeavoring to fulfill his mission.

Soon after he reached his room, a servant called him upstairs for tea. Mariette, in a multi-colored dress, was sitting beside the Countess, sipping tea. On Nekhludoff's entering the room, Mariette had just dropped some funny, indecent joke. Nekhludoff noticed it by the character of their laughter. The good-natured, mustached Countess Catherine Ivanovna was shaking in all her stout body with laughter, while Mariette, with a particularly mischievous expression, and her energetic and cheerful face somewhat bent to one side, was silently looking at her companion.

"You will be the death of me," said the Countess, in a fit of coughing.

No sooner had Nekhludoff seated himself than Mariette, noticing the serious and slightly displeased expression on his face, immediately changed not only her expression, but her frame of mind. This was with the intention she had in mind since she first saw him—to get him to like her. She suddenly became grave, dissatisfied with her life, seeking something, striving after something. She not merely feigned, but actually induced in herself a state of mind similar to that in which Nekhludoff was, although she would not be able to say what it consisted of. In a sympathetic conversation about the injustice of the strong, the poverty of the people, the awful condition of the prisoners, she succeeded in rousing in him the least expected feeling of physical attraction, and under the din of conversation their eyes plainly queried, "Can you love me?" and they answered, "Yes, I can."

On leaving, she told him that she was always ready to be of service to him, and asked him to visit her at the theatre the next day, if only for a minute, saying that she wished to have a talk with him on a matter of importance.

"When will I see you again?" she added, sighing, and carefully putting the gloves on her ring-bedecked hand. "Tell me that you will come."

Nekhludoff promised to come.

For a long time that night Nekhludoff could not fall asleep. When he recalled Maslova, the decision of the Senate, and his determination to follow her; when he recalled his relinquishment of his right to the land, there suddenly appeared before him, as if in answer to these questions, the face of Mariette; her sigh and glance when she said, "When will I see you again?" and her smile—all so distinct that she seemed to stand before him, and he smiled himself. "Would it be proper for me to follow her to Siberia? And would it be proper to deprive myself of my property?" he asked himself.

And the answers to these questions on that bright St. Petersburg night were indefinite. His mind was all in confusion. He called forth his former trend of thought, but those thoughts had lost their former power of conviction.

"And what if all my ideas are due to an over-wrought imagination, and I should be unable to live up to them? If I should repent of what I have done?" he asked himself, and, being unable to find answers to these questions, he was stricken with such sadness and despair as he had rarely experienced before, and he fell into that deep slumber which had been habitual with him after heavy losses at cards.

CHAPTER XVI.

Nekhludoff's first feeling on rising the following morning was that he had committed something abominable the preceding evening.

He began to recall what had happened. There was nothing abominable; he had done nothing wrong. He had only thought that all his present intentions—that of marrying Katiousha, giving the land to the peasants—artificial, unnatural, and that he must continued to live as he had lived before.

He could recall no wrong act, but he remembered what was worse than a wrong act—there were the bad thoughts in which all bad acts have their origin. Bad acts may not be repeated; one may repent of them, while bad thoughts give birth to bad acts.

A bad act only smooths the way to other bad acts, while bad thoughts irresistibly lead toward them.

Recalling his thoughts of the day before, Nekhludoff wondered how he could have believed them. How so novel and difficult might be that which he intended to do, he knew that it was the only life possible to him now, and that, however easy it might be for him to return to his old mode of life, he knew that that was death, not life. This temptation of the day before was similar to that of a man who, after a night's sound sleep, feels like taking his ease on the soft mattress for a while, although he knows that it is time to be up and away on an important affair.

Nekhludoff would have left the same evening but for his promise to Mariette to visit her at the theatre. Though he knew that it was wrong to do it, he went there, contrary to the dictates of his own conscience, considering himself bound to keep his word. Besides his wish to see Mariette again, he also wished, as he thought, to measure himself against that world lately so near, but now so strange to him.

"Could I withstand these temptations?" he thought, but not with entire sincerity. "I will try it for the last time."

Attired in a dress-coat, he arrived in the theatre where the eternal "Dame aux Camelias" was being played. A French actress was showing in a novel way how consumptive women die.

Nekhludoff was shown to the box occupied by Mariette. In the corridor a liveried servant bowed and opened the door for him.

All the spectators in the circle of boxes—sitting and standing, gray-haired, bald and pomaded heads—were intently following the movements of a slim actress making wry faces and in an unnatural voice reading a monologue. Some one hissed when the door was opened, and two streams of cold and warm air were wafted on Nekhludoff's face.

In the box he found Mariette and a strange lady with a red mantle over her shoulders and high head-dress, and two men—a general, Mariette's husband, a handsome, tall man with a high, artificial, military breast, and a flaxen haired, bald-headed man with shaved chin and solemn side-whiskers. Mariette, graceful, slim, elegant, decolette, with her strong, muscular shoulders sloping down from the neck, at the jointure of which was a darkening little mole, immediately turned around, and, pointing with her fan to a chair behind her, greeted him with a welcome, grateful, and, as it seemed to Nekhludoff, significant smile. Her husband calmly, as was

286

his wont, looked at Nekhludoff and bowed his head. In the glance which he exchanged with his wife, as in everything else, he looked the master, the owner, of a beautiful woman.

There was a thunder of applause when the monologue ended. Mariette rose, and, holding in one hand her rustling silk skirt, walked to the rear of the box and introduced Nekhludoff to her husband. The general incessantly smiled with his eyes, said he was glad, and remained calm and mute.

"I had to leave to-day, but I promised you," said Nekhludoff, turning to Mariette.

"If you don't wish to see me, you will see a remarkable actress," Mariette said, answering the meaning of his words. "Wasn't she great in the last scene?" she turned to her husband.

The general bowed his head.

"That does not affect me," said Nekhludoff. "I have seen so much real misfortune to-day that——"

"Sit down and tell us what you have seen."

The husband listened, and ironically smiled with his eyes.

"I went to see that woman who has been released. She is entirely broken down."

"That is the woman of whom I have spoken to you," Mariette said to her husband.

"Yes; I was very glad that she could be released," he calmly said, nodding his head and smiling ironically, as it seemed to Nekhludoff, under his mustache. "I will go to the smoking-room."

Nekhludoff waited, expecting that Mariette would tell him that something which she said she had to tell him, but instead she only jested and talked of the performance, which, she thought, ought to affect him particularly.

Nekhludoff understood that the only purpose for which she had brought him to the theatre was to display her evening toilet with her shoulders and mole, and he was both pleased and disgusted. Now he saw what was under the veil of the charm that at first attracted him. Looking on Mariette, he admired her, but he knew that she was a prevaricator who was living with her career-making husband; that what she had said the other day was untrue, and that she only wished—and neither knew why—to make him love her. And, as has been said, he was both pleased and disgusted. Several times he attempted to leave, took his hat but still remained. But finally, when the general, his thick mustache reeking with tobacco, returned to the box and glanced at Nekhludoff patronizingly disdainful, as if he did not recognize him, Nekhludoff walked out before the door closed behind the general, and, finding his overcoat, left the theatre.

On his way home he suddenly noticed before him a tall, well-built, loudly-dressed woman. Every passer-by turned to look at her. Nekhludoff walked quicker than the woman, and also involuntarily looked her in the face. Her face, probably rouged, was pretty; her eyes flashed at him, and she smiled. Nekhludoff involuntarily thought of Mariette, for he experienced the same feeling of attraction and disgust which took hold of him in the theatre. Passing her hastily, Nekhludoff turned the corner of the street, and, to the surprise of the policeman, began to walk up and down the water-front.

"That one in the theatre also smiled that way when I entered," he thought, "and the smile of the former conveyed the same meaning as that of the latter. The only difference between them is that this one speaks openly and plainly, while the other pretends to be exercising higher and refined feelings. But in reality they are alike. This one is at least truthful, while the other is lying." Nekhludoff recalled his relations with the wife of the district commander, and a flood of shameful recollections came upon him. "There is a disgusting bestiality in man," he thought; "but when it is in a primitive state, one looks down upon and despises it, whether he is carried away with or withstands it. But when this same bestiality hides itself under a so-called aesthetic, poetic cover, and demands to be worshiped, then, deifying the beast, one gives himself up to it, without distinguishing between the good and the bad. Then it is horrible."

As there was no soothing, rest-giving darkness that night, but instead there was a hazy, cheerless, unnatural light, so even was there no rest-giving darkness—ignorance—for Nekhludoff's soul. Everything was clear. It was plain that all that is considered important and useful is really insignificant and wicked, and that all that splendor and luxury were hiding old crimes, familiar to every one, and not only stalking unpunished, but triumphing and adorned with all the allurements man is capable of conceiving.

Nekhludoff wished to forget it, not to see it, but he could no longer help seeing it. Although he did not see the source of the light which revealed these things to him, as he did not see the source of the light which spread over St. Petersburg, and though this light seemed to him hazy, cheerless and unnatural, he could not help seeing that which the light revealed to him, and he felt at the same time both joy and alarm.

CHAPTER XVII.

Immediately upon his arrival in Moskow, Nekhludoff made his way to the prison hospital, intending to make known to Maslova the Senate's decision and to tell her to prepare for the journey to Siberia.

Of the petition which he brought for Maslova's signature, he had little hope. And, strange to say, he no longer wished to succeed. He had accustomed himself to the thought of going to Siberia, and living among the exiles and convicts, and it was difficult for him to imagine how he should order his life and that of Maslova if she were freed.

The door-keeper at the hospital, recognizing Nekhludoff, immediately informed him that Maslova was no longer there.

"Where is she, then?"

"Why, again in the prison."

"Why was she transferred?" asked Nekhludoff.

"Your Excellency knows their kind," said the door-keeper, with a contemptuous smile. "She was making love to the assistant, so the chief physician sent her back."

Nekhludoff did not suspect that Maslova and her spiritual condition were so close to him. This news stunned him. The feeling he experienced was akin to that which people experience when hearing suddenly of some great misfortune. He was deeply grieved. The first feeling he experienced was that of shame. His joyful portraying of her spiritual awakening now seemed to him ridiculous. Her reluctance to accept his sacrifice, the reproaches and the tears, were the mere cunning, he thought, of a dissolute woman who wished to make the most use of him. It seemed to him now that at his last visit he had seen in her the symptoms of incorrigibility which were now evident. All this flashed through his mind at the time he instinctively donned his hat and left the hospital.

"But what's to be done now?" he asked himself. "Am I bound to her? Am I not released now by this, her act?"

But no sooner did he form the question than he understood that in considering himself released and leaving her to her fate he would be punishing not her, which he desired, but himself, and he was terrified.

"No! That will not alter my decision—it will only strengthen it. Let her do whatever her soul prompts her to do; if she would make love to the assistant, let her do so. It is her business. It is my business to do what my conscience demands," he said to himself. "And my conscience demands that I sacrifice my liberty in expiation of my sin, and my decision to marry her, although but fictitiously, and follow her wherever she may be sent, remains unaltered," he said to himself, with spiteful obstinacy, and, leaving the hospital, he made his way with resolute step to the prison gate.

Coming to the gate, he asked the officer on duty to tell the inspector that he wished to see Maslova. The officer knew Nekhludoff, and told him an important piece of prison news. The captain had resigned, and another man, who was very strict, had taken his place.

The inspector, who was in the prison at the time, soon made his appearance. He was tall, bony, very slow in his movements, and gloomy.

"Visitors are allowed only on certain days," he said, without looking at

Nekhludoff.

"But I have a petition here which she must sign."

"You may give it to me."

"I must see the prisoner myself. I was always permitted to see her before."

"That was before," said the inspector, glancing at Nekhludoff.

"I have a pass from the Governor," Nekhludoff insisted, producing his pocket-book.

"Let me see it," said the inspector, without looking in Nekhludoff's eyes, and taking the document with his skinny, long, white hand, on the index finger of which there was a gold ring, he slowly read it. "Walk into the office, please," he said.

On this occasion there was no one in the office. The inspector seated himself at the table, looking through the papers that lay on it, evidently intending to stay through the meeting. When Nekhludoff asked him if Bogodukhovskaia could be seen, he answered: "Visiting the politicals is not allowed," and again buried his head in the papers.

When Maslova entered the room, the inspector raised his eyes, and, without looking either at Maslova or Nekhludoff, said: "You may go ahead," and continued to busy himself with his papers.

Maslova was again dressed in a white skirt, waist and 'kerchief. Coming near Nekhludoff and seeing his cold, angry face, her own turned a purple color, and, with downcast eyes, she began to pick a corner of her waist. Her confusion Nekhludoff considered as confirmation of the hospital porter's words.

So abhorent was she to him now that he could not extend his hand to her, as he desired.

"I bring you bad news," he said in an even voice, without looking at her. "The Senate affirmed the verdict."

"I knew it would be so," she said in a strange voice, as if choking.

If it had happened before, Nekhludoff would have asked her why she knew it; now he only looked at her. Her eyes were filled with tears, but this not only did not soften him, but made him even more inflamed against her.

The inspector rose and began to walk up and down the room.

Notwithstanding the abhorence Nekhludoff felt for Maslova, he thought it proper to express his regret at the Senate's action.

"Do not despair," he said. "This petition may be more successful, and I hope that——"

"Oh, it is not that," she said, looking at him with the tearful and squinting eyes.

"What, then?"

"You have been in the hospital, and they must have told you there about me."

"What of it? That is your business," frowning, Nekhludoff said with indifference. The cruel feeling of offended pride rose in him with greater force at her mention of the hospital. "I, a man of the world, whom any girl of the upper class would be only too happy to marry, offered to become the husband of that woman, and she could not wait, but made love to the assistant surgeon," he thought, looking at her with hatred.

"Sign this petition," he said, and, taking from his pocket a large envelope, placed it on the table. She wiped her tears with a corner of her 'kerchief, seated herself at the table, and asked him where to sign.

He showed her where, and she, seating herself, smoothed with her left hand the sleeve of the right. He stood over her, silently looking at her back bent over the table, and now and then shaking from the sobs she tried to suppress, and his soul was convulsed by a struggle between good and evil, between offended pride and pity for her sufferings. The feeling of pity conquered.

Whether it was the feeling of pity that first asserted itself, or the recollection of his own deeds of the same character for which he reproached her, he scarcely knew, but suddenly he felt himself guilty and pitied her.

Having signed the petition and wiped her soiled fingers on her skirt, she rose and glanced at him.

"Whatever the result, and no matter what happens, I shall keep my word," said Nekhludoff.

The thought that he was forgiving her strengthened in him the feeling of pity and tenderness for her, and he wished to console her.

"I will do what I said. I will be with you wherever you may be."

"That's no use," she hastened to say, and her face became radiant.

"Make note of what you need for the road."

"Nothing particular, I think. Thank you."

The inspector approached them, and Nekhludoff, without waiting to be told that the time was up, took leave of her, experiencing a new feeling of quiet happiness, calmness and love for all mankind. It was the consciousness that no act of Maslova could alter his love for her that raised his spirit and made him feel happy. Let her make love to the assistant—that was her business. He loved her not for himself, but for her and for God.

The love-making for which Maslova was expelled from the hospital, and to which Nekhludoff gave credence, consisted only in that, when Maslova, coming to the drug department for some pectoral herbs, prescribed by her superior, she found there an assistant, named Ustinoff. This Ustinoff had been pursuing her with his attentions for a long time, and as he tried to embrace her she pushed him away with such force that he struck the shelving, and two bottles came crashing to the floor.

The chief physician was passing at the time, and, hearing the sound of the breaking glass, and seeing Maslova running out, all flushed, he angrily shouted to her:

"Well, girl, if you begin to flirt here, I will send you back. What is the matter?" he turned to the assistant, sternly looking over his spectacles.

The assistant, smiling, began to apologize. The doctor, without hearing him to the last, raised his head so that he began to look through the glasses, and walked into the ward. On the same day he asked the inspector to send a more sedate nurse in place of Maslova. Maslova's expulsion from the hospital on the ground of flirting was particularly painful to her by reason of the fact that, after her meeting with Nekhludoff, all association with men, which had been so repugnant to her, became even more disgusting.

The fact that, judging her by her past and present condition, everybody, including the pimpled assistant, thought that they had the right to insult her, and were surprised when she refused their attentions, was very painful to her and called forth her tears and pity for herself. Now, coming out to see Nekhludoff, she wished to explain the injustice of the charge which he had probably heard. But as she attempted to do so, she felt that he would not believe her; that her explanation would only tend to corroborate the suspicion, and her tears welled up in her throat, and she became silent.

Maslova was still thinking, and continued to assure herself that, as she had told him on his second visit, she had not forgiven him; that she hated him, but, in reality, she had long since begun to love him again, and loved him so that she involuntarily carried out his wishes. She ceased to drink and smoke, she gave up flirting, and willingly went as servant to the hospital. All this she did because she knew he wished it. Her repeated refusal to accept his sacrifice was partly due to the fact that she wished to repeat those proud words which she had once told him, and mainly because she knew that their marriage would make him unhappy. She was firmly resolved not to accept his sacrifice, and yet it was painful for her to think that he despised her; that he thought her to be the same as she had been, and did not see the change she was undergoing. The fact that he was at that moment thinking that she did something wrong in the hospital pained her more than the news that she was finally sentenced to hard labor.

CHAPTER XVIII.

Maslova might be sent away with the first party of exiles; hence Nekhludoff was preparing for departure. But he had so many things to attend to that he felt that he could never get through with them, no matter how much time there might be left for preparations. It was different in former times. Then it was necessary to devise something to do, and the interest in all his affairs centered in Dmitri Ivanovich Nekhludoff. But though all interest in life centered in Dmitri Ivanovich, he always suffered from ennui. Now, however, all his affairs related to people other than Dmitri Ivanovich, and were all interesting and attractive, as well as inexhaustible.

Besides, formerly the occupation with the affairs of Dmitri Ivanovich always caused vexation and irritation; while these affairs of others for the most part put him in a happy mood.

Nekhludoff's affairs were now divided into three parts. He himself, in his habitual pedantism, thus divided them, and according placed them in three different portfolios.

The first was that of Maslova. This consisted in efforts to obtain a successful result in the pending petition, and preparations for departure to Siberia.

The second part related to the settlement of his estates. The Panov land was granted to the peasants on condition of their paying a rent to be used for common necessities. But, in order to complete that arrangement, it was necessary to sign an agreement and also make his will. The arrangement made for the Kusminskoie estate was to remain in force, only there remained to be determined what part of the rent he was to appropriate to himself, and what was to be left for the benefit of the peasants. Without knowing what his necessary disbursements would be on his trip to Siberia, he could not make up his mind to deprive himself of his income, although he reduced it by one-half.

The third part related to aid to prisoners, who were now applying to him more and more frequently.

At first, when written to for aid, he proceeded immediately to intercede for the applicants, endeavoring to relieve their condition, but in the end their number became so great that he found it impossible to help every one, and was involuntarily brought to a fourth matter, which had of late occupied him more than either of the others.

His fourth concern consisted in solving the question, Why, how and whence came that remarkable institution called the Criminal Court, to which was due the existence of that prison, with the inmates of which he had become somewhat familiar, and all those places of confinement, beginning with the fortress dedicated to two saints, Peter and Paul, and ending with the island of Saghalin, where hundreds and thousands of victims of that wonderful criminal law were languishing?

From personal contact with prisoners, and from information received from the lawyer, the prison chaplain, the inspector, and from the prison register, Nekhludoff came to the conclusion that the prisoners, so-called criminals, could be divided into five classes. The first class consisted of people entirely innocent, victims of judicial mistakes, such as that would-be incendiary, Menshov, or Maslova, and others. There were comparatively few people of this class, according to the observations of the chaplain—about seven per cent.—but their condition attracted particular attention. The second class consisted of people convicted for offenses committed under exceptional circumstances, such as anger, jealousy, drunkenness, etc.—offenses which, under similar circumstances, would almost invariably have been committed by all those who judged and punished them. This class made up, according to Nekhludoff's observations, more than one-half of all the prisoners. To the third class belonged those who committed, according to their own ideas, the most indifferent or even good acts, but which were considered criminal by people—entire strangers to them—who were making the laws. To this class belonged all those who carried on a secret trade in wine, or were bringing in contraband goods, or were picking herbs, or gathering wood, in private or government forests. To this class also belonged the predatory mountaineers.

The fourth class consisted of people who, according to Nekhludoff, were reckoned among the criminals only because they were morally above the average level of society. Among these the percentage of those who resisted interference with their affairs, or were sentenced for resisting the authorities, was very large.

The fifth class, finally, was composed of people who were more sinned against by society than they sinned themselves. These were the helpless people, blunted by constant oppression and temptation, like that boy with the mats, and hundreds of others whom Nekhludoff saw both in and out of prison, and the conditions of those whose lives systematically drove them to the necessity of committing those acts which are called crimes. To these people belonged, according to Nekhludoff's observations, many thieves and murderers, with some of whom Nekhludoff had come in contact. Among these Nekhludoff found, on close acquaintance, those spoiled and depraved people whom the new school calls the criminal type, and the existence of which in society is given as the reason for the necessity of criminal law and punishment. These so-called depraved types, deviating from the normal, were, according to Nekhludoff, none other than those very people who have sinned less against society than society has sinned against them, and against whom society has sinned, not directly, but through their ancestors.

Nekhludoff's attention was attracted by a habitual thief, Okhotin, who came under this head. He was the son of a fallen woman; had grown up in lodging-houses, and till the age of thirty had never met a moral man. In childhood he had fallen in with a gang of thieves, but he possessed a humorous vein which attracted people to him. While asking Nekhludoff for aid he jested at himself, the judges, the prison and all the laws, not only criminal, but even divine. There was also a fine-looking man, Fedorff, who, in company with a gang of which he was the leader, had killed and robbed an old official. This one was a peasant whose father's house had been illegally taken from him, and who, while in the army, suffered for falling in love with an officer's mistress. He was attractive and passionate. His sole desire in life was to enjoy himself, and he had never met any people who, out of any consideration, tempered their passions, nor had he ever heard that there was any other aim in life than personal enjoyment. It was plain to Nekhludoff that these two were richly endowed by nature, and were only neglected and mutilated as plants are sometimes neglected and mutilated. He also came across a vagabond, and a woman, whose stupidity and apparent cruelty were repulsive, but he failed to find in them that criminal type spoken of by the Italian school. He only saw in them people who were disagreeable to him personally, like some he had met in dress-coats, uniforms, and laces.

297

Thus the investigation of the question: Why are people of such great variety of character confined in prisons, while others, no different than those, enjoy freedom and even judge those people? was the fourth concern of Nekhludoff.

At first he hoped to find an answer to this question in books, and bought every book bearing on the subject. He bought the works of Lombroso, Garofalo, Ferri, Mandsley and Tard, and read them carefully. But the more he read them, the greater was his disappointment. The same thing happened with him that happens with people who appeal to science with direct, simple, vital questions, and not with a view of playing the part of an expounder, writer or teacher in it. Science solved a thousand and one various abstruse, complicated questions bearing on criminal law, but failed to give an answer to the question he had formed. His question was very simple: Why and by what right do some people confine, torture, exile, flog and kill other people no different than they are themselves? And in answer they argued the questions: Whether or not man is a free agent? Can a criminal be distinguished by the measurements of his cranium? To what extent is crime due to heredity? What is morality? What is insanity? What is degeneracy? What is temperament? How does climate, food, ignorance, emulation, hypnotism, passion affect crime? What is society? What are its duties? etc., etc.

These arguments reminded Nekhludoff of an answer he had once received from a schoolboy. He asked the boy whether he had learned the declension of nouns. "Yes," answered the boy. "Well, then decline 'Paw.'" "What paw? A dog's paw?" the boy answered, with a sly expression on his face. Similar answers in the form of questions Nekhludoff found in scientific books to his one basic question.

He found there many wise, learned and interesting things, but there was no answer to his principal question: By what right do some people punish others? Not only was there no answer, but all reasoning tended to explain and justify punishment, the necessity of which was considered an axiom. Nekhludoff read much, but only by fits and starts, and the want of an answer he ascribed to such superficial reading. He, therefore, refused to believe in the justice of the answer which constantly occurred to him.

CHAPTER XIX.

The deportation of the party of convicts to which Maslova belonged was set for the fifth of July, and Nekhludoff was prepared to follow her on that day. The day before his departure his sister, with her husband, arrived in town to see him.

Nekhludoff's sister, Natalie Ivanovna Ragojhinsky, was ten years his senior. He had grown up partly under her influence. She loved him when he was a boy, and before her marriage they treated each other as equals; she was twenty-five and he was fifteen. She had been in love then with his deceased friend, Nikolenka Irtenieff. They both loved Nikolenka, and loved in him and in themselves the good that was in them, and which unifies all people.

Since that time they had both became corrupted—he by the bad life he was leading; she by her marriage to a man whom she loved sensually, but who not only did not love all that which she and Dimitri at one time considered most holy and precious, but did not even understand it, and all those aspirations to moral perfection and to serving others, to which she had once devoted herself, he ascribed to selfishness and a desire to show off before people.

Ragojhinsky was a man without reputation or fortune, but a clever fortune hunter, who, by skillful manœuvering between liberalism and conservatism, availing himself of that dominating tendency which promised bitter results in life, but principally by something peculiar which attracted women to him, he succeeded in making a relatively brilliant judicial career. He was already past his youth when he met Nekhludoff abroad, made Natalie, who was also not very young, to fall in love with him, and married her almost against the wish of her mother, who said that it would be a mésalliance. Nekhludoff, although he concealed it from himself and struggled against the feeling, hated his brother-in-law. He disliked his vulgar feelings, his self-confident narrowness of mind, but, principally, because of his sister, who should so passionately, egotistically and sensually love such a poor nature, and to please whom she should stifle all her noble sentiments. It was always painful to Nekhludoff to think of Natalie as the wife of that hairy, self-confident man, with shining bald head. He could not even suppress his aversion to his children. And whenever he heard that she was about to become a mother, he experienced a feeling of compassion for her being again infected with something bad by the man who was so unlike all of them.

The Ragojhinskys arrived without their children, and engaged the best suite in the best hotel. Natalie Ivanovna immediately went to the old home of her mother, and learning there that her brother had moved to furnished rooms, she went to his new home. The dirty servant, meeting her in the dark, ill-smelling corridor, which was lit up by a lamp during the day, announced that the Prince was away.

Desiring to leave a note, Natalie Ivanovna was shown into his apartments. She closely examined the two small rooms. She noticed in every corner the familiar cleanliness and order, and she was struck by the modesty of the appointments. On the writing table she saw a familiar paper-press, with the bronze figure of a dog, neatly arranged portfolios, papers, volumes of the Criminal Code and an English book of Henry George, and a French one by Tard, between the leaves of which was an ivory paper knife.

She left a note asking him to call on her the same evening, and, shaking her head in wonder at what she had seen, returned to her hotel.

There were two questions relating to her brother that interested Natalie Ivanovna—his marriage to Katiousha, of which she had heard in her city, where it was a matter of common gossip, and the distribution by him of his land to the peasants, upon which some people looked as something political and dangerous. From one point of view, she rather liked the idea of his marrying Katiousha. She admired his resolution, seeing in it herself and him as they had been before her marriage. At the same time, she was horror-stricken at the thought that her brother was to marry such an awful woman. The latter feeling was the stronger, and she decided to dissuade him from marrying her, although she knew how hard that would be.

The other affair, that of his parting with his land, she did not take so close to heart, but her husband was indignant at such folly, and demanded that she influence her brother to abandon the attempt. Ignatius Nikiforovitch said that it was the height of inconsistency, foolhardiness and pride; that such an act could only be explained, if at all, by a desire to be odd, to have something to brag about, and to make people talk about one's self.

"What sense is there in giving the land to the peasants and making them pay rent to themselves?" he said. "If his mind was set on doing it, he could sell them the land through the bank. There would be some sense in that. Taking all in all, his act is very eccentric," said Ignatius Nikiforovitch, already considering the necessity of a guardianship, and he demanded that his wife should seriously speak to her brother of this, his strange intention.

CHAPTER XX.

In the evening Nekhludoff went to his sister. Ignatius Nikiforovitch was resting in another room, and Natalie Ivanovna alone met him. She wore a tight-fitting black silk dress, with a knot of red ribbon, and her hair was done up according to the latest fashion. She was evidently making herself look young for her husband. Seeing her brother, she quickly rose from the divan, and, rustling with her silk skirt, she went out to meet him. They kissed and, smiling, looked at each other. There was an exchange of those mysterious, significant glances in which everything was truth; then followed an exchange of words in which that truth was lacking. They had not met since the death of their mother.

"You have grown stout and young," he said.

Her lips contracted with pleasure.

"And you have grown thin."

"Well, how is Ignatius Nikiforovitch?" asked Nekhludoff.

"He is resting. He has not slept all night."

A great deal should have been said here, but their words said nothing, and their glances said that that which interested them most was left unsaid.

"I have been at your lodging."

"Yes, I know it. I have moved from the house. I am so lonely and

301

weary. I do not need any of those things, so you take them—the furniture—everything."

"Yes, Agrippina Petrovna told me. I have been there. I thank you very much. But——"

At that moment the servant brought in a silver tea service. Natalie Ivanovna busied herself with making the tea. Nekhludoff was silent.

"Well, Dimitri, I know everything," Natalie said, resolutely, glancing at him.

"I am very glad that you know."

"Do you think it possible to reform her after such a life?"

He was sitting erect on a small chair, attentively listening to her, prepared to answer satisfactorily her every question. He was still in that frame of mind which, after his last meeting with Maslova, filled his soul with tranquil happiness and love for all mankind.

"It is not her that I intend to reform, but myself," he answered.

Natalie Ivanovna sighed.

"There are other means besides marriage."

"And I think that that is the best. Besides, that will bring me into that world in which I can be useful."

"I do not think," said Natalie Ivanovna, "that you could be happy."

"It is not a question of my happiness."

"Of course; but if she possesses a heart, she cannot be happy—she cannot even desire it."

"She does not."

"I understand, but life—demands something different."

"Life only demands that we do what is right," said Nekhludoff, looking

302

at her face, still beautiful, although covered with fine wrinkles around the eyes and mouth.

"Poor dear! How she has changed!" thought Nekhludoff, recalling Natalie as she had been before her marriage, and a tender feeling, woven of countless recollections of their childhood, rose in his breast toward her.

At that moment Ignatius Nikiforovitch, as usual holding his head high and projecting his broad chest, entered the room, with shining eye-glasses, bald head and black beard.

"How do you do? How do you do?" he greeted Nekhludoff, unnaturally accentuating his words.

They pressed each other's hand, and Ignatius Nikiforovitch lowered himself into an arm-chair.

"Am I disturbing you?"

"No, I do not conceal anything I say or do from anybody."

As soon as Nekhludoff saw that face, those hairy hands and heard that patronizing tone, his gentle disposition immediately disappeared.

"Yes, we have been speaking about his intention," said Natalie Ivanovna. "Shall I pour out some tea for you?" she added, taking the tea-pot.

"Yes, if you please. What intention do you refer to?"

"My intention of going to Siberia with that party of convicts, among whom there is a woman I have wronged," said Nekhludoff.

"I heard that you intended more than that."

"Yes, and marry her, if she only desires it."

"I see! And may I ask you to explain your motives, if it is not unpleasant to you? I do not understand them."

"My motives are that that woman—that the first step on her downward career——" Nekhludoff became angry because he could not find the proper expression. "My motives are that I am guilty, while she is punished."

"If she is punished, then she is also, probably, guilty."

"She is perfectly innocent."

And, with unnecessary agitation, Nekhludoff related the whole case.

"Yes, that was an omission by the presiding justice. But in such cases there is the Senate."

"The Senate sustained the verdict."

"Ah, then there were no grounds of appeal," said Ignatius Nikiforovitch, evidently sharing the well-known opinion that truth is the product of court proceedings. "The Senate cannot go into the merits of a case. But if there is really a judicial error, a petition should be made to the Emperor."

"That was done, but there is no chance of success. Inquiries will be made at the Ministry, which will refer them to the Senate, and the Senate will repeat its decision, and, as usual, the innocent will be punished."

"In the first place, the Ministry will not refer to the Senate," and Ignatius Nikiforovitch smiled condescendingly, "but will call for all the documents in the case, and, if it finds an error, will so decide. In the second place, an innocent person is never, or, at least, very seldom punished. Only the guilty is punished."

"And I am convinced that the contrary is true," said Nekhludoff, with an unkind feeling toward his brother-in-law. "I am convinced that the majority of the people convicted by courts are innocent."

"How so?"

"They are innocent in the ordinary sense of the word, as that woman was innocent of poisoning; as that peasant is innocent of the murder which he has not committed; as that mother and son are innocent of the arson which was committed by the owner himself, and for which they came near being convicted."

"Of course, there always have been and always will be judicial errors.

Human institutions cannot be perfect."

"And, then, a large part of the innocent, because they have been brought up amid certain conditions, do not consider the acts committed by them criminal."

"Pardon me; that is unfair. Every thief knows that stealing is wrong; that theft is immoral," Ignatius Nikiforovitch said, with the calm, self-confident, and, at the same time, somewhat contemptuous, smile which particularly provoked Nekhludoff.

"No, he does not know. He is told not to steal, but he sees and knows that the employers steal his labor, keep back his pay, and that the officials are constantly robbing him."

"That is anarchism," Ignatius calmly defined the meaning of his brother-in-law's words.

"I do not know what it is, but I am speaking of facts," Nekhludoff continued. "He knows that the officials are robbing him. He knows that we, the landlords, own the land which ought to be common property, and when he gathers some twigs for his oven we send him to jail and try to convince him that he is a thief."

"I do not understand, and if I do, I cannot agree with you. The land cannot be nobody's property. If you divide it," Ignatius Nikiforovitch began, being fully convinced that Nekhludoff was a socialist, and that the theory of socialism demands that all the land should be divided equally; that such division is foolish, and that he can easily refute it. "If you should divide the land to-day, giving each inhabitant an equal share, to-morrow it will again find its way into the hands of the more industrious and able among them——"

"Nobody even thinks of dividing the land into equal shares. There ought to be no property in land, and it ought not to be the subject of purchase and sale or renting."

"The right of property is a natural right. Without property right there would be no interest in cultivating the land. Destroy property right and we will return to the condition of the savage," authoritatively said Ignatius Nikiforovitch.

"On the contrary, only then will land not lie idle, as it is now."

"But, Dimitri Ivanovich, it is perfect madness! Is it possible in our time to destroy property in land? I know it is your old hobby. But permit me to tell you plainly——" Ignatius Nikiforovitch turned pale and his voice trembled. The question was evidently of particular concern to him. "I would advise you to consider that question well before attempting its practical solution."

"You are speaking of my personal affairs?"

"Yes. I assume that we are all placed in a certain position, and must assume the duties that result from that position, must support those conditions of existence into which we were born, which we have inherited from our forefathers, and which we must hand over to our posterity."

"I consider it my duty——"

"Excuse me," continued Ignatius Nikiforovitch, who would not be interrupted. "I am not speaking of myself and my children. The fortune of my children is secure, and I earn enough to live in easy circumstances, and, therefore, my protest against your, permit me to say, ill-considered actions is not based on personal interest, but on principle. And I would advise you to give it a little more thought, to read——"

"You had better let me decide my own affairs. I think I know what to read and what not to read," said Nekhludoff, turning pale, and, feeling that he could not control himself, became silent and began to drink his tea.

CHAPTER XXI.

"Well, how are the children?" Nekhludoff asked his sister, having calmed down.

Thus the unpleasant conversation was changed. Natalie became calm and talked about her children. She would not speak, however, about those things which only her brother understood in the presence of her husband,

and in order to continue the conversation she began to talk of the latest news, the killing of Kanesky in the duel.

Ignatius Nikiforovitch expressed his disapproval of the condition of things which excluded the killing in a duel from the category of crimes.

His remark called forth Nekhludoff's reply, and a hot discussion followed on the same subject, neither expressing fully his opinion, and in the end they were again at loggerheads.

Ignatius Nikiforovitch felt that Nekhludoff condemned him, hating all his activity, and he wished to prove the injustice of his reasoning. Nekhludoff, on the other hand, to say nothing of the vexation caused him by his brother-in-law's interference in his affairs (in the depth of his soul he felt that his brother-in-law, his sister and their children, as heirs, had the right to do so), was indignant at the calm and confident manner of that narrow-minded man who continued to consider legal and just that which to Nekhludoff was undoubtedly foolish. This self-confidence irritated him.

"What should the court do?" asked Nekhludoff.

"Sentence one of the duelists, as it would a common murderer, to hard labor."

Nekhludoff's hands again turned cold, and he continued with warmth:

"Well, what would be then?"

"Justice would be done."

"As if the aim of courts was to do justice!" said Nekhludoff.

"What else?"

"Their aim is to support class interests. Courts, according to my idea, are only instruments for the perpetuation of conditions profitable to our class."

"That is an entirely new view," said Ignatius Nikiforovitch, smiling calmly. "Usually somewhat different aims are ascribed to courts."

"In theory, but not in practice, as I have learned. The only aim of the courts is to preserve the existing state of things, and for this reason they persecute and kill all those who are above the common level and who wish to raise it as well as those who are below it."

"I cannot agree with the view that criminals are executed because they are above the level of the average. For the most part they are the excrescence of society, just as perverted, though in a different manner, as are those criminal types whom you consider below the level of the average."

"And I know people who are far above their judges."

But Ignatius Nikiforovitch, not accustomed to being interrupted when speaking, did not listen to Nekhludoff, which was particularly irritating to the latter, and continued to talk while Nekhludoff was talking.

"I cannot agree with you that the aim of courts is to support the existing order of things. The courts have their aims: either the correction——"

"Prisons are great places for correction," Nekhludoff put in.

"Or the removal," persistently continued Ignatius Nikiforovitch, "of those depraved and savage people who threaten the existence of society."

"That is just where the trouble is. Courts can do neither the one nor the other. Society has no means of doing it."

"How is that? I don't understand——" asked Ignatius Nikiforovitch, with a forced smile.

"I mean to say that there are only two sensible modes of punishment—those that have been used in olden times: corporal punishment and capital punishment. But with the advance of civilization they have gone out of existence."

"That is both new and surprising to hear from you."

"Yes, there is sense in inflicting pain on a man that he might not repeat that for which the pain was inflicted; and it is perfectly sensible to cut the head off a harmful and dangerous member of society. But what sense is there in imprisoning a man, who is depraved by idleness and bad example, and keeping him in secure and compulsory idleness in the society of the most depraved people? Or to transport him, for some reason, at an expense to the government of five hundred roubles, from the District of Tula to the District of Irkutsk, or from Kursk——"

"But people seem to fear these journeys at government expense. And were it not for these journeys, we would not be sitting here as we are sitting now."

"Prisons cannot secure our safety, because people are not imprisoned for life, but are released. On the contrary, these institutions are the greatest breeders of vice and corruption—i. e., they increase the danger."

"You mean to say that the penitentiary system ought to be perfected?"

"It cannot be perfected. Perfected prisons would cost more than is spent on popular education and would be a new burden on the populace."

"But the deficiencies of the penitentiary system do not invalidate the judicial system," Ignatius Nikiforovitch again continued, without listening to his brother-in-law.

"These deficiencies cannot be corrected," said Nekhludoff, raising his voice.

"What then? Would you kill? Or, as a certain statesman suggested, pluck out their eyes?" said Ignatius Nikiforovitch, smiling triumphantly.

"Yes; that would be cruel, but expedient. What we are doing now is both cruel and inexpedient."

"And I am taking part in it," said Ignatius Nikiforovitch, paling.

"That is your business. But I do not understand it."

"I think there are many things you do not understand," said Ignatius Nikiforovitch, with a quiver in his voice.

"I saw a public prosecutor in court trying his utmost to convict an unfortunate boy, who could only arouse compassion in any unperverted man——"

"If I thought so, I should give up my position," said Ignatius Nikiforovitch, rising.

Nekhludoff noticed a peculiar glitter under his brother-in-law's eye-glasses. "Can it be tears?" thought Nekhludoff. They really were tears. Ignatius Nikiforovitch was offended. Going toward the window, he drew a handkerchief from his pocket, coughed, and began to wipe his eye-glasses, and, removing them, he also wiped his eyes. Returning to the couch, Ignatius Nikiforovitch lit a cigar and spoke no more. Nekhludoff was pained and ashamed at the grief that he had caused his brother-in-law and sister, especially as he was leaving the next day and would not see them again. In great agitation he took leave of them and departed.

"It is quite possible that what I said was true. At any rate, he did not refute me. But it was wrong to speak that way. Little have I changed if I could insult him and grieve poor Natalie," he thought.

CHAPTER XXII.

The party of convicts, which included Maslova, was to leave on the three o'clock train, and in order to see them coming out of the prison and follow them to the railroad station Nekhludoff decided to get to the prison before twelve.

While packing his clothes and papers, Nekhludoff came across his diary and began to read the entry he had made before leaving for St. Petersburg. "Katiusha does not desire my sacrifice, but is willing to sacrifice herself," it ran. "She has conquered, and I have conquered. I am rejoicing at that inner change which she seems to me to be undergoing. I fear to believe it, but it appears to me that she is awakening." Immediately after this was the following entry: "I have lived through a very painful and very joyous experience. I was told that she had misbehaved in the hospital. It was very painful to hear it. Did not think it would so affect me. Have spoken to her with contempt and hatred, but suddenly remembered how often I myself have been guilty— am even now, although only in thought, of that for which I hated her, and suddenly I was seized with disgust for myself and pity for her, and I became very joyful. If we would only see in time the beam in our own eye, how much kinder we would be." Then he made the following entry for the day: "Have seen Katiusha, and, because of my self-content, was unkind and angry, and departed with a feeling of oppression. But what can I do? A new life begins to-morrow. Farewell to the old life! My mind is filled with numberless impressions, but I cannot yet reduce them to order."

On awakening the following morning, Nekhludoff's first feeling was one of sorrow for the unpleasant incident with his brother-in-law.

"I must go to see them," he thought, "and smooth it over."

But, looking at the clock, he saw that there was no time left, and that he must hasten to the prison to see the departure of the convicts. Hastily packing up his things and sending them to the depot, Nekhludoff hired a trap and drove to the prison.

The hot July days had set in. The stones of the street, the houses, and the tins of the roofs, failing to cool off during the suffocating night, exhaled their warmth into the hot, still air. There was no breeze, and such as rose every now and then was laden with dust and the stench of oil paint. The few people that were on the streets sought shelter in the shade of the houses. Only sun-burnt street-pavers in bast shoes were sitting in the middle of the street, setting boulders into the hot sand; gloomy policemen in unstarched blouses and carrying revolvers attached to yellow cords, were lazily shuffling about, and tram-cars with drawn blinds on the sides exposed to the sun, and drawn by white-hooded horses, were running up and down the street.

When Nekhludoff arrived at the prison, the formal delivery and acceptance of the departing convicts, which began at four in the morning, were still going on. The party consisted of six hundred and twenty-three men and sixty-four women; all had to be counted, the weak and sick had to be separated, and they were to be delivered to the convoy. The new inspector, two assistants, a physician, his assistant, the officer of the convoy and a clerk were sitting in the shade around a table with papers and documents, calling and examining each convict and making entries in their books.

One-half of the table was already exposed to the sun. It was getting warm and close from want of air, and from the breathing of the convicts standing near by.

"Will there ever be an end?" said a tall, stout, red-faced captain of the convoy, incessantly smoking a cigarette and blowing the smoke through the moustache which covered his mouth. "I am exhausted. Where have you taken so many? How many more are there?"

The clerk consulted the books.

"Twenty-four men and the women."

"Why are you standing there? Come forward!" shouted the captain to the crowding convicts.

The convicts had already been standing three hours in a broiling sun, waiting their turn.

All this was taking place in the court-yard of the prison, while without the prison stood the usual armed soldier, about two dozen trucks for the baggage, and the infirm convicts, and on the corner a crowd of relatives and friends of the convicts, waiting for a chance to see the exiles as they emerged from the prison, and, if possible, to have a last few words with them, or deliver some things they had brought for them. Nekhludoff joined this crowd.

He stood there about an hour. At the end of the hour, from behind the gates came the clatter of chains, the tramping of feet, voices of command, coughing and the low conversation of a large crowd. This lasted about five minutes, during which time prison officers flitted in and out through the wicket. Finally there was heard a sharp command.

The gates were noisily flung open, the clatter of the chains became more distinct, and a detachment of guardsmen in white blouses and shouldering guns marched forth and arranged themselves, evidently as a customary manœuvre, in a large semi-circle before the gates. Again a command was heard, and the hard-labor convicts, in pairs, began to pour out. With pancake-shaped caps on their shaved heads, and sacks on their shoulders, they dragged their fettered legs, holding up the sacks with one hand and waving the other.

First came the men convicts, all in gray trousers and long coats with diamond aces on their backs. All of them—young, old, slim, stout, pale, and red-faced, dark-haired, moustached, bearded and beardless, Russians, Tartars, Jews—came, clanging their chains and briskly waving their hands as though going on a long journey; but after making about ten steps they stopped and humbly arranged themselves in rows of four. Immediately behind these came another contingent, also with shaved heads and similarly dressed, without leg-fetters, but handcuffed to each other. These were exiles. They walked as briskly as the others, stopped, and formed in rows of four. Then came the women in the same order, in gray coats and 'kerchiefs, those sentenced to hard labor coming first; then the exiles, and finally those voluntarily following their husbands, in their native costumes. Some of the women carried infants under the skirts of their coats.

Children—boys and girls—followed them on foot, hanging on to the skirts of their mothers. The men stood silently, coughing now and then, or exchanging remarks, while the women carried on incessant conversation. Nekhludoff thought that he saw Maslova as she was coming out, but she was soon lost in the large crowd, and he only saw a lot of gray creatures almost deprived of all womanly features, with their children and sacks, grouping themselves behind the men.

Although the convicts had been counted within the walls of the prison, the guard began to count them over again. This counting took a long time, because the convicts, moving from one place to another, confused the count of the officers. The officers cursed and pushed the humbly but angrily compliant convicts and counted them again. When the counting was finally over, the officer of the guard gave some command, and suddenly all became confusion in the crowd. Infirm men, women and children hastened to the trucks, on which they first placed their sacks, then climbed in themselves, the infants crying in their mothers' arms, the children quarreling about the places, the men looking gloomy and despondent.

Some of the convicts, removing their caps, approached the officer and made some request. As Nekhludoff afterward learned, they were asking to be taken on the wagons. The guard officer, without looking at the applicants, silently inhaled the smoke of his cigarette, then suddenly swung his short hand at one of the convicts that approached him, who dodged and sprang back.

"I will elevate you to the nobility with a rope! You can walk!" shouted the officer.

Only a tall, staggering old man in irons was permitted to ride on a wagon. The old man removed his cap, and making the sign of the cross, dragged himself to the wagon; but his fettered legs prevented his climbing up until an old woman, sitting on the wagon, took his hand and helped him in.

When all the wagons were loaded with sacks and those that were permitted to ride, the guard officer uncovered his bald head, wiped with a handkerchief his pate, forehead and red, stout neck, made the sign of the cross, and gave command to proceed.

There was a clatter of weapons; the convicts, removing their caps, began to make the sign of the cross, some with their left hands; the escorting crowd shouted something, the convicts shouted in answer; a great wailing arose among the women, and the party, surrounded by soldiers in white blouses moved forward, raising a cloud of dust with their fettered feet. They marched in the order in which they formed at the prison gates, in rows of four, preceded by a detachment of soldiers. The rear was brought up by the wagons loaded with the sacks and the infirm. On top of one of the wagons, above all the others, sat a woman, wrapped up in her coat and sobbing incessantly.

CHAPTER XXIII.

When Nekhludoff reached the railroad station the prisoners were already seated in the cars, behind grated windows. There were a few people on the platform, come to see their departing relatives, but they were not allowed to come near the cars. The guards were greatly troubled this day. On the way from the prison to the station five men had died from sunstroke. Three of them had been taken to the nearest police station from the street, while two were stricken at the railroad station.[F] They were troubled not because five men had died while under their guard. That did not bother them; but they were chiefly concerned with doing all that the law required them to do

314

under the circumstances—to make proper transfer of the dead, their papers and belongings, and to exclude them from the list of those that were to be transferred to Nijhni, which was very troublesome, especially on such a warm day.

This it was that occupied the convoy, and this was the reason why Nekhludoff and others were not permitted to approach the cars while the formalities were unfinished. However, upon bribing one of the sergeants, Nekhludoff was permitted to come near the cars, the sergeant asking him to do his errand so that the captain would not see him. There were eighteen cars, and all, except the one reserved for the authorities, were literally packed with prisoners. Passing by the windows, Nekhludoff listened to the sounds within. Everywhere he heard the rattling of chains, bustle, and the hum of conversation, interspersed with stupid profanity; but nowhere did he hear, as he expected, any reference to the dead comrades. Their conversation related more to sacks, drinking-water, and the choice of seats. Looking into the window of one of the cars, Nekhludoff saw some guardsmen removing the handcuffs from the wrists of the prisoners. The prisoners stretched out their hands, while one of the guards with a key opened the locks of the handcuffs, which were collected by another. When Nekhludoff reached the second car occupied by the women he heard a woman's moan, "Oh, heavens! Oh, heavens!"

Nekhludoff passed by and approached one of the windows of the third car, pointed out to him by one of the guards. Overheated air, impregnated with a thick odor of perspiration, assailed his nostrils, and shrill women's voices were distinctly heard. All the benches were occupied by flushed, perspiring women in waists and coats, loudly conversing. His approach attracted their attention. Those sitting nearest to the grated window became silent. Maslova, in a waist and without headgear, was sitting near the opposite window. The smiling Theodosia, who was sitting near Maslova, seeing Nekhludoff, pushed her with her elbow and pointed to Nekhludoff. Maslova hurriedly rose, threw a 'kerchief over her black hair, and, with an animated, red, perspiring and smiling face, came near the window and placed her hands on the grating.

"But how warm it is!" she said, smiling joyously.

"Did you get the things?"

"I did, thank you."

"Do you need anything?" asked Nekhludoff, feeling the heat issuing from the window as from a steam bath.

"I do not need anything. Thank you."

"If we could only get some water," said Theodosia.

"Yes, some water," repeated Maslova.

"I will ask one of the guards," said Nekhludoff. "We will not meet now until we reach Nijhni."

"Why, are you going there?" she said, as if she did not know it, but joyously glancing at Nekhludoff.

"I am going on the next train."

Maslova was silent for a few moments; then sighed deeply.

"Is it true, master, that twelve people have died from the heat?" said a churlish old woman in a hoarse voice.

It was Korableva.

"I don't know that twelve have died. I have seen two," said Nekhludoff.

"They say twelve. They ought to be punished for it, the devils!"

"How is it with the women?" asked Nekhludoff.

"Women are stronger," said another prisoner, smiling. "Only there is one who has taken it into her head to give birth to a child. Listen to her wailing," she said, pointing to the adjacent car, from which the moaning proceeded.

"You asked if anything was needed," said Maslova, endeavoring to restrain a happy smile. "Could not that woman be taken off the train? She suffers so. Won't you tell the authorities?"

"Yes, I will."

"Another thing—could you not get her to see her husband, Tarass?" she added, pointing to the smiling Theodosia. "He is going with you, isn't he?"

At this point the voice of a sergeant was heard reminding Nekhludoff that talking with the prisoners was prohibited. It was not the sergeant who passed Nekhludoff.

Nekhludoff walked off to find the captain, intending to see him about the sick woman and Tarass, but for a long time could not find him, the guards being too busy to answer his inquiries. Some were leading away one of the convicts; others were hurrying away to buy their provisions; still others were attending a lady who was traveling with the captain of the convoy.

Nekhludoff found the captain after the second bell. The captain, wiping his thick moustache with his short hand and raising his shoulders, was reprimanding one of the sergeants.

"What is it you want?" he asked Nekhludoff.

"There is a woman giving birth to a child, so I thought it would be well——"

"Well, let her. When the child is born we will see to it," said the captain, passing to his car.

The conductor came with a whistle in his hand. The third bell sounded, and a loud wailing rose among the female prisoners and their friends and relatives on the platform. Nekhludoff was standing beside Tarass, and watched the cars passing before him, with the grated windows and the shaved heads seen through them. As the one in which Maslova was passed, he saw her standing with others at the window, looking at him and smiling piteously.

FOOTNOTES:

[F] Early in the eighties five prisoners died from sunstroke while being transferred from the Boutyr prison to the Nijhni railroad station.—L. T.

CHAPTER XXIV.

The passenger train which was to carry away Nekhludoff was to start in two hours. Nekhludoff at first thought of utilizing these two hours in visiting his sister, but after the impressions of the morning he felt so excited and exhausted that he seated himself on a sofa in the saloon for first-class passengers. But he unexpectedly felt so drowsy that he turned on his side, placed his palm under his cheek, and immediately fell asleep.

He was awakened by a servant in dress-coat holding a napkin in his hand.

"Mister, mister, are you not Prince Nekhludoff? A lady is looking for you."

Nekhludoff quickly raised himself, rubbing his eyes, and the incidents of the morning passed before his mind's eye—the procession of the convicts, the men who had died from the heat, the grated windows of the cars, and the women huddled behind them, one of whom was laboring in child-birth without aid, and another piteously smiling to him from behind the iron grating. But in reality he saw a table covered with bottles, vases, chandeliers, and fruit stands; nimble servants bustling around the table, and in the depth of the saloon, before the lunch-counter, loaded with viands and fruits, the backs of passengers leisurely eating their luncheon.

While Nekhludoff was raising himself and shaking off the slumber, he noticed that everybody in the saloon was curiously watching the entrance. He turned his eyes in the same direction, and saw a procession of people who bore an arm-chair in which was seated a lady, her head covered with tulle. The first bearer was a lackey who seemed familiar to Nekhludoff. The one behind was also a familiar porter, with white crown lace around his cap. Behind the arm-chair came an elegantly dressed maid-servant with curly hair, carrying a round leather box and a sunshade. Further behind came the short-necked Prince Korchagin, his shoulders thrown back; then Missy, Misha, their cousin, and a diplomat Osten, unfamiliar to Nekhludoff, with his long neck and prominent Adam's apple and an ever cheerful appearance. He walked impressively, but evidently jestingly talking to the smiling Missy. Behind them came the doctor, angrily smoking a cigarette.

The Korchagins were moving from their estate to the Prince's sister, whose estate was situated on the Nijhni road.

318

The procession passed into the ladies' room. The old Prince, however, seating himself at the table, immediately called over a waiter and began to order something. Missy with Osten also stopped in the dining-room, and were about to sit down when they saw an acquaintance in the doorway and went to meet her. It was Natalia Ivanovna. She was escorted by Agrippina Petrovna, and as she entered the dining-room she looked around. At almost the same moment she noticed Missy and her brother. She first approached Missy, only nodding her head to Nekhludoff. But after kissing Missy she immediately turned to him.

"At last I have found you," she said.

After greeting his sister, Nekhludoff entered into conversation with Missy, who told him that their house had burned down, necessitating their removal to her aunt's. Osten began to relate a droll anecdote anent the fire. Nekhludoff, without listening to Osten, turned to his sister:

"How glad I am that you came!"

In the course of their conversation he told her how sorry he felt for having fallen out with her husband; that he had intended to return and confess that he was at fault, but that he knew not how her husband would take it.

"I spoke improperly to him, and it tortured me," he said.

"I knew it. I was sure you didn't intend it," said his sister. "Don't you know——"

The tears welled up in her eyes, and she touched her brother's hand. It was spoken tenderly; he understood her, and was affected. The meaning of her words was that, besides her love for her husband, her love for her brother was dear and important to her, and that any disagreement with him caused her suffering.

"Thank you, thank you. Oh, what I have seen to-day!" he said, suddenly recalling the two dead convicts. "Two convicts have been killed."

"How killed?"

319

"So, simply killed. They have been brought here in this heat, and two of them died from sunstroke."

"Impossible! How? To-day? Just now?"

"Yes, just now. I have seen their corpses."

"Why were they killed? Who killed them?" asked Natalia Ivanovna.

"Those who forcibly brought them here," said Nekhludoff excitedly, feeling that she took the same view of this as her husband.

"Oh, my God!" said Agrippina Petrovna, coming nearer to them.

"Yes, we have no conception of the life these unfortunates are leading, and it is necessary to know it," Nekhludoff added, looking at the old Prince, who, sitting at the table with a napkin tucked under his chin and a large glass before him, at that moment glanced at Nekhludoff.

"Nekhludoff," he shouted. "Won't you take sauce to cool off? It is excellent stuff."

Nekhludoff refused and turned away.

"But what will you do?" continued Natalia Ivanovna.

"I will do what I can. I do not know what, but I feel that I must do something. And I will do what I can."

"Yes, yes, I understand that. And what about him?" she said, smiling and nodding in the direction of Korchagin. "Is it really all over?"

"Yes, it is and I think without regret on either side."

"I am very sorry. I like her. But I suppose it must be so. But why should you bind yourself? Why are you following her?"

"Because it is proper that I should," Nekhludoff said dryly, as though desiring to change the subject.

But he immediately felt ashamed of his coldness to his sister. "Why should I not tell her what I think?" he thought; "and let Agrippina Petrovna also know it," he said to himself, looking at the old servant.

The presence of Agrippina Petrovna only encouraged him to repeat his decision to his sister.

"You are speaking of my intention to marry Katiusha. You see, I have decided to do it, but she firmly and decidedly refused me," he said, and his voice trembled, as it always did when he spoke of it. "She does not desire my sacrifice, and in her position she sacrifices very much, and I could not accept her sacrifice, even if it were only momentary. That is why I am following her, and I will be near her, and will endeavor to relieve her condition as far as I am able."

Natalia Ivanovna was silent. Agrippina Petrovna looked inquiringly at Natalia Ivanovna, shaking her head. At that moment the procession started again from the ladies' room. The same handsome Phillip and the porter were bearing the Princess. She stopped the bearers, beckoned Nekhludoff to her side, and in a piteously languid manner extended her white, ring-bedecked hand, with horror anticipating the hard pressure of his.

"Epouvantable!" she said of the heat. "It is unbearable. Ce climat me tue." And having said a few words of the horrors of the Russian climate, and invited Nekhludoff to visit them, she gave a sign to the bearers. "Don't fail to come, now," she added, turning her long face to Nekhludoff.

Nekhludoff went out on the platform. The procession turned to the right, toward the first-class coaches. Nekhludoff, with a porter who carried his baggage, and Tarass, with his bags, turned to the left.

"That is my comrade," Nekhludoff said to his sister, pointing to Tarass, whose story he had told her before.

"What, are you taking the third class?" asked Natalia Ivanovna, when Nekhludoff stopped before a third-class car and the porter, with Tarass, entered it.

"Yes, I will have it more convenient then. Tarass is with me. Another thing," he added. "I have not yet given the Kusminskoie land to the peasants.

So that, in case of my death, your children will inherit it."

"Dmitri, don't talk that way," said Natalia Ivanovna.

"And if I do give it away, then all I have to tell you is that the remainder will be theirs, for I shall hardly marry. And if I do, there will be no children— so that——"

"Dmitri, please stop it," said Natalia Ivanovna; but Nekhludoff saw that she was glad to hear what he was saying.

The time for parting had come. The conductors were closing the doors, inviting the passengers to take seats, others to leave the cars.

Nekhludoff entered the heated and ill-smelling car and immediately appeared on its platform. Natalia Ivanovna was standing opposite, and evidently wished to say something, but could not find words. She could not say "ecrivez," because they had long been ridiculing the customary phrase of parting friends. The conversation about financial affairs and the inheritance at once destroyed the tender relations they had resumed. They now felt themselves estranged from each other. So that Natalia Ivanovna was glad when the train began to move and she could say, with a smile: "Well, Dmitri, good-by!" As soon as the train left she began to think how to tell her husband of her conversation with her brother, and her face became grave and worried.

And though Nekhludoff entertained the best sentiments toward his sister, and he concealed nothing from her, he now felt estranged from her, and was glad to be rid of her. He felt that the Natasha of old was no more; that there was only a slave of an unpleasant, dark, hairy man with whom he had nothing in common. He plainly saw this, because her face became illumined with peculiar animation only when he spoke of that which interested her husband—of the distribution of the land among the peasants, and of the inheritance. This made him sad.

CHAPTER XXV.

The heat in the large car of the third class, due to its exposure to the scorching sun rays and the large crowd within, was so suffocating that Nekhludoff remained on the platform. But there was no relief even there, and he drew in long breaths when the train rolled out beyond the houses and the movement of the train created a draught. "Yes, killed," he repeated to himself. And to his imagination appeared with unusual vividness the beautiful face of the second dead convict, with a smile on his lips, the forbidding expression of his forehead, and the small, strong ear under the shaved, bluish scalp. "And the worst part of it is that he was killed, and no one knows who killed him. Yet he was killed. He was forwarded, like the others, at the order of Maslenikoff. Maslenikoff probably signed the usual order with his foolish flourish, on a printed letter-head, and, of course, does not consider himself guilty. The prison physician, who inspected the convicts, has still less reason for considering himself guilty. He carefully fulfilled his duties, separated the weak ones, and could not possibly foresee either the terrible heat, or that they would be taken away so late and in such a crowd. The inspector? But the inspector only carried out the order that on such a day so many men and women prisoners should be sent away. No more guilty was the officer of the convoy, whose duty consisted in receiving so many people at such a place and delivering them at another place. He led the party in the usual way, according to instructions, and could not possibly foresee that such strong men, like the two whom Nekhludoff had seen, would succumb and die. No one was guilty, and yet the men were killed by these very people who were innocent of their death.

"All this happened," thought Nekhludoff, "because all those people— the governor, inspector and the other officers—saw before them, not human beings and their duties toward them, but the service and its requirements. Therein lies the difficulty."

In his meditation Nekhludoff did not notice how the weather had changed. The sun had hidden behind a low strip of cloud, and from the southern sky a light-gray mass, from which a slanting rain was already pouring in the distance over the fields and forests, was coming on. Now and then a flash of lightning rent the clouds, and the rattle of the train mingled with the rattle of thunder. The clouds came nearer and nearer, the slanting drops of rain, driven by the wind, pattered on the platform of the car and stained Nekhludoff's overcoat. He moved to the other side, and drawing in the fresh, humid air and the odor of the wheat coming from the parched ground, he looked on the passing gardens, forests; the rye fields just turning yellow, the emerald streaks of oats, and the furrows of the dark-green, flowering potato. Everything looked as if covered with varnish: the green and yellow colors became brighter; the black became blacker.

"More, more," said Nekhludoff, rejoicing at the reviving fields and gardens under the abundant rain.

The heavy rain did not last long. The clouds partly dissipated, and the last fine shower fell straight on the wet ground. The sun came forth again, the earth brightened, and a low but brilliant violet tinged rainbow, broken at one end, appeared in the eastern horizon.

"What was I thinking of?" Nekhludoff asked himself, when all these changes of nature came to an end and the train descended into a vale. "Yes, I was thinking that all those people—the inspector, the guard and all those servants, for the most part gentle, kind people—have become wicked."

He recalled the indifference of Maslenikoff when he told the latter of what was going on in the prison, of the severity of the inspector, the cruelty of the sergeant who refused the use of the wagons to the weak convicts and paid no attention to the suffering of the woman in child-birth. All those people were evidently proof against the feeling of sympathy, "as is this paved ground against rain," he thought, looking at the incline paved with multi-colored stone, from which the water streamed off. "May be it is necessary to lay the stones on the incline, but it is sad to see the soil deprived of vegetation when it could be made to grow grain, grass, shrubs and trees like those seen on those heights. It is the same with people," thought Nekhludoff. "The whole trouble lies in that people think that there are conditions excluding the necessity of love in their intercourse with man, but such conditions do not exist. Things may be treated without love; one may chop wood, make bricks, forge iron without love, but one can no more deal with people without love than one can handle bees without care. The nature of bees is such that if you handle them carelessly you will harm them as well as yourself. It is the same with people. And it cannot be different, because mutual love is the basic law of human life. True, man cannot compel himself to love, as he can compel himself to work, but it does not follow from this that in his dealings with men he can leave love out of consideration, especially if he wants something from them. If you feel no love for people, then keep away from them," Nekhludoff said to himself. "Occupy yourself with things, yourself—anything; only keep away from people. As it is harmful to eat except when one is hungry, so is it harmful to have intercourse with people when one does not love them. If one permits himself to deal with people without having any love for them, as I did yesterday with my brother-in-law, there is no limit to the cruelty and brutality one is liable to display toward others, as I have seen to-day, and there is no limit to one's own suffering, as I have learned from all the experiences of my own life. Yes, yes, that is so," thought Nekhludoff, experiencing the double pleasure of a cool breeze after the intolerable heat, and the consciousness of having reached the highest degree of lucidity in the question which had so long occupied him.

PART THIRD.

CHAPTER I.

The party of convicts to which Maslova belonged had gone about thirty-five hundred miles. It was not until Perm was reached that Nekhludoff succeeded in obtaining Maslova's transfer to the contingent of politicals, as he was advised to do by Bogodukhovskaia, who was among them.

The journey to Perm was very burdensome to Maslova, both physically and morally—physically because of the crowded condition of their quarters, the uncleanliness and disgusting insects, which gave her no rest; morally because of the equally loathsome men who, though they changed at every stopping place, were like the insects, always insolent, intrusive and gave her little rest. The cynicism prevailing among the convicts and their overseers was such that every woman, especially the young women, had to be on the alert. Maslova was particularly subject to these attacks because of her attractive looks and her well-known past. This condition of constant dread and struggle was very burdensome to her. The firm repulse with which she met the impertinent advances of the men was taken by them as an insult and exasperated them. Her condition in this respect was somewhat relieved by the presence of Theodosia and Tarass, who, learning that his wife was subjected to these insults, had himself included among the prisoners, and riding as such from Nijhni, was able to protect her to some extent.

Maslova's transfer to the division of the politicals bettered her situation in every respect. Besides the improvement in the quarters, food and treatment, her condition was also made easier by the fact that the persecution of the men ceased and she was no longer reminded of her past, which she was so anxious to forget now. The principal advantage of the transfer, however, lay in the acquaintance she made of some people who exerted a decisive influence over her.

At stopping places she was permitted to mingle with the politicals, but, being a strong woman, she was compelled to walk with the other prisoners. She thus walked from Tomsk. There were two politicals who traveled on foot with her—Maria Pablovna Stchetinina, the same pretty girl with the sheepish eyes who had attracted Nekhludoff's attention when visiting Bogodukhovskaia, and one Simonson, banished to Yakoutsk—that same shaggy man with deep-set eyes whom Nekhludoff had noticed on the same occasion. Maria Pablovna walked, because she yielded her place on the wagon to a pregnant woman; Simonson, because he would not profit by class advantages. These three started on foot with the other convicts in the early morning, the politicals following them later in wagons. It was at the last stopping place, near a large city, where the party was handed over to another convoy officer.

It was a chill September morning. Snow and rain fell alternately between cold blasts of wind. All the prisoners—400 men and 50 women—were already in the court-yard, some crowding around the chief officer of the convoy, who was paying out money to the overseers for the day's rations; others were buying food of the hucksters who had been admitted into the court-yard. There were a din of prisoners' voices counting money and the shrill conversation of the hucksters.

Katiousha and Maria Pablovna, both in boots and short fur coats and girdled with 'kerchiefs, came into the court-yard from the house and walked toward the hucksters, who were sitting under the northern wall and calling out their wares—fresh meat-pies, fish, boiled shred paste, buckwheat mush, meat, eggs, milk; one woman even offered roasted pig.

Simonson, in rubber jacket and similar galoshes, bound with whip-cord over woolen socks (he was a vegetarian and did not use the skin of animals), was also awaiting the departure of the party. He stood near the entrance of the house, writing down in a note-book a thought that occurred to him. "If," he wrote, "a bacterium were to observe and analyze the nail of a man, it would declare him an inorganic being. Similarly, from an observation of the earth's surface, we declare it to be inorganic. That is wrong."

Having bought eggs, buns, fish and fresh wheat bread, Maslova packed them away in a bag while Maria Pablovna settled for the food, when among the prisoners there arose a commotion. Every one became silent, and the prisoners began to form into ranks. An officer came forth and gave final orders.

Everything proceeded as usual—the prisoners were counted over, the chains were examined and men were handcuffed in pairs.

CHAPTER II.

After six years of luxurious and pampered life in the city and two months in prison among the politicals, her present life, notwithstanding the hard conditions, seemed to Katiousha very satisfactory. The journeys of fifteen or twenty miles on foot between stopping places, the food and day's rest after two days' tramp, strengthened her physically, while her association with her new comrades opened up to her new phases of life of which she had formerly no conception.

She was charmed with all her new comrades. But above all, with Maria Pablovna—nay, she even came to love her with a respectful and exulting love. She was struck by the fact that a beautiful girl of a rich and noble family, and speaking three languages, should conduct herself like a common workingwoman, distribute everything sent her by her rich brother, dress herself not only simply, but poorly, and pay no attention to her appearance. This entire absence of coquetry surprised and completely captivated Maslova. She saw that Maria Pablovna knew, and that it even pleased her to know, that she was pretty, but that so far from rejoicing at the impression she was making on the men, she only feared it, and rather looked at love with disgust and dread. If her male comrades, who knew her, felt any attraction toward her they never showed it. But strangers often attempted familiarities with her, and in such cases her great physical strength stood her in good stead. "Once," she laughingly related, "I was approached by a stranger on the street, whom I could not get rid of. I then gave him such a shaking up that he ran away in fright."

She also said that from childhood she had felt an aversion for the life of the gentry, but loved the common folks, and was often chidden for staying in the servants' quarters, the kitchen and the stable, instead of the parlor.

"But among the cooks and drivers I was always cheerful, while our ladies and gentlemen used to worry me. Afterward, when I began to understand, I saw that we were leading a wicked life. I had no mother, and I did not like my father. At nineteen I left the house with a girl friend and went to work in a factory," she said.

From the factory she went to the country, then returned to the city, where she was arrested and sentenced to hard labor. Maria Pablovna never related it herself, but Katiousha learned from others that she was sentenced to hard labor because she assumed the guilt of another.

Since Katiousha came to know her she saw that Maria Pablovna, everywhere and under all circumstances, never thought of herself, but was always occupied in helping some one else. One of her present comrades, jesting, said of her that she had given herself up to the sport of charity. And that was true. Like a sportsman looking for game, her entire activity consisted in finding occasion for serving others. And this sport became a habit with her, her life's aim. And she did it so naturally that all those that knew her ceased to appreciate it, and demanded it as by right.

When Maslova entered their ranks, Maria Pablovna felt a disgust and loathing for her. Katiousha noticed it. But she also noticed afterward that Maria Pablovna, making some effort, became particularly kind and gentle toward her. The kindness and gentleness of such an uncommon person so affected Maslova that she gave herself up to her with her whole soul, unconsciously acquired her glance and involuntarily imitated her in everything.

They were also drawn together by that disgust which both felt toward physical love. The one hated it, because she had experienced all the horror of it; the other, because not having experienced it, she looked upon it as something strange and at the same time disgusting and offensive to human dignity.

CHAPTER III.

The influence exerted by Maria Pablovna over Katiousha was due to the fact that Katiousha loved Maria Pablovna. There was another influence—that of Simonson, and that was due to the fact that Simonson loved Katiousha.

Simonson decided everything by the light of his reason, and having once decided upon a thing, he never swerved. While yet a student he made up his mind that the wealth of his father, who was an officer of the Commissary Department, was dishonestly accumulated. He then declared to him that his wealth ought to be returned to the people. And when he was reprimanded he left the house and refused to avail himself of his father's means. Having come to the conclusion that all evil can be traced to the people's ignorance, he joined the Democrats, on leaving the university, and obtaining the position of village teacher, he boldly preached before his pupils and the peasants that which he considered to be just, and denounced that which he considered unjust and false.

He was arrested and prosecuted.

During the trial he decided that the court had no right to judge him, and said so. The judges disagreeing with him and proceeding with the trial, he concluded not to answer their questions and remained silent. He was sentenced to exile in the Government of Archangel. There he formulated a religious creed defining all his actions. According to this religious teaching nothing in the world is dead, there is life in everything; all those things which we consider dead, inorganic, are but parts of a huge organic body which we cannot embrace, and that, as a part of a huge organism, man's aim should be to conserve the life of that organism and the lives of all its parts. He therefore considered it a crime to destroy life; was against war, executions, the killing in any manner not only of human beings, but of animals. He also had his theory of marriage, according to which the breeding of people was man's lower function, his higher function consisting in conserving life already existing. He found confirmation of this idea in the existence of phagocites in the blood. Bachelors, according to him, were the same phagocites whose function was to help the weak, sickly parts of the organism. And true to his convictions, he had been performing this function since he became convinced of the truth of the theory, although as a youth he had led a different life. He called himself, as well as Maria Pablovna, a phagocite of the world.

His love for Katiousha did not violate this theory, since it was purely platonic. He assumed that such love not only did not prevent his phagocite

330

activity, but aided it.

And it was this man who, falling in love with Katiousha, had a decisive influence over her. With the instincts of a woman, Maslova soon discovered it, and the consciousness that she could arouse the feeling of love in such a remarkable man raised her in her own estimation. Nekhludoff offered to marry her out of magnanimity, and the obligation for the past, but Simonson loved her as she was now, and loved her simply because he loved her. She felt, besides, that he considered her an unusual woman, distinguished from all other women, and possessing high moral qualities. She did not know exactly what those qualities were, but, at all events, not to deceive him, she endeavored with all her power to call forth her best qualities and, necessarily, be as good as she could be.

CHAPTER IV.

Nekhludoff managed to see Maslova only twice between Nijhni and Perm—once in Nijhni while the prisoners were being placed on a net-covered lighter, and again in the office of the Perm prison. On both occasions he found her secretive and unkind. When he asked her about her prison conditions, or whether she wanted anything, she became confused and answered evasively and, as it seemed to him, with that hostile feeling of reproach which she had manifested before. And this gloomy temper, due only to the persecutions to which she was being subjected by the men, tormented him.

But at their very first meeting in Tomsk she became again as she was before her departure. She no longer frowned or became confused when she saw him, but, on the contrary, met him cheerfully and simply, thanking him for what he had done for her, especially for bringing her in contact with her present company.

After two months of journey from prison to prison, this change also manifested itself in her appearance. She became thin, sun-burnt and apparently older; wrinkles appeared on her temples and around her mouth; she no longer curled her hair on her forehead, but wore a 'kerchief on her head, and neither in her dress, coiffure, nor in her conduct were there any signs of her former coquetry. And this change called forth in Nekhludoff a particularly joyous feeling. The feeling he now experienced toward her was unlike any he had experienced before. It had nothing in common with his first poetic impulse, nor with that sentimental love which he felt afterward, nor even with that consciousness of a duty performed, coupled with self-admiration, which impelled him, after the trial, to resolve on marrying her. It was that same simple feeling of pity and contrition which he experienced at their first meeting in the prison and afterward, with greater force, when he conquered his disgust and forgave her conduct with the physician's assistant in the hospital (the injustice he had done her had subsequently become plain). It was the same feeling with the difference that, while it was temporary then, now it was permanent.

During this period, because of Maslova's transfer to the politicals, Nekhludoff became acquainted with many political prisoners. On closer acquaintance he was convinced that they were not all villains, as many people imagined them to be, nor all heroes, as some of them considered the members of their party, but that they were ordinary people, among whom, as in other parties, some were good, some bad, the others indifferent.

He became particularly attached to a consumptive young man who was on his way to a life term at hard labor. The story of the young man was a very short one. His father, a rich Southern landlord, died while he was a child. He was the only son, and was brought up by his mother. He was the best scholar in the university, making his specialty mathematics. He was offered a chair in the university and a course abroad. But he hesitated. There was a girl of whom he became enamored, so he contemplated marriage and political activity. He wished everything, but resolved on nothing. At that time his college chums asked him for money for a common cause. He knew what that common cause was, and at the time took no interest in it whatever, but from a feeling of fellowship and egoism gave the money, that it might not be thought that he was afraid. Those who took the money were arrested; a note was found from which it was learned that the money had been given by Kryltzoff. He was arrested, taken to the police station, then to the prison.

After his discharge he traveled now South, now to St. Petersburg, then abroad, and again to Kieff and to Odessa. He was denounced by a man in whom he placed great faith. He was arrested, tried, kept in prison two years and finally death sentence was imposed on him, but was afterward commuted to hard labor for life.

He was stricken with consumption while in prison, and under the present circumstances had but a few months to live, and he knew it.

CHAPTER V.

At last Nekhludoff succeeded in obtaining permission to visit Maslova in her cell among the politicals.

While passing the dimly-lighted court-yard from the officers' headquarters to "No. 5," escorted by a messenger, he heard a stir and buzzing of voices coming from the one-story dwelling occupied by the prisoners. And when he came nearer and the door was opened, the buzzing increased and turned into a Babel of shouting, cursing and laughing. A rattling of chains was heard, and a familiar noisome air was wafted from the doorway. The din of voices with the rattle of chains, and the dreadful odor always produced in Nekhludoff the tormenting feeling of some moral nausea, turning into physical nausea. These two impressions, mingling, strengthened each other.

The apartment occupied by the political prisoners consisted of two small cells, the doors of which opened into the corridor, partitioned off from the rest. As Nekhludoff got beyond the partition he noticed Simonson feeding a billet of pine wood into the oven.

Spying Nekhludoff he looked up without rising and extended his hand.

"I am glad you came; I want to see you!" he said, with a significant glance, looking Nekhludoff straight in the eyes.

"What is it?" asked Nekhludoff.

"I will tell you later; I am busy now."

And Simonson again occupied himself with making the fire, which he did according to his special theory of the greatest conservation of heat energy.

Nekhludoff was about to enter the first door when Maslova, broom in hand, and sweeping a heap of dirt and dust toward the oven, emerged from the second door. She wore a white waist and white stockings and her skirt was tucked up under the waist. A white 'kerchief covered her head to her very eyebrows. Seeing Nekhludoff, she unbent herself and, all red and animated, put aside the broom, and wiping her hands on her skirt, she stood still.

"You are putting things in order?" asked Nekhludoff, extending his hand.

"Yes, my old occupation," she answered and smiled. "There is such dirt here; there is no end to our cleaning."

"Well, is the plaid dry?" she turned to Simonson.

"Almost," said Simonson, glancing at her in a manner which struck Nekhludoff as very peculiar.

"Then I will fetch the furs to dry. All our people are there," she said to Nekhludoff, going to the further room and pointing to the nearest door.

Nekhludoff opened the door and walked into a small cell, dimly lighted by a little metallic lamp standing on a low bunk. The cell was cold and there was an odor of dust, dampness and tobacco. The tin lamp threw a bright light on those around it, but the bunks were in the shade and vacillating shadows moved along the walls. In the small room were all the prisoners, except two men who had gone for boiling water and provisions. There was an old acquaintance of Nekhludoff, the yellow-faced and thin Vera Efremovna, with her large, frightened eyes and a big vein on her forehead. She was sitting nervously rolling cigarettes from a heap of tobacco lying on a newspaper in front of her.

In the far corner there was also Maria Pablovna.

"How opportune your coming! How you seen Katia?" she asked Nekhludoff.

There was also Anatolie Kryltzoff. Pale and wasted, his legs crossed under him, bending forward and shivering, he sat in the far corner, his hands hidden in the sleeves of his fur jacket, and with feverish eyes looked at

Nekhludoff. Nekhludoff was about to approach him, but to the right of the entrance, sorting something in a bag and talking to the pretty and smiling Grabetz, sat a man with curly red hair, in a rubber jacket and with spectacles. His name was Novodvoroff, and Nekhludoff hastened to greet him. Of all political prisoners, Nekhludoff liked him best. Novodvoroff glanced over his spectacles at Nekhludoff and, frowning, he extended his thin hand.

"Well, are you enjoying your journey?" he said, evidently in irony.

"Yes, there are many interesting things," answered Nekhludoff, pretending not to see the irony, and treating it as a civility. Then he went over to Kryltzoff. In appearance Nekhludoff seemed to be indifferent, but in reality he was far from being so to Novodvoroff. These words of Novodvoroff, and his evident desire to say something unpleasant, jarred upon his kindly sentiments, and he became gloomy and despondent.

"Well, how is your health?" he said, pressing Kryltzoff's cold and trembling hand.

"Pretty fair, only I cannot get warm; I am all wet," said Kryltzoff, hastily hiding his hand in the sleeve of his coat. "Those windows are broken." He pointed to the windows behind the iron gratings. "Why did you not come before?"

Expecting to have a private conversation with Katiousha, Nekhludoff sat conversing with Kryltzoff. Kryltzoff listened attentively, fixedly gazing at Nekhludoff.

"Yes," he said, suddenly, "I have often thought that we were going into exile with those very people on account of whom we were banished. And yet we not only do not know them, but do not wish to know them. And, worse of all, they hate us and consider us their enemies. This is dreadful."

"There is nothing dreadful about it," said Novodvoroff, overhearing the conversation. "The masses are always churlish and ignorant."

At that moment there was an outburst of curses behind the partition wall, followed by a jostling and banging against walls, a clatter of chains, screaming and shouting. Some one was being beaten; some one shouted "Help!"

"See those beasts! What have they in common with us?" calmly asked Novodvoroff.

"You call them beasts, but you should have heard Nekhludoff telling of the conduct of one of them," Kryltzoff said excitedly.

"You are sentimental!" Novodvoroff said, ironically. "It is hard for us to understand the emotions of these people and the motives of their acts. Where you see magnanimity, there may only be envy."

"Why is it you do not wish to see good in others?" said Maria Pablovna, suddenly becoming excited.

"I cannot see that which does not exist."

"How can you say it does not exist when a man risks a terrible death?"

"I think," said Novodvoroff, "that if we wish to serve our cause effectively it is necessary that we stop dreaming and look at things as they are. We must do everything for the masses, and expect nothing from them. The masses are the object of our activity, but they cannot be our collaborators while they are as inert as they are now. And it is, therefore, perfectly illusive to expect aid from them before they have gone through the process of development—that process of development for which we are preparing them."

"What process of development?" said Kryltzoff, becoming red in the face. "We say that we are against the use of force, but is this not force in its worst form?"

"There is no force here," calmly said Novodvoroff. "I only said that I know the path the people must follow, and can point it out."

"But how do you know that yours is the right path? Is it not the same despotism which gave rise to the Inquisition and the executions of the Great Revolution? They, too, knew the only scientific path."

"The fact that people erred does not prove that I am erring. Besides, there is a great difference between the ravings of ideologists and the data of positive economic science."

Novodvoroff's voice filled the entire cell. He alone was speaking; all the others were silent.

"Those eternal discussions!" said Maria Pablovna at a momentary lull.

"And what do you think of it?" Nekhludoff asked Maria Pablovna.

"I think that Anatolie is right—that we have no right to force our ideas on the people."

"That is a strange conception of our ideas," said Novodvoroff, and he began to smoke angrily.

"I cannot talk to them," Kryltzoff said in a whisper, and became silent.

"And it is much better not to talk," said Nekhludoff.

CHAPTER VI.

An officer entered the cell and announced that the time for departing had arrived. He counted every prisoner, pointing at every one with his finger. When he reached Nekhludoff he said, familiarly:

"It is too late to remain now, Prince; it is time to go."

Nekhludoff, knowing what that meant, approached him and thrust three rubles into his hand.

"Nothing can be done with you—stay here a while longer."

Simonson, who was all the while silently sitting on his bunk, his hands clasped behind his head, firmly arose, and carefully making his way through those sitting around the bunk, went over to Nekhludoff.

"Can you hear me now?" asked Simonson.

"Certainly," said Nekhludoff, also rising to follow him.

Maslova saw Nekhludoff rising, and their eyes meeting, she turned red in the face and doubtfully, as it seemed, shook her head.

"My business with you is the following," began Simonson, when they reached the corridor. "Knowing your relations toward Catherine Michaelovna," and he looked straight into Nekhludoff's face, "I consider it my duty——" But at the very door two voices were shouting at the same time.

"I tell you, heathen, they are not mine," shouted one voice.

"Choke yourself, you devil!" the other said, hoarsely.

At that moment Maria Pablovna entered the corridor.

"You cannot talk here," she said. "Walk in here; only Verotchka is there." And she opened the door of a tiny cell, evidently intended for solitary confinement, and now at the disposal of the political prisoners. On one of the bunks lay Vera Efremovna, with her head covered.

"She is ill and asleep; she cannot hear you, and I will go," said Maria Pablovna.

"On the contrary, stay here," said Simonson. "I keep nothing secret, especially from you."

"Very well," said Maria Pablovna, and childishly moving her whole body from side to side, and thus getting into a snug corner of the bunks, she prepared to listen, at the same time looking somewhere in the distance with her beautiful, sheepish eyes.

"Well, then, knowing your relations toward Catherine Michaelovna, I consider it my duty to let you know my relations to her."

"Well, go on," said Nekhludoff, involuntarily admiring Simonson's simplicity and straightforwardness.

"I wished to tell you that I would like to marry Catherine Michaelovna——"

"Remarkable!" exclaimed Maria Pablovna, fixing her gaze on Simonson.

"And I have decided to ask her to be my wife," continued Simonson.

"What, then, can I do? It depends on her," said Nekhludoff.

"Yes; but she would not decide the matter without you."

"Why?"

"Because, while the question of your relations remains undecided, she cannot choose."

"On my part the question is definitely decided. I only wished to do that which I considered it my duty to do, and also to relieve her condition, but in no case did I intend to influence her choice."

"Yes; but she does not wish your sacrifice."

"There is no sacrifice."

"And I also know that her decision is irrevocable."

"Why, then, talk to me?" said Nekhludoff.

"It is necessary for her that you should also approve of it."

"I can only say that I am not free, but she is free to do what she wishes."

Simonson began to ponder.

"Very well, I will tell her so. Do not think that I am in love with her," he continued. "I admire her as a good, rare person who has suffered much. I wish nothing from her, but I would very much like to help her, to relieve her——"

Simonson's trembling voice surprised Nekhludoff.

"To relieve her condition," continued Simonson. "If she does not wish to accept your help, let her accept mine. If she consented, I would ask permission to join her in prison. Four years is not an eternity. I would live near her, and perhaps lighten her fate——" His emotion again compelled him to stop.

"What can I say?" said Nekhludoff. "I am glad that she has found such a protector."

"That is just what I wanted to know," continued Simonson. "I wished to know whether you, loving her and seeking her good, could approve of her marrying me?"

"Oh, yes," Nekhludoff answered, decisively.

"It is all for her; all I wish is that that woman, who had suffered so much, should have some rest," said Simonson, with a childlike gentleness that no one would expect from a man of such gloomy aspect.

Simonson rose, took Nekhludoff's hand, smiled bashfully and embraced him.

"Well, I will so tell her," he said, and left the room.

CHAPTER VII.

"What do you think of him?" said Maria Pablovna. "In love, and earnestly in love! I never thought that Vladimir Simonson could fall in love in such a very stupid, childish fashion. It is remarkable, and to tell the truth, sad," she concluded, sighing.

"But Katia? How do you think she will take it?" asked Nekhludoff.

"She?" Maria Pablovna stopped, evidently desiring to give a precise answer. "She? You see, notwithstanding her past, she is naturally of a most moral character. And her feelings are so refined. She loves you—very much so—and is happy to be able to do you the negative good of not binding you to herself. Marriage with you would be a dreadful fall to her, worse than all her past. For this reason she would never consent to it. At the same time, your presence perplexes her."

"Ought I then to disappear?" asked Nekhludoff.

Maria Pablovna smiled in her pleasant, childish way.

"Yes, partly."

"How can I partly disappear?"

"I take it back. But I will tell you that she probably sees the absurdity of that exalted love of his (he has not spoken to her about it), is flattered by it,

340

and fears it. You know that I am not competent in these matters, but I think that his love is that of the ordinary man, although it is masked. He says that it rouses his energy and that it is a platonic love; but it has nothing but nastiness for its basis."

"But what am I to do?" asked Nekhludoff.

"I think it is best that you have a talk with her. It is always better to make everything clear. Shall I call her?" said Maria Pablovna.

"If you please," answered Nekhludoff, and Maria Pablovna went out.

Nekhludoff was seized with a strange feeling when, alone in the small cell, he listened to the quiet breathing of Vera Efremovna, interrupted by an occasional moan, and the constant din coming from the cells of the convicts.

That which Simonson had told him freed him from his self-imposed obligation, which, in a moment of weakness, seemed to him burdensome and dreadful; and yet it was not only unpleasant, but painful. The offer of Simonson destroyed the exclusiveness of his act, minimized in his own and other people's eyes the value of the sacrifice he was making. If such a good man as Simonson, who was under no obligation to her, wished to join his fate to hers, then his own sacrifice was no longer so important. Maybe there was also the ordinary feeling of jealousy; he was so used to her love that he could not think that she was capable of loving any one else. Besides, his plans were now shattered, especially the plan of living near her while she served her sentence. If she married Simonson, his presence was no longer necessary, and that required a rearrangement of his projects. He could scarcely collect his thoughts, when Katiousha entered the cell.

With quick step she approached him.

"Maria Pablovna sent me," she said, stopping near him.

"Yes, I would like to talk with you. Take a seat. Vladimir Ivanovitch spoke to me."

She seated herself, crossed her hands on her knees, and seemed calm. But as soon as Nekhludoff pronounced Simonson's name, her face turned a purple color.

"What did he tell you?" she asked.

"He told me that he wishes to marry you."

Her face suddenly became wrinkled, evidencing suffering, but she remained silent, only looking at the floor.

"He asked my consent or advice. I told him that it all rests with you; that you must decide."

"Oh, what is it all for?" she said, and looked at Nekhludoff with that squinting glance that always peculiarly affected him. For a few seconds they looked silently at each other. That glance was significant to both.

"You must decide," repeated Nekhludoff.

"Decide what?" she said. "It has all been decided long ago. It is you who must decide whether you will accept the offer of Vladimir Ivanovitch," she continued, frowning.

"But if a pardon should come?" said Nekhludoff.

"Oh, leave me alone. It is useless to talk any more," she answered, and, rising, left the cell.

Gaining the street, Nekhludoff stopped, and, expanding his chest, drew in the frosty air.

The following morning a soldier brought him a note from Maria Pablovna, in which she said that Kryltzoff's condition was worse than they thought it to be.

"At one time we intended to remain here with him, but they would not allow it. So we are taking him with us, but we fear the worst. Try to so arrange in town that if he is left behind some one of us shall remain with him. If it is necessary for that purpose that I should marry him, then, of course, I am ready to do it."

Nekhludoff obtained horses and hastened to catch up with the party of prisoners. He stopped his team near the wagon carrying Kryltzoff on a bed of hay and pillows. Beside Kryltzoff sat Maria Pablovna. Kryltzoff, in a fur coat and lambskin cap, seemed thinner and more pale than before. His beautiful eyes seemed particularly larger and sparkling. Weakly rolling from side to side from the jostling of the wagon, he steadily looked at Nekhludoff, and in answer to questions about his health, he only closed his eyes and angrily shook his head. It required all his energy to withstand the jostling of the wagon. Maria Pablovna exchanged glances with Nekhludoff, expressing apprehension concerning Kryltzoff's condition.

"The officer seems to have some shame in him," she shouted, so as to be heard above the rattling of the wheels. "He removed the handcuffs from Bouzovkin, who is now carrying his child. With him are Katia, Simonson and, in my place, Verotchka."

Kryltzoff, pointing at Maria Pablovna, said something which could not, however, be heard. Nekhludoff leaned over him in order to hear him. Then Kryltzoff removed the handkerchief, which was tied around his mouth, and whispered:

"Now I am better. If I could only keep from catching cold."

Nekhludoff nodded affirmatively and glanced at Maria Pablovna.

"Have you received my note, and will you do it?" asked Maria Pablovna.

"Without fail," said Nekhludoff, and seeing the dissatisfied face of Kryltzoff, went over to his own team, climbed into the wagon, and holding fast to the sides of it, drove along the line of gray-coated and fettered prisoners which stretched for almost a mile.

Nekhludoff crossed the river to a town, and his driver took him to a hotel, where, notwithstanding the poor appointments, he found a measure of comfort entirely wanting in the inns of his stopping places. He took a bath, dressed himself in city clothes and drove to the governor of the district. He alighted at a large, handsome building, in front of which stood a sentry and a policeman.

The general was ill, and did not receive. Nekhludoff, nevertheless, asked the porter to take his card to the general, and the porter returned with a favorable answer:

"You are asked to step in."

The vestibule, the porter, the messenger, the shining floor of the hall—everything reminded him of St. Petersburg, only it was somewhat dirtier and more majestic. Nekhludoff was admitted to the cabinet.

The general, bloated, with a potato nose and prominent bumps on his forehead, hairless pate and bags under his eyes, a man of sanguine temperament, was reclining in a silk morning gown, and with a cigarette in his hand, was drinking tea from a silver saucer.

"How do you do, sir? Excuse my receiving you in a morning gown; it is better than not receiving at all," he said, covering his stout, wrinkled neck with the collar of his gown. "I am not quite well, and do not go out. What brought you into these wilds?"

"I was following a party of convicts, among whom is a person near to me," said Nekhludoff. "And now I come to see Your Excellency about that person, and also another affair."

The general inhaled the smoke of his cigarette, took a sip of tea, placed his cigarette in a malachite ash-holder, and steadily gazing with his watery, shining eyes at Nekhludoff, listened gravely. He only interrupted Nekhludoff to ask him if he wished to smoke.

Nekhludoff told the general that the person in whom he was interested was a woman, that she was unjustly convicted, and that His Majesty's clemency had been appealed to.

"Yes. Well?" said the general.

"I was promised in St. Petersburg that the news of this woman's fate would be sent to this place not later than this month."

Looking steadily at Nekhludoff, the general asked:

"Anything else?"

"My second request would be concerning the political prisoner who is going to Siberia with this detachment."

"Is that so?" said the general.

"He is very sick—he is a dying man. And he will probably be left here in the hospital; for this reason one of the female prisoners would like to remain with him."

"Is she a relative of his?"

"No. But she wishes to marry him, if it will allow her to stay with him."

The general looked sharply at Nekhludoff from his shining eyes, and, smoking continually, he kept silence, as if wishing to confound his companion.

When Nekhludoff had finished he took a book from the table, and frequently wetting the fingers with which he turned the leaves, he lighted on the chapter treating of marriage and perused it.

"What's her sentence?" he asked, lifting his eyes from the book.

"Hers? Hard labor."

"If this is the case, the sentence cannot be changed by marriage."

"But——"

"I beg your pardon! If a free man would marry her she would have to serve her sentence all the same. Whose sentence is harder, his or hers?"

"Both are sentenced to hard labor."

"So they are quits," the general said, laughing. "An equal share for both of them. He may be left here on account of his sickness," he continued, "and, of course, everything will be done to ameliorate his condition, but she, even if she should marry him, cannot remain here. Anyhow, I will think it over. What are their names? Write them down here."

Nekhludoff did as he was asked.

"And this I cannot do either," said the general, concerning his request to see the patient. "Of course I don't suspect you, but you are interested in them and in others. You have money, and the people here are corrupt. How, then, is it possible for me to watch a person who is five thousand miles distant from me? There he is king, as I am here," and he began to laugh. "You have surely seen the political prisoners. You have surely given them money," he added, smiling. "Isn't it so?"

"Yes, it is true."

"I understand that you must act in this way. You want to see the political prisoner, and you all sorrow for him, and the soldier on guard will surely take money, because he has a family, and his salary amounts to something less than nothing; he cannot afford to refuse. I would do the same were I in yours or his place. But, being situated as I am now, I cannot permit myself to disobey one iota of the law, for the very reason that I, too, am no more than a man, and am liable to yield to pity. They confide in me under certain conditions, and I, by my actions, must prove that I am trustworthy. So this question is settled. Well, now tell me what is going on at the metropolis?"

Then the general put various questions, as if he would like to learn some news.

"Well, tell me now whom you are stopping with—at Duke's? It is unpleasant there. Come to us to dinner," he said, finally, dismissing Nekhludoff, "at five. Do you speak English?"

"Yes, sir."

"Well, that is good. You see, there is an English traveler here. He is studying the exile system, and the prisons in Siberia. So he will dine with us, and you come, too. We dine at five, and madam wants us to be punctual. I will let you know what will be done with that woman, and also with the patient. Maybe it will be possible to leave somebody with him."

Having taken leave of the general, Nekhludoff drove to the postoffice. Receiving his mail, he walked up to a wooden bench, on which a soldier was sitting, probably waiting for something; he sat down beside him, and started to look through the letters. Among them he found a registered letter in a beautiful, large envelope, with a large seal of red wax on it. He tore open the envelope, and, seeing a letter from Selenin with some official document, he felt the blood mounting to his cheeks, and his heart grow weak. This document was the decision concerning Katiousha's trial. What was it? Was it possible that it contained a refusal? Nekhludoff hastily ran over the letter, written in small, hardly legible, broken handwriting, and breathed freely. The decision was a favorable one.

"Dear friend," wrote Selenin, "our last conversation made a strong impression upon me. You were right concerning Maslova. I have looked through the accusation. This could be corrected only through the Commission for Petitions, to which you sent your petition. They let me have a copy of the pardon, and here I send it to you, to the address which the Countess Catherine Ivanovna gave me. I press your hand in friendship."

The news was pleasant and important. All that Nekhludoff could wish for Katiousha and himself was realized. True, those changes in his life changed his relations to her. But now, he thought, all that was most important was to see her as quick as possible and bring her the good news of her freedom. He thought that the copy he had in his hand was sufficient for that. So he bade the cabman drive at once to the prison.

The superintendent of the prison told him that he could not admit him without a permit from the general. The copy of the petition from their majesty's bureau also did not prevail with the superintendent. He positively refused admittance. He also refused to admit him to see Kryltzoff.

CHAPTER VIII.

After the disappointment at the prison, Nekhludoff drove down to the Governor's Bureau to find out whether they had received there any news concerning the pardon of Maslova. There was no news there, so he drove back to his hotel, and wrote at once to the lawyer and to Selenin concerning it. Having finished the letters, he glanced at his watch; it was already time to go to the general.

On the way he thought again of how he might hand over the pardon to Katiousha; of the place she would be sent to, and how he would live with her.

At dinner in the general's house all were not only very friendly to Nekhludoff, but, as it seemed, very favorably inclined to him, as he was a new, interesting personality. The general, who came in to dinner with a white cross on his breast, greeted Nekhludoff like an old friend. On the general's inquiry as to what he had done since he saw him in the morning, Nekhludoff answered that he had been at the postoffice, that he had found out the facts concerning the pardoning of the person they were talking of in the morning, and he asked permission to visit her.

The general seemed displeased, began to frown and said nothing.

"Will you have some whisky?" he said in French to the Englishman who had walked up to him. The Englishman took some, and related that he had been to see the cathedral of the city, and the factory, and expressed the desire to see the great jail in which criminals were confined on their way to Siberia.

"This idea is excellent!" exclaimed the general, turning to Nekhludoff. "You may go together. Give them a pass!" he added, turning to his lieutenant.

"What time do you wish to go?" Nekhludoff asked the Englishman.

"I prefer to visit prisons in the evening," the Englishman replied. "All are then at home, and there are no preparations."

After dinner, Nekhludoff followed her into the ante-chamber, where the Englishman was already waiting for him to visit the prison, as they had agreed. Having taken leave of the whole family, he walked out, followed by the Englishman.

The sombre looking prison, the soldier on guard, the lantern behind the gate, notwithstanding the pure white layer of snow which had covered everything—the sidewalk, the roof and the walls—made a gloomy impression. The proud looking superintendent, walking out to the gate and glancing at Nekhludoff's pass in the light of the lantern, shrugged his broad shoulders, but obeyed the order and invited the visitors to follow him. He first led them to the yard, and then to a door on the right hand and up the stairs leading to the office. Offering them seats, he asked them in what way he could serve them, and learning from Nekhludoff that he wished to see Maslova, he sent the jailer for her and prepared himself to answer the questions which the Englishman wished to ask him, before going to the cell.

Nekhludoff translated the Englishman's questions. While they were conversing they heard approaching footsteps, the door opened and the jailer entered, followed by Katiousha in her prison garb, with a scarf tied around her head.

Nekhludoff rose and made a few steps toward her. She said nothing, but her excited expression surprised him. Her face was lit up with a wonderful decision. He had never seen her look like that. Now the blood rushed to her face, and now she turned pale; now her fingers twisted convulsively the edges of her jacket, now she looked at him, and now she dropped her eyes.

"You know what I called you for?" asked Nekhludoff.

"Yes, he told me. But now I am decided. I will ask permission to go with Vladimir Ivanovitch." She said this quickly, as if she had made up her mind before what to say.

"How with Vladimir Ivanovitch?" asked Nekhludoff. But she interrupted him.

"But if he wants me to live with him?" Here she stopped in fear, and added, "I mean to stay with him. I could expect nothing better, and perhaps I may be useful to him and others. What difference does it make to me?"

One of the two things had happened—either she had fallen in love with Simonson and did not wish his sacrifice, which weighed so heavily on him, or she was still in love with Nekhludoff and renounced him for his own good, burning all bridges behind her, and throwing her fortunes in the same scale with those of Simonson. Nekhludoff understood it, and felt ashamed.

"If you are in love with him," he said.

"I never knew such people, you know. It is impossible not to love them. And Vladimir is entirely unlike any person I have ever known."

"Yes, certainly," said Nekhludoff. "He is an excellent man, and I think——"

Here she interrupted him, as if she were afraid that he would speak too much, or she would not say everything.

"You will forgive me for doing that which you did not wish. You, too, must love."

She said the very thing that he had just said to himself.

But now he was no longer thinking so, but felt altogether different. He felt not only shame, but pity.

"Is it possible that all is at an end between us?" he said.

"Yes, it looks like it," she answered, with a strange smile.

"But nevertheless I would like to be useful to you."

"To us," she said, glancing at Nekhludoff. "We don't need anything. I am very much obliged to you. If it were not for you"—she wished to say something, but her voice began to tremble.

"I don't know which of us is under greater obligation to the other. God will settle our accounts," said Nekhludoff.

"Yes, God will settle them," she whispered.

"Are you ready?" asked the Englishman.

"Directly," answered Nekhludoff, and then he inquired of her what she knew of Kryltzoff.

She quieted down and calmly told him:

"Kryltzoff became very weak on the road and was taken to the hospital. Maria Pablovna wanted to become a nurse, but there is no answer yet."

"Well, may I go?" she asked, noticing the Englishman who was waiting for him.

"I am not yet taking leave of you," said Nekhludoff, holding out his hand to her.

"Pardon me," she said in a low tone.

Their eyes met, and in that strange, stern look, and in that pitiful smile, with which she said not "good-by," but "pardon me," Nekhludoff understood, that of the two suppositions concerning her decision the latter was the right one. She still loved him and thought she would mar his life by a union with him, and would free him by living with Simonson.

She pressed his hand, turned quickly, and left the room.

CHAPTER IX.

Passing through the hall and the ill-smelling corridors, the superintendent passed into the first building of the prison in which those condemned to hard labor were confined. Entering the first room in that building they found the prisoners stretched on their berths, which occupied the middle of the room. Hearing the visitors enter they all jumped down, and, clinking their chains, placed themselves beside their berths, while their half-shaven heads were distinctly set off against the gloom of the prison. Only two of the prisoners remained at their places. One of them was a young man whose face was evidently heated with fever; the other was an old man, who never left off groaning.

The Englishman asked whether the young man had been sick for a long time. The superintendent replied that he had been taken sick that very same morning, that the old man had had convulsions for a long time, and that they kept him in prison because there was no place for him in the hospital.

The Englishman shook his head discontentedly, said that he would like to say a few words to the prisoners, and asked Nekhludoff to translate his remarks. It turned out that, besides the aim of his journey, which was the description of the exile system—he had another one—the preaching of the gospel, of salvation through faith.

"Tell them that Christ pitied and loved them," he said to Nekhludoff, "and that He died for them. He who will believe in Him will be saved."

While he was saying this, all the prisoners were standing erect with their hands by their sides.

"Tell them," continued the Englishman, "that all I said will be found in this book. Are there any among them who can read?" It turned out that there were more than twenty who could.

The Englishman took out a few leather-bound Bibles from his traveling bag, and soon a number of muscular hands, terminating in long black nails, were stretched out toward him, pushing each other aside in order to reach the Testaments. He left two Testaments in this room, and went to the next one.

There the same thing occurred. There prevailed the same dampness and ill-smells. But in this room, between the windows, an image of the Virgin, before which a small lamp burned dimly, was hung up. To the left side of the door stood the large vat. Here the prisoners were stretched out on their berths, and in the same way they rose and placed themselves in a row. Three of them remained in their places. Two of these three lifted themselves and sat up, but the third one remained stretched out, and did not even look at the visitors. These latter ones were sick. The Englishman addressed them in the same manner, and left two Testaments.

From the cells in which those condemned to hard labor were imprisoned, they passed over to the cells of the exiles, and finally those in which the relatives who escorted the prisoners to Siberia were awaiting the day appointed to start hence.

Everywhere the same cold, hungry, idling, sickly, degraded, brutalized human beings could be seen.

The Englishman distributed his Bibles, and, being tired out, he walked through the rooms saying "All right" to whatever the superintendent told him concerning the prisons.

They went out into the corridor.

The Englishman, pointing to an open door, asked what that room was for.

"This is the prison morgue."

"Oh!" exclaimed the Englishman, and he expressed a desire to enter. This room was an ordinary room. A small lamp, fastened to the wall, lit up the four bodies which were stretched on berths, with their heads toward the wall and the feet protruding toward the door. The first body, in a plain shirt, was that of a tall young man, with a small, pointed beard and half-shaven head. The corpse was already chilled, and its blue hands were folded over the breast. Beside him, in a white dress and jacket, lay a bare-footed old woman, with thin hair and wrinkled, yellowish face. Beside this old woman lay a corpse, attired in blue.

This color recalled something in Nekhludoff's memory.

"And who is this third one?" he asked, mistrusting his own eyesight.

"This one is a gentleman who was sent hither from the hospital," replied the superintendent.

Nekhludoff walked up to the body and touched the icy cold feet of Kryltzoff.

CHAPTER X.

Nekhludoff, after parting with the Englishman, went straight to his hotel, and walked about his room for a long time. The affair with Katiousha was at an end. There was something ugly in the very memory of it. But it was not that which grieved him. Some other affair of his was yet unsettled—an affair which tortured him and required his attention. In his imagination rose the gloomy scenes of the hundreds and thousands of human beings pent up in the pestiferous air. The laughter of the prisoners resounded in his ears. He saw again among the dead bodies the beautiful, angry, waxen face of the dead Kryltzoff; and the question whether he was mad, or all those who commit those evils and think themselves wise were mad, bore in upon his mind with renewed power, and he found no answer to it. The principal difficulty consisted in finding an answer to the principal question, which was: What should be done with those who became brutalized in the struggle for life?

When he became tired walking about the room he sat down on the lounge, close by the lamp, and mechanically opened the Bible which the

Englishman had presented him, and which he had thrown on the table while emptying his pockets. They say, he thought, that this Bible contains the solution to all questions. So, opening it, he began to read at the place at which it opened itself—Matt. x., 8. After a while he inclined close to the lamp and became like one petrified. An exultation, the like of which he had not experienced for a long time, took possession of his soul, as though, after long suffering and weariness, he found at last liberty and rest. He did not sleep the whole night. As is the case with many who read the Bible for the first time, he now, on reading it again, grasped the full meaning of words which he had known long ago, but which he had not understood before. Like a sponge that absorbs everything, so he absorbed everything that was important, necessary and joyful.

"That is the principal thing," thought Nekhludoff. "We all live in the silly belief that we ourselves are the lords of our world, that this world has been given us for our enjoyment. But this is evidently untrue. Somebody must have sent us here for some reason. And for this reason it is plain that we will suffer like those laborers suffer who do not fulfill the wishes of their Master. The will of the Lord is expressed in the teachings of Christ. Let man obey Him, and the Kingdom of the Lord will come on earth, and man will derive the greatest possible good.

"Seek the truth and the Kingdom of God, and the rest will come of itself. We seek that which is to come, and do not find it, and not only do we not build the Kingdom of God, but we destroy it.

"So this will henceforth be the task of my life!"

And indeed, from that night a new life began for Nekhludoff; not so much because he had risen into a new stage of existence, but because all that had happened to him till then assumed for him an altogether new meaning.

THE END.

About Author

In the 1870s Tolstoy experienced a profound moral crisis, followed by what he regarded as an equally profound spiritual awakening, as outlined in his non-fiction work A Confession (1882). His literal interpretation of the ethical teachings of Jesus, centering on the Sermon on the Mount, caused him to become a fervent Christian anarchist and pacifist. Tolstoy's ideas on nonviolent resistance, expressed in such works as The Kingdom of God Is Within You (1894), were to have a profound impact on such pivotal 20th-century figures as Mahatma Gandhi and Martin Luther King Jr. Tolstoy also became a dedicated advocate of Georgism, the economic philosophy of Henry George, which he incorporated into his writing, particularly Resurrection (1899).

Origins

The Tolstoys were a well-known family of old Russian nobility who traced their ancestry to a mythical nobleman named Indris described by Pyotr Tolstoy as arriving "from Nemec, from the lands of Caesar" to Chernigov in 1353 along with his two sons Litvinos (or Litvonis) and Zimonten (or Zigmont) and a druzhina of 3000 people. While the word "Nemec" has been long used to describe Germans only, at that time it was applied to any foreigner who didn't speak Russian (from the word nemoy meaning mute). Indris was then converted to Eastern Orthodoxy under the name of Leonty and his sons – as Konstantin and Feodor, respectively. Konstantin's grandson Andrei Kharitonovich was nicknamed Tolstiy (translated as fat) by Vasily II of Moscow after he moved from Chernigov to Moscow.

Because of the pagan names and the fact that Chernigov at the time was ruled by Demetrius I Starshy some researches concluded that they were Lithuanians who arrived from the Grand Duchy of Lithuania, then part of the State of the Teutonic Order. At the same time, no mention of Indris was ever found in the 14th – 16th-century documents, while the Chernigov Chronicles used by Pyotr Tolstoy as a reference were lost. The first documented members of the Tolstoy family also lived during the 17th century, thus Pyotr

Tolstoy himself is generally considered the founder of the noble house, being granted the title of count by Peter the Great.

Life and career

Tolstoy was born at Yasnaya Polyana, a family estate 12 kilometres (7.5 mi) southwest of Tula, Russia, and 200 kilometers (120 mi) south of Moscow. He was the fourth of five children of Count Nikolai Ilyich Tolstoy (1794–1837), a veteran of the Patriotic War of 1812, and Countess Mariya Tolstaya (née Volkonskaya; 1790–1830). After his mother died when he was two and his father when he was nine, Tolstoy and his siblings were brought up by relatives. In 1844, he began studying law and oriental languages at Kazan University, where teachers described him as "both unable and unwilling to learn." Tolstoy left the university in the middle of his studies, returned to Yasnaya Polyana and then spent much of his time in Moscow, Tula and Saint Petersburg, leading a lax and leisurely lifestyle. He began writing during this period, including his first novel Childhood, a fictitious account of his own youth, which was published in 1852. In 1851, after running up heavy gambling debts, he went with his older brother to the Caucasus and joined the army. Tolstoy served as a young artillery officer during the Crimean War and was in Sevastopol during the 11-month-long siege of Sevastopol in 1854–55, including the Battle of the Chernaya. During the war he was recognised for his bravery and courage and promoted to lieutenant. He was appalled by the number of deaths involved in warfare, and left the army after the end of the Crimean War.

His conversion from a dissolute and privileged society author to the non-violent and spiritual anarchist of his latter days was brought about by his experience in the army as well as two trips around Europe in 1857 and 1860–61. Others who followed the same path were Alexander Herzen, Mikhail Bakunin and Peter Kropotkin. During his 1857 visit, Tolstoy witnessed a public execution in Paris, a traumatic experience that would mark the rest of his life. Writing in a letter to his friend Vasily Botkin: "The truth is that the State is a conspiracy designed not only to exploit, but above all to corrupt its citizens ... Henceforth, I shall never serve any government anywhere." Tolstoy's concept of non-violence or Ahimsa was bolstered when he read a

German version of the Tirukkural. He later instilled the concept in Mahatma Gandhi through his A Letter to a Hindu when young Gandhi corresponded with him seeking his advice.

His European trip in 1860–61 shaped both his political and literary development when he met Victor Hugo, whose literary talents Tolstoy praised after reading Hugo's newly finished Les Misérables. The similar evocation of battle scenes in Hugo's novel and Tolstoy's War and Peace indicates this influence. Tolstoy's political philosophy was also influenced by a March 1861 visit to French anarchist Pierre-Joseph Proudhon, then living in exile under an assumed name in Brussels. Apart from reviewing Proudhon's forthcoming publication, La Guerre et la Paix (War and Peace in French), whose title Tolstoy would borrow for his masterpiece, the two men discussed education, as Tolstoy wrote in his educational notebooks: "If I recount this conversation with Proudhon, it is to show that, in my personal experience, he was the only man who understood the significance of education and of the printing press in our time."

Fired by enthusiasm, Tolstoy returned to Yasnaya Polyana and founded 13 schools for the children of Russia's peasants, who had just been emancipated from serfdom in 1861. Tolstoy described the school's principles in his 1862 essay "The School at Yasnaya Polyana". Tolstoy's educational experiments were short-lived, partly due to harassment by the Tsarist secret police. However, as a direct forerunner to A.S. Neill's Summerhill School, the school at Yasnaya Polyana can justifiably be claimed the first example of a coherent theory of democratic education.

Towards the end of his career, Tolstoy was selected to receive the first Nobel Prize in Literature in 1901, but turned down the honor in October of the same year, worrying that the prize money would bring unwanted complications to his life.

Personal life

The death of his brother Nikolay in 1860 had an impact on Tolstoy, and led him to a desire to marry. On 23 September 1862, Tolstoy married Sophia Andreevna Behrs, who was 16 years his junior and the daughter of a court physician. She was called Sonya, the Russian diminutive of Sofia, by her family and friends. They had 13 children, eight of whom survived childhood:

Count Sergei Lvovich Tolstoy (1863–1947), composer and ethnomusicologist

Countess Tatyana Lvovna Tolstaya (1864–1950), wife of Mikhail Sergeevich Sukhotin

Count Ilya Lvovich Tolstoy (1866–1933), writer

Count Lev Lvovich Tolstoy (1869–1945), writer and sculptor

Countess Maria Lvovna Tolstaya (1871–1906), wife of Nikolai Leonidovich Obolensky

Count Peter Lvovich Tolstoy (1872–1873), died in infancy

Count Nikolai Lvovich Tolstoy (1874–1875), died in infancy

Countess Varvara Lvovna Tolstaya (1875–1875), died in infancy

Count Andrei Lvovich Tolstoy (1877–1916), served in the Russo-Japanese War

Count Michael Lvovich Tolstoy (1879–1944)

Count Alexei Lvovich Tolstoy (1881–1886)

Countess Alexandra Lvovna Tolstaya (1884–1979)

Count Ivan Lvovich Tolstoy (1888–1895)

The marriage was marked from the outset by sexual passion and emotional insensitivity when Tolstoy, on the eve of their marriage, gave her his diaries detailing his extensive sexual past and the fact that one of the serfs on his estate had borne him a son. Even so, their early married life was happy and allowed Tolstoy much freedom and the support system to compose War and Peace and Anna Karenina with Sonya acting as his secretary, editor, and financial manager. Sonya was copying and handwriting his epic works time after time. Tolstoy would continue editing War and Peace and had to have clean final drafts to be delivered to the publisher.

However, their later life together has been described by A.N. Wilson as one of the unhappiest in literary history. Tolstoy's relationship with his wife deteriorated as his beliefs became increasingly radical. This saw him seeking to reject his inherited and earned wealth, including the renunciation of the copyrights on his earlier works.

Some of the members of the Tolstoy family left Russia in the aftermath of the 1905 Russian Revolution and the subsequent establishment of the Soviet Union, and many of Leo Tolstoy's relatives and descendants today live in Sweden, Germany, the United Kingdom, France and the United States. Among them are Swedish jazz singer Viktoria Tolstoy and the Swedish landowner Christopher Paus, whose family owns the major estate Herresta outside Stockholm.

One of his great-great-grandsons, Vladimir Tolstoy (born 1962), is a director of the Yasnaya Polyana museum since 1994 and an adviser to the President of Russia on cultural affairs since 2012. Ilya Tolstoy's great-grandson, Pyotr Tolstoy, is a well-known Russian journalist and TV presenter as well as a State Duma deputy since 2016. His cousin Fyokla Tolstaya (born Anna Tolstaya in 1971), daughter of the acclaimed Soviet Slavist Nikita Tolstoy (ru) (1923–1996), is also a Russian journalist, TV and radio host.

Novels and fictional works

Tolstoy is considered one of the giants of Russian literature; his works include the novels War and Peace and Anna Karenina and novellas such as Hadji Murad and The Death of Ivan Ilyich.

Tolstoy's earliest works, the autobiographical novels Childhood, Boyhood, and Youth (1852–1856), tell of a rich landowner's son and his slow realization of the chasm between himself and his peasants. Though he later rejected them as sentimental, a great deal of Tolstoy's own life is revealed. They retain their relevance as accounts of the universal story of growing up.

Tolstoy served as a second lieutenant in an artillery regiment during the Crimean War, recounted in his Sevastopol Sketches. His experiences in battle helped stir his subsequent pacifism and gave him material for realistic depiction of the horrors of war in his later work.

His fiction consistently attempts to convey realistically the Russian society in which he lived. The Cossacks (1863) describes the Cossack life and people through a story of a Russian aristocrat in love with a Cossack girl. Anna Karenina (1877) tells parallel stories of an adulterous woman trapped by the conventions and falsities of society and of a philosophical landowner (much like Tolstoy), who works alongside the peasants in the fields and seeks to reform their lives. Tolstoy not only drew from his own life experiences but also created characters in his own image, such as Pierre Bezukhov and Prince Andrei in War and Peace, Levin in Anna Karenina and to some extent, Prince Nekhlyudov in Resurrection.

War and Peace is generally thought to be one of the greatest novels ever written, remarkable for its dramatic breadth and unity. Its vast canvas includes 580 characters, many historical with others fictional. The story moves from family life to the headquarters of Napoleon, from the court of Alexander I of Russia to the battlefields of Austerlitz and Borodino. Tolstoy's original idea for the novel was to investigate the causes of the Decembrist revolt, to which it refers only in the last chapters, from which can be deduced that Andrei Bolkonsky's son will become one of the Decembrists. The novel explores Tolstoy's theory of history, and in particular the insignificance of individuals such as Napoleon and Alexander. Somewhat surprisingly, Tolstoy did not consider War and Peace to be a novel (nor did he consider many of the great Russian fictions written at that time to be novels). This view becomes less surprising if one considers that Tolstoy was a novelist of the realist school who considered the novel to be a framework for the examination of social and political issues in nineteenth-century life. War and Peace (which is to Tolstoy really an epic in prose) therefore did not qualify. Tolstoy thought that Anna Karenina was his first true novel.

After Anna Karenina, Tolstoy concentrated on Christian themes, and his later novels such as The Death of Ivan Ilyich (1886) and What Is to Be Done? develop a radical anarcho-pacifist Christian philosophy which led to his excommunication from the Russian Orthodox Church in 1901. For all the praise showered on Anna Karenina and War and Peace, Tolstoy rejected the two works later in his life as something not as true of reality.

In his novel Resurrection, Tolstoy attempts to expose the injustice of man-made laws and the hypocrisy of institutionalized church. Tolstoy also explores and explains the economic philosophy of Georgism, of which he had become a very strong advocate towards the end of his life.

Tolstoy also tried himself in poetry with several soldier songs written during his military service and fairy tales in verse such as Volga-bogatyr and Oaf stylized as national folk songs. They were written between 1871 and 1874 for his Russian Book for Reading, a collection of short stories in four volumes (total of 629 stories in various genres) published along with the New Azbuka textbook and addressed to schoolchildren. Nevertheless, he was skeptical about poetry as a genre. As he famously said, "Writing poetry is like ploughing and dancing at the same time". According to Valentin Bulgakov, he criticised poets, including Alexander Pushkin, for their "false" epithets used "simply to make it rhyme".

Critical appraisal by other authors

Tolstoy's contemporaries paid him lofty tributes. Fyodor Dostoyevsky, who died thirty years before Tolstoy's death, thought him the greatest of all living novelists. Gustave Flaubert, on reading a translation of War and Peace, exclaimed, "What an artist and what a psychologist!" Anton Chekhov, who often visited Tolstoy at his country estate, wrote, "When literature possesses a Tolstoy, it is easy and pleasant to be a writer; even when you know you have achieved nothing yourself and are still achieving nothing, this is not as terrible as it might otherwise be, because Tolstoy achieves for everyone. What he does serves to justify all the hopes and aspirations invested in literature." The 19th-century British poet and critic Matthew Arnold opined that "A novel by Tolstoy is not a work of art but a piece of life."

Later novelists continued to appreciate Tolstoy's art, but sometimes also expressed criticism. Arthur Conan Doyle wrote "I am attracted by his earnestness and by his power of detail, but I am repelled by his looseness of construction and by his unreasonable and impracticable mysticism." Virginia

Woolf declared him "the greatest of all novelists." James Joyce noted that "He is never dull, never stupid, never tired, never pedantic, never theatrical!" Thomas Mann wrote of Tolstoy's seemingly guileless artistry: "Seldom did art work so much like nature." Vladimir Nabokov heaped superlatives upon The Death of Ivan Ilyich and Anna Karenina; he questioned, however, the reputation of War and Peace, and sharply criticized Resurrection and The Kreutzer Sonata.

Religious and political beliefs

After reading Schopenhauer's The World as Will and Representation, Tolstoy gradually became converted to the ascetic morality upheld in that work as the proper spiritual path for the upper classes: "Do you know what this summer has meant for me? Constant raptures over Schopenhauer and a whole series of spiritual delights which I've never experienced before. ... no student has ever studied so much on his course, and learned so much, as I have this summer"

In Chapter VI of A Confession, Tolstoy quoted the final paragraph of Schopenhauer's work. It explained how the nothingness that results from complete denial of self is only a relative nothingness, and is not to be feared. The novelist was struck by the description of Christian, Buddhist, and Hindu ascetic renunciation as being the path to holiness. After reading passages such as the following, which abound in Schopenhauer's ethical chapters, the Russian nobleman chose poverty and formal denial of the will:

But this very necessity of involuntary suffering (by poor people) for eternal salvation is also expressed by that utterance of the Savior (Matthew 19:24): "It is easier for a camel to go through the eye of a needle, than for a rich man to enter into the kingdom of God." Therefore, those who were greatly in earnest about their eternal salvation, chose voluntary poverty when fate had denied this to them and they had been born in wealth. Thus Buddha Sakyamuni was born a prince, but voluntarily took to the mendicant's staff; and Francis of Assisi, the founder of the mendicant orders who, as a youngster at a ball, where the daughters of all the notabilities were sitting together, was asked: "Now Francis, will you not soon make your choice from these beauties?"

and who replied: "I have made a far more beautiful choice!" "Whom?" "La povertà (poverty)": whereupon he abandoned every thing shortly afterwards and wandered through the land as a mendicant.

In 1884, Tolstoy wrote a book called What I Believe, in which he openly confessed his Christian beliefs. He affirmed his belief in Jesus Christ's teachings and was particularly influenced by the Sermon on the Mount, and the injunction to turn the other cheek, which he understood as a "commandment of non-resistance to evil by force" and a doctrine of pacifism and nonviolence. In his work The Kingdom of God Is Within You, he explains that he considered mistaken the Church's doctrine because they had made a "perversion" of Christ's teachings. Tolstoy also received letters from American Quakers who introduced him to the non-violence writings of Quaker Christians such as George Fox, William Penn and Jonathan Dymond. Tolstoy believed being a Christian required him to be a pacifist; the consequences of being a pacifist, and the apparently inevitable waging of war by government, are the reason why he is considered a philosophical anarchist.

Later, various versions of "Tolstoy's Bible" would be published, indicating the passages Tolstoy most relied on, specifically, the reported words of Jesus himself.

Tolstoy believed that a true Christian could find lasting happiness by striving for inner self-perfection through following the Great Commandment of loving one's neighbor and God rather than looking outward to the Church or state for guidance. His belief in nonresistance when faced by conflict is another distinct attribute of his philosophy based on Christ's teachings. By directly influencing Mahatma Gandhi with this idea through his work The Kingdom of God Is Within You (full text of English translation available on Wikisource), Tolstoy's profound influence on the nonviolent resistance movement reverberates to this day. He believed that the aristocracy were a burden on the poor, and that the only solution to how we live together is through anarchism.

He also opposed private property in land ownership and the institution of marriage and valued the ideals of chastity and sexual abstinence (discussed in Father Sergius and his preface to The Kreutzer Sonata), ideals also held by the young Gandhi. Tolstoy's later work derives a passion and verve from the depth of his austere moral views. The sequence of the temptation of Sergius in Father Sergius, for example, is among his later triumphs. Gorky relates how Tolstoy once read this passage before himself and Chekhov and that Tolstoy was moved to tears by the end of the reading. Other later passages of rare power include the personal crises that were faced by the protagonists of The Death of Ivan Ilyich, and of Master and Man, where the main character in the former or the reader in the latter are made aware of the foolishness of the protagonists' lives.

Tolstoy had a profound influence on the development of Christian anarchist thought. The Tolstoyans were a small Christian anarchist group formed by Tolstoy's companion, Vladimir Chertkov (1854–1936), to spread Tolstoy's religious teachings. Philosopher Peter Kropotkin wrote of Tolstoy in the article on anarchism in the 1911 Encyclopædia Britannica:

Without naming himself an anarchist, Leo Tolstoy, like his predecessors in the popular religious movements of the 15th and 16th centuries, Chojecki, Denk and many others, took the anarchist position as regards the state and property rights, deducing his conclusions from the general spirit of the teachings of Jesus and from the necessary dictates of reason. With all the might of his talent, Tolstoy made (especially in The Kingdom of God Is Within You) a powerful criticism of the church, the state and law altogether, and especially of the present property laws. He describes the state as the domination of the wicked ones, supported by brutal force. Robbers, he says, are far less dangerous than a well-organized government. He makes a searching criticism of the prejudices which are current now concerning the benefits conferred upon men by the church, the state, and the existing distribution of property, and from the teachings of Jesus he deduces the rule of non-resistance and the absolute condemnation of all wars. His religious arguments are, however, so well combined with arguments borrowed from a dispassionate observation of the present evils, that the anarchist portions of his works appeal to the religious and the non-religious reader alike.

During the Boxer Rebellion in China, Tolstoy praised the Boxers. He was harshly critical of the atrocities committed by the Russians, Germans, Americans, Japanese, and other western troops. He accused them of engaging in slaughter when he heard about the lootings, rapes, and murders, in what he saw as Christian brutality. Tolstoy also named the two monarchs most responsible for the atrocities; Nicholas II of Russia and Wilhelm II of Germany. Tolstoy, a famous sinophile, also read the works of Chinese thinker and philosopher, Confucius. Tolstoy corresponded with the Chinese intellectual Gu Hongming and recommended that China remain an agrarian nation and warned against reform like what Japan implemented.

The Eight-Nation Alliance intervention in the Boxer Rebellion was denounced by Tolstoy as were the Philippine–American War and the Second Boer War between the British Empire and the two independent Boer republics. The words "terrible for its injustice and cruelty" were used to describe the Czarist intervention in China by Tolstoy. Confucius's works were studied by Tolstoy. The attack on China in the Boxer Rebellion was railed against by Tolstoy. The war against China was criticized by Leonid Andreev and Gorkey. To the Chinese people, an epistle, was written by Tolstoy as part of the criticism of the war by intellectuals in Russia. The activities of Russia in China by Nicholas II were described in an open letter where they were slammed and denounced by Leo Tolstoy in 1902. Tolstoy corresponded with Gu Hongming and they both opposed the Hundred Day's Reform by Kang Youwei and agreed that the reform movement was perilous. Tolstoys' ideology on non violence shaped the anarchist thought of the Society for the Study of Socialism in China. Lao Zi and Confucius's teachings were studied by Tolstoy. Chinese Wisdom was a text written by Tolstoy. The Boxer Rebellion stirred Tolstoy's interest in Chinese philosophy. The Boxer and Boxer wars were denounced by Tolstoy.

In hundreds of essays over the last 20 years of his life, Tolstoy reiterated the anarchist critique of the state and recommended books by Kropotkin and Proudhon to his readers, whilst rejecting anarchism's espousal of violent revolutionary means. In the 1900 essay, "On Anarchy", he wrote; "The Anarchists are right in everything; in the negation of the existing order, and in the assertion that, without Authority, there could not be worse violence than that of Authority under existing conditions. They are mistaken only in thinking that Anarchy can be instituted by a revolution. But it will be instituted only by there being more and more people who do not require the protection of governmental power ... There can be only one permanent revolution—a moral one: the regeneration of the inner man." Despite his misgivings about anarchist violence, Tolstoy took risks to circulate the prohibited publications of anarchist thinkers in Russia, and corrected the proofs of Kropotkin's "Words of a Rebel", illegally published in St Petersburg in 1906.

Tolstoy was enthused by the economic thinking of Henry George, incorporating it approvingly into later works such as Resurrection (1899), the book that played a major factor in his excommunication.

In 1908, Tolstoy wrote A Letter to a Hindu outlining his belief in non-violence as a means for India to gain independence from British colonial rule. In 1909, a copy of the letter was read by Gandhi, who was working as a lawyer in South Africa at the time and just becoming an activist. Tolstoy's letter was significant for Gandhi, who wrote Tolstoy seeking proof that he was the real author, leading to further correspondence between them.

Reading Tolstoy's The Kingdom of God Is Within You also convinced Gandhi to avoid violence and espouse nonviolent resistance, a debt Gandhi acknowledged in his autobiography, calling Tolstoy "the greatest apostle of non-violence that the present age has produced". The correspondence between Tolstoy and Gandhi would only last a year, from October 1909 until Tolstoy's death in November 1910, but led Gandhi to give the name Tolstoy Colony to his second ashram in South Africa. Besides nonviolent resistance, the two men shared a common belief in the merits of vegetarianism, the subject of several of Tolstoy's essays.

Tolstoy also became a major supporter of the Esperanto movement. Tolstoy was impressed by the pacifist beliefs of the Doukhobors and brought their persecution to the attention of the international community, after they burned their weapons in peaceful protest in 1895. He aided the Doukhobors in migrating to Canada. In 1904, during the Russo-Japanese War, Tolstoy condemned the war and wrote to the Japanese Buddhist priest Soyen Shaku in a failed attempt to make a joint pacifist statement.

Towards the end of his life, Tolstoy become more and more occupied with the economic theory and social philosophy of Georgism. He spoke of great admiration of Henry George, stating once that "People do not argue with the teaching of George; they simply do not know it. And it is impossible to do otherwise with his teaching, for he who becomes acquainted with it cannot but agree." He also wrote a preface to George's Social Problems. Tolstoy and George both rejected private property in land (the most important source of income of the passive Russian aristocracy that Tolstoy so heavily criticized) whilst simultaneously both rejecting a centrally planned socialist economy. Some assume that this development in Tolstoy's thinking was a move away from his anarchist views, since Georgism requires a central administration to collect land rent and spend it on infrastructure. However, anarchist versions of Georgism have also been proposed since. Tolstoy's 1899 novel Resurrection explores his thoughts on Georgism in more detail and hints that Tolstoy indeed had such a view. It suggests the possibility of small communities with some form of local governance to manage the collective land rents for common goods; whilst still heavily criticising institutions of the state such as the justice system.

Death

Tolstoy died in 1910, at the age of 82. Just prior to his death, his health had been a concern of his family, who were actively engaged in his care on a daily basis. During his last few days, he had spoken and written about dying. Renouncing his aristocratic lifestyle, he had finally gathered the nerve to separate from his wife, and left home in the middle of winter, in the dead of night. His secretive departure was an apparent attempt to escape unannounced from Sophia's jealous tirades. She was outspokenly opposed to many of his teachings, and in recent years had grown envious of the attention which it seemed to her Tolstoy lavished upon his Tolstoyan "disciples".

Tolstoy died of pneumonia at Astapovo train station, after a day's rail journey south. The station master took Tolstoy to his apartment, and his personal doctors were called to the scene. He was given injections of morphine and camphor.

The police tried to limit access to his funeral procession, but thousands of peasants lined the streets. Still, some were heard to say that, other than knowing that "some nobleman had died", they knew little else about Tolstoy.

According to some sources, Tolstoy spent the last hours of his life preaching love, nonviolence, and Georgism to his fellow passengers on the train. (Source: Wikipedia)